Japanese-American Civilian Prisoner Exchanges and Detention Camps, 1941–45

This book considers the negotiation and conduct of civilian prisoner exchanges between the United States and Japan during the Second World War. To locate Japanese citizens and American citizens of Japanese descent willing to be repatriated, during early 1942 the United States government gathered approximately 120,000 Japanese-Americans into relocation centers. Critics have often attacked these relocation centers for serving no purpose, except perhaps to humiliate and punish innocent persons of Japanese descent. This book reveals that there was a very pressing motive for establishing the relocation centers—to facilitate the Japanese-American official and non-official exchange program —and they accomplished this goal superbly.

Utilizing recently released archival documents, this book examines the details of the diplomatic negotiations, the actual mechanics underlying the two successful exchanges, the reasons for the termination of the exchange program, and its final outcome. It highlights the important links between the civilian prisoner exchange negotiations and Washington's decision to employ the Japanese-American war relocation centers to identify suitable candidates for repatriation. It provides compelling evidence that the war relocation centers were created and administered in a manner that sought to satisfy Japan's concerns over reciprocity and its subsequent demand that the U.S. government provide for the safety and well-being of the Japanese, even those who had refused repatriation.

Overall, this book provides a thorough and insightful examination of the hitherto little-known, but fascinating, story of Japanese-American civilian prisoner exchanges during the Second World War.

Bruce Elleman is Associate Professor at the Maritime History Department of the U.S. Naval War College. He received a BA from UC Berkeley, and the MA, MPhil and PhD from Columbia University. His published research includes numerous articles on the USSR's and China's secret diplomacy surrounding the Chinese Eastern Railway, Outer Mongolia, and the United Front policy. He is the author of *Modern Chinese Warfare, 1795–1989* (2001), and other books on Sino-Soviet relations and Chinese military and naval history.

Routledge studies in the modern history of Asia

The Police in Occupation Japan
Control, corruption and resistance to reform
Christopher Aldous

Chinese Workers
A new history
Jackie Sheehan

The Aftermath of Partition in South Asia
Tai Yong Tan and Gyanesh Kudaisya

The Australia-Japan Political Alignment
1952 to the present
Alan Rix

Japan and Singapore in the World Economy
Japan's economic advance into Singapore, 1870–1965
Shimizu Hiroshi and Hirakawa Hitoshi

The Triads as Business
Yiu Kong Chu

Contemporary Taiwanese Cultural Nationalism
A-chin Hsiau

Religion and Nationalism in India
The case of the Punjab
Harnik Deol

Japanese Industrialisation
Historical and cultural perspectives
Ian Inkster

War and Nationalism in China
1925–1945
Hans J. van de Ven

Hong Kong in Transition
One country, two systems
Edited by Robert Ash, Peter Ferdinand, Brian Hook and Robin Porter

Japan's Postwar Economic Recovery and Anglo-Japanese Relations, 1948–1962
Noriko Yokoi

Japanese Army Stragglers and Memories of the War in Japan, 1950–1975
Beatrice Trefalt

Ending the Vietnam War
The Vietnamese Communists' perspective
Ang Cheng Guan

The Development of the Japanese Nursing Profession
Adopting and adapting Western influences
Aya Takahashi

Women's Suffrage in Asia
Gender nationalism and democracy
Louise Edwards and Mina Roces

The Anglo-Japanese Alliance, 1902–1922
Phillips Payson O'Brien

The United States and Cambodia, 1870–1969
From curiosity to confrontation
Kenton Clymer

Japanese-American Civilian Prisoner Exchanges and Detention Camps, 1941–45

Bruce Elleman

Routledge
Taylor & Francis Group

LONDON AND NEW YORK

First published 2006
by Routledge
2 Park Square, Milton Park, Abingdon, Oxon OX14 4RN

Simultaneously published in the USA and Canada
by Routledge
605 Third Avenue, New York, NY 10017

Routledge is an imprint of the Taylor & Francis Group, an informa business

Typeset in Times New Roman by
Rosemount Typing Services, Auldgirth, Dumfriesshire

British Library Cataloguing in Publication Data
A catalogue record for this book is available from British Library

Library of Congress Cataloging in Publication Data
Elleman, Bruce, 1951-
Japanese-American civilian prisoner exchanges and detention camps, 1941-45 / Bruce Elleman.
    p. cm. – (Routledge studies in the modern history of Asia ; 37)
Includes bibliographical references and index.
1. World War, 1939-1945–Prisoners and prisons, American. 2. Japanese Americans–Evacuation and relocation, 1942-1945. 3. World War, 1939-1945–Prisoners and prisons, Japanese. 4. World War, 1939-1945–Diplomatic history. 5. Prisoners of war–United States–History–20th century. 6. Prisoners of war–Japan–History–20th century. I. Title. II. Series.
D769.8.A6E56 2006
940.53'17'089956073–dc22

                                                              2005024459

ISBN13: 978–0–415–46192–4 (pbk)

To Donald Goodwin, my Sanderson High School
social studies teacher, who taught me never to accept
written history at face value.

Contents

Introduction

There have been hundreds, even thousands, of books published about the relocation of Japanese-Americans during World War II.[1] Those condemning this program argue: "Racism, wartime hysteria, and failed political leadership resulted in the incarceration of U.S. citizens and legal residents in concentration camps located in desolate and barren regions."[2] On the other side of the debate, those who have defended the relocation program, for example a woman whose husband died in a Japanese camp in the Philippines, say: "Although nothing in the Geneva Convention dictates that a 'family camp' must be established for enemy aliens, the United States, in the interest of humane treatment and understanding, permitted Japanese nationals (enemy aliens) to be interned at the civilian War Relocation Authority centers."[3]

As access to classified materials has increased over the years, more books have been published explaining the rationale behind the war relocation program. One study of the Japanese diplomatic code (MAGIC) intercepts has concluded that decoded messages from Japan did show "the existence of widespread Japanese espionage operations, particularly on the West Coast."[4] After the September 11, 2001 attacks, which resulted in racial profiling of many U.S. residents from the Middle East, there has been renewed discussion about racial profiling in wartime: "Ethnic Japanese forced to leave the West Coast of the United States and relocate outside of prescribed military zones after the Pearl Harbor attack endured a heavy burden, but they were not the only ones who suffered and sacrificed. Enemy aliens from all Axis nations—not just Japan—were subjected to curfews, registration, censorship, and exclusion from sensitive areas."[5]

Another aspect of the war relocation program was the U.S.–Japanese civilian exchange program. In 1987, P. Scott Corbett's *Quiet Passages* was the first book to examine the question of official and non-official exchanges between the United States and Japan. Although his book is very useful from the U.S. perspective, Corbett himself admitted: "In one sense, only half the story of the exchanges is told here … A similar study from the Japanese perspective, using Foreign Office records, particularly those of the Foreign Interest Section, is needed to round out the story. Such a study would shed light on such issues as the degree of Japanese commitment to the exchange process."[6]

The present book utilizes not just American sources on the U.S.–Japanese exchange, but also the diplomatic records of the Foreign Ministry Archives in Tokyo, Japan. As this new documentation reveals, the negotiations to determine the exact conditions for exchanging government officials and non-officials between Japan and the United States were on-going and divisive. As a direct consequence of the U.S.–Japanese exchanges, virtually all American government officials, as well as thousands of ordinary American citizens, were able to return from Japan, Manchuria, and occupied China, as were many officials and non-officials from Canada, Central America, and South America; these countries were included on the American side of the exchange, while Japan's allies—such as Thailand and Japanese-occupied French Indochina—were included on the Japanese side.

Reciprocity was a key feature of these exchanges. For every American who returned to the United States one Japanese had to be repatriated to Japan. In total, some 2,700 U.S. citizens, plus 300 citizens from other American nations, were able to return safely to the Western Hemisphere during 1942 and 1943, right as some of the worst fighting of the Pacific War raged around them. This was a notable accomplishment, since it represented almost twice the number of Americans—some 1,200—who were repatriated from Europe during the war, mainly during July 1942 in exchange for German-Americans and Italian-Americans living in the United States.[7]

There has long been a basic misunderstanding of the treatment of Japanese-Americans compared with the German- and Italian-American communities. Prior to 18 February 1942, which is one day before President Roosevelt signed Executive Order 9066, a total of 267 Italian, 1,396 German, and 2,209 Japanese "alien enemies" had already been arrested by local authorities. On the East Coast and in the mid-West, the number of Germans and Italians arrested far outnumbered Japanese; only in New York City was there a preponderance of Japanese—275 Japanese were arrested there, compared to 212 Germans, and 86 Italians. Meanwhile, in Hawaii, 389 Japanese were arrested, as compared to 11 Italians and 79 Germans, while in most of the West Coast cities, including San Diego, Los Angeles, San Francisco, and Seattle, the Japanese arrested far outnumbered Germans and Italians; in Portland, Oregon, interestingly, the numbers were almost equal, with 39 Japanese arrested and 35 Germans taken into custody.[8]

These statistics suggest that there was no organized movement to mistreat only Japanese-Americans, but rather there was a general concern applying to all nationals from enemy countries. While much attention has been focused on the plight of the Japanese-American community in the United States, similar relocation and exchange programs were established for German-Americans and Italian-Americans. This story has largely been overlooked or distorted. One historian of the Japanese-Americans relocation falsely stated: "A similar plan to relocate German and Italian aliens aroused such widespread protest that the government canceled it, explaining that it would effect the nation's economic structure and lower morale among citizens of those nationalities."[9]

In fact, the relocation program for Germans and Italians was not canceled; rather German-Americans were treated exactly the same as Japanese-Americans. The plight of the Japanese-Americans, however, has over-shadowed that of the Germans: "Most misunderstood was the arrest and internment of over 10,000 members of America's German community as dangerous enemy aliens and enemy sympathizers."[10] Similar to those Japanese-Americans who expressed their loyalty to Japan, not all of these American-Germans who were interned were loyal to America, but included those who had rediscovered their "Germanness," "foolhardy nationalists and ideologues," and "devoted German nationalists."[11]

Throughout World War II, the U.S. government did not just focus on the Japanese, or even just on the Japanese and the Germans, the two strongest Axis powers, but also authorized the relocation and exchange of Italian-Americans. The Italian-American community has felt equally mistreated, not by the internment alone, but also by the failure of the U.S. government to apologize to them as it did to the Japanese-Americans: "If Americans can grasp the deep sense of personal humiliation that goes with being told you are an enemy of your country, as explained so eloquently by Japanese Americans over the years, is it so difficult then to understand that for Italian Americans what happened to them during nine months in 1942 is also a matter of dignity and pride?"[12]

If nothing else, a more thorough history of the U.S.–Japanese exchanges during World War II will show that the Japanese-Americans were not singled out for mistreatment. Rather, this treatment applied generally to nationals of all enemy countries. The internment of Japanese-Americans, as well as of German- and Italian-Americans, was part of a diplomatically negotiated exchange program to repatriate citizens and their families from the U.S. back to a number of enemy countries in return for repatriating American citizens from enemy territory back to the United States.

Unfortunately, even though the two U.S.–Japanese exchanges that took place in 1942 and 1943 were highly successful, this still left approximately 6,000 other American citizens interned in Japanese camps in Japan, Manchukuo, China, and other Southeast Asian nations. By 1 May 1944, out of the approximately 112,000 Japanese-Americans interned in the U.S. war relocation centers, a total of 20,161 Japanese citizens and American citizens of Japanese ancestry—almost one-fifth—had applied to be repatriated to Japan; most had to wait until the end of the war until their cases could be considered.[13]

This book will examine not only the fate of those people who were fortunate enough to be repatriated during the war, but also what happened to those unfortunate people who, because of a breakdown in the U.S.–Japanese negotiations, were forced to remain in the detention centers for the duration of the hostilities. While almost all of the Japanese-Americans in U.S. centers survived the war and remained healthy and well-fed throughout, the same could not be said for the American citizens interned by Japan; although exact numbers are difficult to discern, anywhere from one-third to one-half of the Americans in some Japanese camps died of mistreatment and starvation.

* * *

Negotiations resulting in the U.S.–Japanese official and non-official (i.e. civilian) exchanges began almost immediately after the onset of hostilities. The conditions for the first exchange were negotiated during the winter of 1941 and the spring of 1942. The Swiss government, through its consulate in Tokyo, represented the United States in these exchanges, while the Spanish government, through its embassy in Washington, represented Japan. On 10 December 1941, only three days after Japan's attack on Pearl Harbor, the Swiss Minister to Japan, Camille Gorge, wrote to Foreign Minister Shigenori Togo passing on a query of 8 December from the U.S. government asking if "the Japanese Government would consent, in principle, to exchanging the Japanese consular 'officers' and diplomats, as well as other Japanese subjects blockaded [*bloqués*] in the United States, in return for the American consular 'officers' and diplomats, as well as those American citizens blockaded [*bloqués*] in the Empire of Japan, in occupied China, as well as in Manchuria." This U.S. letter ended with the assurance that if the Japanese government concurred with these principles, then the U.S. government would be willing to consider "with goodwill" [*avec bienveillance*] any proposal that would serve to bring about the "transfer of the persons in question."[14]

The American original of this letter, reprinted in the series *Foreign Relations of the United States,* makes it even more clear that the State Department was determined to make the exchanges a reality. This version stated "the Department will be glad to consider any means that the Japanese Government may wish to propose by which to effect such a transfer."[15] With the assistance of the Swiss and Spanish governments acting as intermediaries, U.S.–Japanese negotiations were quickly opened and a process for exchanging official and non-official evacuees was soon established between the Japanese government and the United States government.

These early negotiations were not without problems. The very generality of the U.S. proposal allowed the Japanese government to set the specific terms for the U.S.–Japanese exchanges. A series of written negotiations were undertaken beginning in late 1941 and continuing into early 1942. By the spring of 1942, most of the details of the U.S.–Japanese exchanges had been discussed and a *modus operandi* for conducting the planned transfers decided. Although the Japanese government agreed to exchange non-officials as well as officials, it focused on very specific groups of non-officials: Japanese "treaty merchants," scholars, and students. In general, this corresponded to businessmen, missionaries, and educators on the American side. This opened the door to widen the U.S.–Japanese exchange to include ordinary citizens.

By early 1942, there was hope that thousands of American citizens trapped in Japan, or being held in Japanese detention camps in Manchuria or China, might be able to come home. The negotiation of a U.S.–Japanese exchange program appeared to offer perhaps the only viable method during wartime for guaranteeing their safe return. However, one important question remained unanswered: Where was the United States government going to find an equivalent number of Japanese in the U.S. to exchange for its citizens being detained in Japan?

* * *

Reciprocity was the price Japan demanded for the safe return of all of the American citizens. In order to conform to Japanese views of reciprocity, it was first necessary to locate an equal number of Japanese citizens and American citizens of Japanese ancestry who wished to be repatriated to Japan.[16] Because of the need to maintain reciprocity, the U.S.–Japanese exchange program soon became intimately linked with the Japanese-American war relocation centers, which were responsible for maintaining statistics on those Japanese citizens and American citizens of Japanese ancestry who had been evacuated from the West Coast. Although these centers have been criticized for not having any purpose except to abuse Japanese-Americans, in fact, the war relocation centers played a vital role in the U.S.–Japanese exchange effort.

Based on MAGIC intercepts, the U.S. government believed that the Japanese military had devised war plans that included attacking the West Coast. Espionage is a major part of warfare. Japan had earlier demonstrated its prowess in this field during the Russo-Japanese War of 1904–5, when it helped to fund revolutionary movements in Russia.[17] Later, during the 1930s, Japan conducted highly effective intelligence operations in China. There was every reason to believe that Japan would try to do the same in the United States. To counter this possibility, during March 1942, the United States government ordered that 112,000 Japanese-Americans, some 70,000 of them U.S. citizens by birth—although of this number some 9,000 had grown up or been educated mainly in Japan—to evacuate from their homes in Washington, Oregon, California, and southern Arizona to inland war relocation centers.[18]

The rationale for the war relocation centers was threefold: First, based on the assumption that any Japanese spies or sympathizers would be concentrated in the Japanese-American community, putting them in relocation centers would keep them far from the anticipated battlefield on the West Coast and under U.S. surveillance. In one fell swoop Japanese espionage in the U.S. would be rendered ineffective.[19] Second, relocation in guarded camps would prevent vigilante reprisals, either as payback for Pearl Harbor, or especially once the anticipated attacks by Japan against the West Coast took place. Third, the war relocation centers served as the clearing houses for the U.S.–Japanese exchange program, quickly becoming one of the most important instruments for locating, interviewing, and identifying those Japanese citizens and American citizens of

Japanese ancestry who wished to return to Japan as distinct from those Japanese who stated their loyalty to the United States government and expressed their desire to remain in the United States.

The urgent need to locate as quickly as possible Japanese citizens and Americans of Japanese ancestry willing to be repatriated helps to explain not only the rationale for the war relocation centers, but also many of the centers' actions, such as the intensive interviews, the loyalty oaths, and the questionnaires concerning repatriation, which many critics have condemned as signs of anti-Japanese racism or bureaucratic ineptitude. As a result of this effort, thousands of Japanese citizens and American citizens of Japanese ancestry of the more than 20,000 who had requested repatriation were gradually located, segregated from the loyal Japanese-American population in the centers, and then eventually moved to the Tule Lake Segregation Center in northern California pending their return to Japan.

On 15 November 1942, the Wartime Civil Control Administration (WCCA) handed over full control to the War Relocation Authority (WRA) for processing Japanese citizens and American citizens of Japanese ancestry who had applied for repatriation. Just nine days earlier, Assistant Secretary of State Breckinridge Long had emphasized in a memorandum how some of these Japanese-Americans could be exchanged for Americans being held by Japan.[20] Unfortunately, U.S.–Japanese exchange negotiations became increasingly acrimonious and only two exchanges ever took place. In the end, only 4 Japanese from the relocation centers were included on the first exchange in 1942, while 314 others were included in the 1943 exchange.[21]

The more than 20,000 Japanese citizens and American citizens of Japanese ancestry who had requested repatriation remained in the relocation centers throughout the rest of the war, with a large number of them being segregated at the Tule Lake center. After the war ended, 4,406 of those who had requested repatriation were quickly returned to Japan.[22] However, most of those who had asked to be repatriated—over 15,000 people—eventually changed their minds, requested that they be allowed to continue living in the U.S., and were allowed to remain.

As a result of these two exchanges, approximately 2,700 United States citizens and another 300 Canadian, Mexican, Central American, and South American citizens were able to return home, while 3,000 Japanese citizens and loyalists were able to return to Japan. Unfortunately, a third exchange was never carried out, for reasons that will be discussed more fully below. Therefore, even though the U.S.–Japanese exchanges ground to a halt in 1943, and even though the majority of the U.S. and Japanese civilians were not exchanged during the war, the war relocation centers did play a crucial role in assisting the two exchanges that occurred during the war, and in assisting 4,406 others to return to Japan after the war ended.

In the case of the Americans who were able to return home, based on the survival rates of those who remained interned in Japan, approximately one-third might have died had they remained in Japanese custody. Seen in this perspective, the U.S.–Japanese exchange program can truly be called a success for those Americans who managed to get home. The program is in many ways the formerly "missing link" that helps not only to explain why the war relocation centers were established in the first place, but also why they adhered to such policies as the administration of loyalty oaths and the segregation of repatriates and expatriates. These activities were linked to the exchange program.

* * *

This book will examine the details of the diplomatic negotiations, the actual mechanics underlying the two successful exchanges, the reasons for the termination of the exchange program, and the final outcome of the U.S.–Japanese wartime exchange program. Interesting as the personal experiences of the exchangees are, this work will not attempt to tell their stories in depth. Nor will it examine in great detail the bureaucratic infighting underlying the American side of the exchanges, a task that has largely been accomplished already.[23] Unlike previous studies, this book *will* strive to highlight the important links between the U.S.–Japanese exchange negotiations and Washington's decision to employ the Japanese-American war relocation centers to identify suitable candidates for repatriation.

This book will show that during interviews conducted at the war relocation centers a total of 20,161 Japanese citizens and American citizens of Japanese ancestry offered to participate in the official U.S.–Japanese exchange program by returning to Japan. This number equals approximately 18 percent of the total of the Japanese-Americans housed in the war relocation centers, or approximately 10 percent of the entire Japanese-American population in the United States. Most of the Japanese who participated in the first two exchanges were Japanese diplomats, East Coast detainees, and Japanese citizens who had been relocated to the United States from Canada, Central America, and South America, while it was thought that any future exchange would focus most heavily on the Japanese housed in the war relocation centers.

Finally, this work will also provide compelling evidence that the war relocation centers were created and administered in a manner that sought to satisfy Japan's concerns over *reciprocity*—by exchanging one Japanese for every American allowed to return home—and its subsequent demand that the U.S. government provide for the safety and well-being of the Japanese, even those who had refused repatriation. Although the premature termination of the exchange program in 1943 meant that the vast majority of the remaining Japanese loyalists were never exchanged, under better circumstances their repatriation might have allowed an equal number of American citizens held by Japan the chance to return home.

1 The origin of the Japanese–American exchange program

On 8 December 1941, only one day after the Japanese attack on Pearl Harbor, the U.S. government transmitted through the Swiss Minister in Tokyo its initial proposal for the treatment and eventual exchange of Japanese government officials in return for American government officials. The Japanese responded positively and diplomatic negotiations via written communications were soon opened. Over time, these intensive diplomatic negotiations resulted in a gentleman's agreement that allowed all American officials from Japan, Manchukuo (formerly Manchuria), and Japanese-occupied China to return home to the United States; later, French Indochina (Vietnam), Thailand, and Singapore were included as well. Other countries, including Canada, most Central American states, and several countries in South America were also included in these exchanges on the American side, while Thailand and French Indochina joined in on the Japanese side; Great Britain and its colonies participated as well, but conducted their negotiations with Tokyo separately from the United States.[1]

As a result of these successful exchanges, all Japanese officials throughout the Western Hemisphere were soon able to return to Japan. However, the impact of these early U.S.–Japanese negotiations was actually much greater than merely exchanging government officials. Instead of limiting the exchanges just to diplomatic personnel, their families, and the embassy staff, from the beginning Washington recommended including interned non-officials as well. This would allow ordinary American citizens, including businessmen, teachers, missionaries, and tourists, to return home safely even in the midst of war.

Tokyo immediately agreed to the American suggestion. The Japanese government gave high priority to able-bodied men, and especially "treaty merchants," professors, and students, all of whom could potentially play an important role in the war effort. The American government, by contrast, put a premium on first repatriating women and children, especially from those Asian countries occupied by Japanese forces—such as Manchukuo and occupied China—where the conditions in the detention camps were marginal at best. Only after these vulnerable American citizens were returned home, were Americans detained in Japan proper to be exchanged. The most reliable U.S. estimate of how many American citizens were being held in all of the Japanese detention camps by early 1942 was around 6,000.

Many of the terms and conditions that were initially negotiated just for exchanging government officials were eventually applied across the board to the return of non-officials as well. This solution was both good and bad. On the positive side, many non-official citizens from each country were indeed given an opportunity to return home, which might not have happened otherwise. One unexpected negative consequence, however, was that since the official exchanges were termed "reciprocal," the exchange of non-officials also became reciprocal. In other words, one American citizen had to be traded either for a Japanese citizen or for an American citizen of Japanese ancestry willing to be repatriated.

Washington unwittingly obligated itself to locate suitable candidates to offer in exchange for the return of American citizens. This limitation was to result in many unforeseen consequences, including quite possibly the creation of war relocation centers as one means of locating Japanese-Americans willing to be repatriated to Japan. On 18 March 1942, the U.S. government established the war relocation centers for West Coast Japanese-Americans. In these centers were collected approximately 112,000 Japanese citizens and American citizens of Japanese ancestry who had refused to move voluntarily from the Pacific coast region in response to a special presidential Public Proclamation 1 of 2 March 1942 ordering them to relocate.

Very few of the Japanese-Americans who moved voluntarily out of the Western Defense Command Zone—estimates range as high as 9,000 total— before the four-week deadline were ever included in the war relocation program. Some who did relocate voluntarily were turned back at the Nevada border, or had difficulty buying gasoline for their vehicles.[2] By 29 March, however, the period of voluntary evacuation ended by military order.[3] During this four-week delay, the United States government was under constant criticism from Canada and Mexico, which had already largely relocated their Japanese nationals from coastal areas, as well as from the governors of western states adjacent to the Pacific zones, who were afraid that thousands of fleeing Japanese-Americans would come pouring into their states.

The 13 December 1941 U.S. exchange proposal

On 13 December 1941, only six days after the outbreak of war, Washington sent a fuller proposal detailing a possible exchange program. This proposal, which was transferred from the Foreign Office at Berne to the Swiss Minister at Tokyo on 16 December 1941, eventually became the basis of the U.S.–Japanese exchange of government officials.[4] Several sections of this early proposal, especially the promise that the exchanges would be "reciprocal," arguably also were to have an important impact on the exchange of non-officials. This promise, which might have appeared innocuous at the time, was to affect directly the formation and functions of the U.S. government war relocation centers for removing Japanese citizens and American citizens of Japanese ancestry to a safe distance from the Pacific Coast; these relocation centers were created on 18 March 1942, long after negotiations to exchange government officials had already been initiated.

The U.S. government's 13 December 1941 proposal was divided into three general parts. First, there were several sections pertaining to treatment of government officials still in their host country, including a guarantee to protect their personal safety. Second, there were detailed instructions on how often and through what intermediaries these government officials could communicate with their home government. Third, there were detailed regulations concerning how the actual exchange process might be organized.

With regard to the personnel of the "former Japanese embassy" in Washington and to Japanese consulates throughout the United States, the U.S. government agreed to accord them "correct and liberal treatment in accordance with international law and with the pertinent precedents." It furthermore promised to provide "them and the members of their families with adequate protection" in addition to assuring "their comfort as long as they remain within the jurisdiction of the United States." Meanwhile, members of the Japanese embassy would be allowed to live in the embassy if they were unmarried, or with their families in their normal housing if married. Married personnel could "visit the Embassy daily," while unmarried officials could visit their non-embassy residences, but only "for the purpose of packing their personal effects."[5]

Prior to Japan's agreement to accept this formal proposal, the U.S. treatment of the Japanese embassy staff in Washington was less than exemplary. On 17 December 1941, Breckinridge Long, the Special Assistant Secretary of State in charge of war problems, recounted how they had "been pretty tough on the Japs. For six days they slept 40 in the embassy prepared to sleep 10. They had no mattresses, no bedclothes, no clean linen."[6] However, in general the Japanese officials' "international status required that they be accorded above-minimal treatment," in particular since the United States government "hoped its diplomatic officials would receive similar treatment."[7]

As for purchasing necessities, while confined to their embassy they would designate one staff member to "circulate within the city for the purpose of making any desired purchases for the comfort and convenience of the Embassy staff." Officials, their families, and all members of the staff would be afforded police protection, but "no police officer will be stationed within the Embassy." Furthermore, communications would be conducted by an intermediate country— with Spain representing Japan and Switzerland the U.S.—and these countries' representatives would "have free access to the Embassy." Meanwhile, the embassy would be provided with telephone communications with the Spanish representative and with the U.S. State Department. Direct communication with Tokyo by telegraph was forbidden, however, and: "The Embassy will be permitted to communicate freely with the Japanese Foreign Office [only] through the intermediary of the protecting Power."[8]

Finally, and arguably most importantly, the largest section described in detail the mechanics of the actual exchange. According to the American proposal, the "Japanese diplomatic and consular personal [sic] and their families will proceed on an appropriate passenger vessel provided by this government to Lourenço Marques," in the Portuguese portion of South Africa, where they would meet ships from Japan carrying all of the American officials, their families, and staff: "the vessels [would] exchange passengers and baggage at Lourenço Marques and return to their respective countries."[9]

For funding, the U.S. government stated that "all expenses of the Japanese mentioned above for travel and subsistence from their former posts of duty . . . . will be borne by the United States Government." Furthermore: "It is assumed that the Japanese Government will agree to accord similar treatment on reciprocal basis to American nationals possessed of official status within the Japanese Empire and in the Japanese occupied territories while such American nationals remain there, and in all that appertains to facilitating their departure and transit homeward."[10]

All of these terms and conditions appeared relatively straightforward and easy to carry out. With regard to government officials, this largely proved to be the case. However, as soon as these terms were applied across the board to non-officials, the situation suddenly became much more complicated. In particular, the exact phraseology of one section—"It is assumed that the Japanese Government will agree to accord similar treatment on a reciprocal basis . . ."— might suggest that the U.S. Government was attempting at this early stage to push Japan into matching its generally good treatment of Japanese officials.

Over time, however, the exact meaning of the term "reciprocal"—in terms of numbers of exchangees, providing security guarantees, and financing for future exchanges—became a major stumbling block during negotiations, as well as in the actual implementation of the exchange program for non-officials. By referring to this term, the Japanese could insist that the U.S. government had to repatriate one Japanese citizen or American citizen of Japanese ancestry for every American citizen allowed to return home. Moreover, trying to exchange persons of equivalent social status, in terms of education and employment, also became a consideration. Such limitations were destined to make the exchange program extraordinarily complicated.

The meaning of "reciprocal" in the U.S.–Japanese exchanges

The term "reciprocal" proved to be very important during both the negotiations and the actual conduct of the U.S.–Japanese exchanges. Although it was never stated directly, by agreeing to "reciprocal" funding the United States and Japan also implied that there should be exactly equal numbers of each countries' citizens included in the exchanges, because otherwise the cost of supporting the exchange program could not possibly be shared equally. In addition, in Japan the word "reciprocal" had a special social meaning that American counterparts might not have fully understood, since social status in Japan was so clearly demarcated. Full reciprocity could entail the exchange of persons of equivalent social value. Not only did the numbers of exchangees have to be equal, but to some degree even the value—in terms of family background, social status, education, etc.—of the exchangees had to be calculated and deemed to be "equal."

For Americans, whose Declaration of Independence states that "all men are equal," even to imagine trying to judge the social value or worth of those persons involved in the exchange program would be considered impossible. According to European and American traditions, during emergencies—such as a ship sinking— women and children were always evacuated first. In Japan, by contrast, women and children (especially female children) were considered to be on the lowest rung of the social ladder. Therefore, in the U.S.–Japanese exchanges, the Japanese government ranked women and female children as the lowest priority. Such divergent differences in Japan's and America's social structures would prove to be an active deterrent to the on-going negotiations, especially for exchanging non-officials.

Why were the Japanese officials so sensitive to these factors? When the Western nations became actively involved in the Far East in the mid-nineteenth century, they imposed their own treaty port system on Japan. This unequal treaty system guaranteed Westerners privileges in Japan with no corresponding privileges for Japan in the West. The overriding policy objective of the new Meiji government had been the abolition of this unreciprocal treaty system, which it finally succeeded in achieving during the 1890s.

Later, at the 1919 Paris peace talks, Japan put forward an anti-racist clause— proclaiming that all nations should be treated equally—and this clause was voted down by the predominantly European and American delegates. Although the Japanese diplomats obtained their primary objectives at Versailles—including the handover of the German concession in Shandong—their inability to obtain promises of equal treatment grated on them. It appeared to suggest that Japan was still not considered to be a great nation.

Finally, at the 1921–22 Washington conference, a naval agreement between Great Britain, the United States, and Japan gave parity to the British and American fleets, but required that Japan's navy remain at 60 percent the size of its competitors. Although this smaller number left Japan dominant in the Pacific, since both the United States and Britain had to deploy their fleets in two or more oceans, to Japanese this unequal ratio smacked of mistreatment. Many Japanese pointed to this example as yet one more proof that Japan was not treated equally.

In all three of these cases, the Japanese felt that they had not received reciprocal treatment. Thus, in the U.S.–Japanese negotiations to exchange officials the exact meaning of "reciprocity" would prove to be of great importance to Japan. In the midst of World War II, the Japanese negotiators were determined not to allow any inequalities between enemies. To make matters worse, at the beginning of the war there were many more American officials and ordinary citizens being detained by Japan than there were Japanese officials and citizens being held in custody by the United States. This made a truly "reciprocal" exchange very difficult. To make up the difference, especially in the numbers of non-officials, the Japanese government expected Washington to locate additional Japanese citizens willing to repatriate and to match their approximate social value with those Americans being held in Japan—who included such categories as businessmen, teachers, missionaries, and tourists.

Unfortunately, many of these people chose to remain in the United States, where their Western education and technical training guaranteed a high standard of living. By contrast, those Japanese on the lowest rungs of the social ladder, including shop-keepers, tenant farmers, and day laborers, appear to have sought repatriation to Japan at a higher rate. What this meant in terms of qualitative reciprocity was that the United States government was trying to exchange farmers and day laborers for teachers and missionaries. Since such social groups were considered by the Japanese government to be at the opposite extremes of the social scale, the Japanese thought they were not socially equal to the American citizens awaiting repatriation. Therefore, "qualitative reciprocity" was to become an equally important, albeit largely subsurface factor, in league with "quantitative reciprocity," during negotiations to establish the exchange program.

The terms for exchanging officials also led to three important problems when applied to non-officials. First, at this early stage the only Americans and Japanese being included in the exchange were government officials. The number of these officials was something that each country knew exactly. It was sensible, therefore, that each government should be responsible for financing the security, the travel, and the subsistence of their counterpart's official evacuees. By contrast, no non-officials were as yet specifically included in the exchange, and certainly there were no numbers available for the many non-officials residing in each country.

Second, from the point of view of geography, such an agreement was not unduly difficult to execute vis-à-vis each other's embassies and consulates, which after all were stationary buildings. However, once non-officials—for example, journalists, and later even ordinary civilians were included in the exchange—then the process of simply locating and taking care of the non-officials became a logistical nightmare. It was hard enough for Japan, which had put virtually all American citizens irrespective of their status in detention camps soon after the war started, but this task would be even more complicated in the United States, which in addition to the problems of its physical size, had a population of well over 200,000 Japanese-Americans, among whom were interspersed those Japanese loyalists who wished to be repatriated to Japan. Clearly, some method was needed to identify which Japanese-Americans wanted to remain and which wanted to return to Japan.

Third, guaranteeing the security of each other's citizens proved to be extremely difficult. For example, while it was relatively easy to protect the Japanese embassy in Washington or Japan's regional consulates, it was much more difficult for the U.S. government to provide sufficient police officers—

especially in wartime—to insure the personal safety of thousands of non-official Japanese, each living in a different location; again, Japan had already solved this problem by putting many foreigners in detention camps. Clearly, a viable means of applying these security guarantees to non-officials had yet to be created.

As early as 13 December 1941, less than a week after Japan's attack on Pearl Harbor, there were several looming problems linked to the reciprocal exchange of official representatives. While these conditions made perfect sense when applied to government officials, they were not feasible when applied to non-officials. In particular, determining the numbers, the geographical location, and providing security for non-officials would prove to be enormously difficult. Matching quantitative and qualitative reciprocity would be even more of a challenge. As a result, the U.S.–Japanese exchange negotiations would quickly become much more complicated once non-officials were added and especially once it was determined that these above-mentioned guarantees and restrictions should also be applied to them.

Including non-officials under the 1929 Geneva Convention on POWs

Almost as soon as the war began, the question of exchanging non-officials was raised. On 10 December 1941, Tokyo received the United States government proposal that "American citizens blocked in the Japanese empire, in occupied China, or in Manchuria" should be exchanged along with government officials.[11] The Japanese government appeared to agree with this proposal, and an early draft provided a list of its preferred exchangees—listing not only government officials, but also journalists, businessmen, students, teachers, and then finally women and children, in that order. Absolutely no mention was made of small businessmen, farmers, or day laborers. This early list appears in the Japanese archives under the date 16 December 1941.[12]

From the very beginning the best method for conducting such a non-official exchange was questioned. It was still unclear at this early stage whether non-officials could be traded under the auspices of the 1929 Geneva Convention. On 17 December 1941, Max Huber, President of the International Red Cross Committee, answered a Japanese inquiry on this very point: "We think that [the] fact Japan is not party 1929 convention relative to war prisoners does not prevent carrying out above-mentioned scheme provided reciprocity agreed upon by parties of war or provided these parties declare themselves prepared apply de facto provisions contained in 1929 war prisoners convention."[13]

The 27 July 1929 Geneva Convention was not written to apply to civilians, but to prisoners of war. However, there was one provision, Article 81, that could be stretched to include civilians. This article stated: "Persons who follow the armed forces without directly belonging thereto, such as correspondents, newspaper reporters, sutlers, or contractors, who fall into the hands of the enemy, and whom the latter think fit to detain, shall be entitled to be treated as prisoners of war, provided they are in possession of an authorization from the military authorities of the armed forces which they were following."[14]

In addition to this article, which might adequately cover the exchange of certain non-officials such as journalists, there were several other sections of the 1929 Convention pertaining to the treatment of POWs and civilians. These discussed matters such as work restrictions, expense of repatriation, and locales where POWs and civilians could not be detained. Many of these points would eventually come into play in the U.S.–Japanese non-official exchanges. For example, prisoners of war could be asked to work, although there could be "no direct connection with the operations of the war." In addition, if POWs were repatriated, the expenses for travel, upkeep, etc., would be paid by the soldier's mother country, not the country that had taken him prisoner. Finally, there were limits on where POWs could be detained, and "no prisoner may at any time be sent to an area where he would be exposed to the force of the fighting zone, or be employed to render by his presence certain points or areas immune from bombardment."[15]

On 27 December 1941, the United States government clearly stated in a note to Japan that it was willing to apply the terms of the Geneva Convention "to any civilian enemy aliens that may be interned insofar as the provisions of that convention may be adaptable thereto."[16] On 29 January 1942, the Japanese government agreed, stating that Japan would "stictly observe" (*observe strictement*) the Geneva Convention of 27 July 1929.[17] In line with the Convention, therefore, Japan requested that the non-officials not be forced to conduct labor and that detention camps not be placed in strategic locations. However, instead of Japan agreeing to pay to regain its citizens from the U.S., it was mutually decided that each country would pay for its own side of the exchange on a reciprocal basis.

Thus, while the structure of the U.S.–Japanese non-official exchanges followed the basic format of the 1929 Geneva Convention, it did not conform exactly to all of the specific points, especially with regard to money. In practice, this meant that when friction later arose over the conduct and continuation of the non-official exchanges, neither party could turn to the Geneva Convention for a ready solution. Instead, every dispute had to be negotiated *de novo*. Such limitations ultimately hindered the success of the exchange program.

The term "reciprocity" and the numbers, location, and security of non-officials all soon became important factors in the exchange negotiations. In a memorandum dated 5 January 1942, the term reciprocity was not yet specifically emphasized in a U.S. government note, nor was the term security.[18] However, by 12 February 1942 the phrase "basis of reciprocity" had appeared in negotiating records that pertained to non-officials.[19] Later, in a note dated 24 March 1942, the Japanese government clarified the meaning of reciprocity by stating that the terms of the Geneva Convention "will apply on condition of reciprocity."[20] This meant that virtually every facet of the U.S.–Japanese exchanges had to be reciprocal.

Although both terms—reciprocity and security—might appear at first glance to be simple enough, what they came to mean for non-officials was something entirely different from earlier negotiations on the exchange of officials. For reciprocity, the Japanese government insisted that for each American civilian exchangee there would have to be one Japanese civilian, and (even more difficult to fulfill) of approximately equal social status, available to be repatriated. For security, the Japanese government demanded that all non-officials had to be accorded either police or military protection.

In wartime, this goal would be particularly difficult to achieve in the United States, especially due to its large size, the large population of Japanese-Americans, and the dispersion of the Japanese-American community. In Japan, the geographic extent was smaller, the number of American civilians was limited, and they were mostly living in large cities. What is more, as early as August 1941, months before the outbreak of war, Japan had started detaining American citizens seeking to depart Japan in retaliation for the U.S. decision to freeze Japanese assets.[21] By early 1942, most foreigners had already been registered and many of them were rounded up and put into Japanese camps. Thus, the demand to do something quickly put greater pressure on the U.S. government than on the Japanese government.

In practice, the terms reciprocity and security meant that the U.S. government had obliged itself to: (1) locate those Japanese citizens and American citizens loyal to Japan who wanted to be repatriated, (2) provide suitable transportation for bringing them to the point of embarkation, (3) pay for their participation in the exchanges, and (4) guarantee their safety until they boarded the exchange ships. Most importantly, (5) each Japanese-American seeking repatriation had to be matched with an American civilian in Japan.

Under these conditions, the decision to create war relocation centers would prove to be not only a convenient method for locating and gathering those Japanese citizens and American citizens of Japanese ancestry who wished to return to Japan, but the centers would be in charge of transportation, cover living costs, and even more importantly could provide a secure environment for the exchangees to live in prior to their repatriation. During the spring of 1942, the governors of ten Western states had even requested that the Japanese-Americans be "under constant military watch." This meant that the "WRA had no choice but to build centers where evacuees would be concentrated and under constant guard." Furthermore, these locations were "situated away from industrial areas" so that national security might not be put at risk.[22]

One of the most prolific critics of the relocation program points to the opinions expressed at the governors' meeting as a sign of white racism against the Japanese, and concludes that it was at this point that "it seemed clear to [Milton] Eisenhower and other WRA officials that for the majority of the evacuated people close confinement would be necessary." Instead of a rapid evacuation and immediate resettlement, long-term confinement in the relocation centers was necessary. According to this opinion, the fact that the quick option was not tried "was not so much a failure of imagination but rather a direct result of the preconceptions about nonwhites in general and about Japanese in particular held by most Americans, up to and including the Commander in Chief."[23]

Such criticism ignores the commitments made by the U.S. government many weeks prior to the governors' meeting promising the Japanese government to guarantee the security of the Japanese-Americans who requested repatriation to Japan, as well as promising that they would not be housed in strategic areas that might become targets for bombing or some other form of attack. Most importantly, it was at the relocation centers that in-depth interviews could be held in order to determine who wished to be repatriated, and then determine their social background to satisfy the Japanese government.

As later U.S.–Japanese diplomatic exchanges would reveal, the war relocation centers were in many ways a direct outgrowth of these early U.S. promises for reciprocity and to ensure that the Japanese exchangees "at all times be afforded adequate police protection."[24] To protect the evacuees from possible harassment, on 13 August 1942, Henry L. Stimson, Secretary of War, issued Public Proclamation No. WD 1 stating that "No persons" other than the internees and the authorized personnel of the relocation centers "shall enter any of such War Relocation Project Areas except under written authorization . . . [and] which said authorization shall set forth the effective period thereof and the terms and conditions upon and purposes for which it has been granted."[25]

The final U.S.–Japanese exchange agreement

The most comprehensive American exchange proposal was dated 26 December 1941 and arrived in Japan on 5 January 1942. The American proposals were largely adopted in the final U.S.–Japanese exchange agreement. Later, they were also applied across the board to the exchange of South American, Central American, and Canadian diplomats; Great Britain also negotiated its own exchange with Japan based on the U.S. agreement. This early document eventually became the basic plan for the exchange agreement for non-official exchangees as well.

In this 26 December document, the various points were broken down into sixteen distinct sections. Section 1 repeated many of the details of the exchange, as listed above, but did make a new offer: "To the extent that may be desired by the other interested governments, there may be embarked on this vessel the diplomatic, consular, and official personnel of the Japanese Government, together with their dependents, staffs, and personal effects in territory under control of any of the other governments in the Americas including Canada which have now or may by the time of the exchange have broken relations with the Japanese Government."[26]

As time would show, this U.S. offer to negotiate on behalf of the Central American and Canadian governments, in return for Japan including Manchukuo and occupied China on its side of the exchange, would greatly complicate the exchange process. However, when the foreign ministers of most of the Western Hemisphere governments met in Rio de Janeiro in January 1942, they supported this policy. By April 1942 a large number of "enemy aliens, diplomatic and consular personnel, and private citizens" were beginning to arrive in the United States; according to one account, 2,264 Latin-American-Japanese were involved in the program.[27]

The second and third points repeated previous messages, specifying that the evacuees could take their personal belongings, albeit "subject to such limitations as may be imposed by availability of space on the vessel and the arrival of the effects at the point of embarkation in time to be laden aboard the vessel." In addition, none of the government officials would be subject to a search of "any kind" and this "shall likewise be true of their accompanying dependents and staffs and of their personal effects."[28]

Points 4, 5, and 8 were necessarily vague, stating that the exchange would be by ship and that it would "proceed to the point agreed upon and return along courses the detail of which will be later communicated." The selected ship would "proceed unarmed without convoy under the safe conduct of the belligerent governments" to the point of exchange. The U.S. government requested, however, that included among its official personnel should be the "personnel of the United States court at Shanghai, the Marine Guards remaining in China and there under the protection of international agreement, and all employees of the various branches of the Government of the United States in the Far Eastern areas under the military control of the Japanese Government." Finally, the ships "will proceed to the point agreed upon and return along courses the details of which will be later communicated without stopping at any port en route."[29]

Later, when Japan refused to include the Marine Guards among the evacuees, Washington acknowledged Japan's view but stated: "The United States Government may revert to this point at a later date."[30] On 19 February 1942, the Japanese government attempted to confirm the American view on the Marine Guards: "The Japanese Government gather that the United States Government do not insist on inclusion of the Marine Guards in China in the present exchange."[31] In response, on 17 March 1942, the U.S. government said that it "expects the Japanese Government to take cognizance of their true status as diplomatic guards."[32]

However, at almost the same time that they deadlocked on the Marine Guards—on 14 March 1942—the U.S. government asked Japan whether it would be willing to abide by the 1929 Geneva Convention detailing the exchange of prisoners of war. Although the U.S. Marines stationed in Shanghai were not mentioned by name, this might have been what Washington had in mind. In fact, the Japanese government's view that the Marines were military personnel—rather than diplomatic personnel—could have made them eligible for a POW exchange under this provision of the Geneva Convention.[33] It is unclear when a final determination was made regarding the Marine Guards.

Sections 6 and 7 repeated earlier points from December 1941, specifically that the evacuees "will be allowed to take with them their personal effects subject to such limitations as may be imposed by availability of space on the vessel and arrival of the effects at the port or ports of embarkation in time to be laden aboard the vessel." As for searches, since the officials were "representatives of the United States or any of the other American Governments in Japan or elsewhere" the evacuees "will not be subjected by the Japanese Authorities to search of any kind and this shall likewise be true of their accompanying dependents and staffs and of their personal effects."[34]

Points 9, 10, and 11 were new. The first suggested that: "Identical facilities and privileges" should be accorded to representatives of those "American Governments which have now or may before the time of the exchange have broken diplomatic relations with Japan." The second stated that among those to be exchanged would be "accredited representatives of the press including radio reporters and press photographers whose identity shall be suitably notified." Finally, the United States government expressed its agreement "that there take place at the point agreed upon for the exchange of American and Japanese personnel a simultaneous exchange to be negotiated separately by the British and Japanese Governments of British and associated personnel and Japanese and associated personnel."[35] Each of these three new points were to entail enormous complications and delays in the civilian exchange process once they had to be applied in practice.

Points 12, 13, and 14 concerned safe conduct and payment of the exchange vessels. Specifically, point 12 stated that each participating government "shall on its own behalf guarantee safe conduct for the duly notified vessel concerned in the exchange throughout their voyage." In addition, each government would "obtain a similar assurance of safe conduct from other belligerent[s] friendly to it." Point 13 stated that once all proper safe conduct guarantees had been received, then the "Swiss and Spanish Governments ... shall at the proper time notify the Government providing each vessel that all necessary safe conducts have been received in order that such vessel may commence its voyage." Finally, according to point 14: "The Government providing each vessel in the exchange shall meet the expenses incident to the operation of the vessel throughout its voyage."[36]

The final two sections—15 and 16—were also new, and concerned those governments and groups that were to monitor the exchange. According to 15, representatives from the Swiss and Spanish governments "shall travel on each vessel," "shall have unrestricted use of the radio facilities of the vessel for communication in plain language with their respective governments in matters concerning the execution of the exchange agreement and the voyage of the vessel," and: "None of the other passengers shall be permitted any use whatever of the radio facilities of the vessel." Monitoring the entire exchange process would be the Red Cross, and point 16 stated: "There may be accommodated on the vessels traveling in either direction properly accredited personnel of the international red cross committee or other red cross societies."[37]

Although the main goal of the exchange was to return U.S. and Japanese officials and their families to their homelands, the exchange of government officials included citizens of many other allied or occupied countries as well. The Amercian proposals made the extensive nature of the exchange clear when it ended by stating: "A summary of the foregoing will be communicated to all the United States diplomatic Missions in the Americas and to the American Embassy in London with the request that it be communicated where appropriate to the Governments to which those Missions are accredited with the offer to make the arrangement arising therefrom available for the return to America of American and to Europe of British and Associated Diplomatic Consular and other official Personnel with their dependents, staff, and personal effects and the return to Japan of corresponding official personnel of Japan and Associated Governments."[38]

Finally, as a reassurance to Japan that its citizens would be well treated, the U.S. note ended: "The Government of the United States will furthermore suggest that none of the governments in the Americas which may request participation in the arrangements adopt toward the personnel of the Japanese and Associated Governments an attitude less favorable than that which the Government of the United States is extending."[39] This final point was notable in that it was similar to "most-favored-nations" clauses often included in international treaties with Asian countries, except in reverse since the U.S. government was attempting to set a high standard for treatment of the Japanese citizens that the other governments would then be obliged to follow. This offer was later to cause a certain degree of diplomatic friction, since the U.S. government unwittingly obliged itself to assume diplomatic responsibility for the treatment of Japanese nationals by other countries not under the direct authority of Washington.

The U.S. proposal dated 26 December 1941 both "widened" the scope of the exchanges, by including Japanese from Central American and South American countries, and "deepened" it, by offering to include POWs in the exchange. In addition to allowing virtually unlimited luggage and promising that there would be no searches, this proposal offered to provide "safe conduct" to all ships involved in the exchange. While easily accomplished during the first exchange of government officials, such promises were to be harder and harder to honor as the war developed.

Geographical considerations

Geography was to play a large role in the U.S.–Japanese exchange program, since Japanese-Americans on the East Coast of the continental U.S. were too few in number, but transporting large numbers of Japanese-Americans from Hawaii all the way to New York City was simply not feasible in wartime. Statistics on the Japanese-American population along the West Coast may have helped government officials decide to make this area the focus of their efforts to find Japanese-Americans willing to volunteer for repatriation.

Many of the West Coast Japanese-Americans considered themselves to be temporary residents in the United States. According to one study conducted in the mid-1930s, 76 percent of Japanese farm laborers, 53 percent of Japanese urban workers, 40 percent of Japanese farm owners, and only 38 percent of the Japanese businessmen living in the U.S. stated that their intention was to return to Japan.[40] Virtually all of the Japanese-American farmers and farm laborers lived on the West Coast, with the highest single number in California, so the greatest source of volunteers would clearly need to be there; Hawaii was also a good source, of course, but the cost of transport to the East Coast embarkation site was prohibitively expensive and the trip was too time-consuming and dangerous.

There may have been a correlation between education levels and loyalty, with the more educated Japanese on the average preferring the U.S. over Japan. As early as 1914, this correlation was commented on by one American scholar, who noted that while Japanese who studied in Europe "returned to Japan confirmed in their patriotism and highly critical of other lands, … those who had studied in America were highly critical of Japan and laudatory of America." Furthermore, this affected "Japanese merchants and farmers, too, who have spent a number of years in America or Hawaii, [and] find their ideals of life so transformed that a return to their own land is accompanied with no little pain."[41] According to one study published in 1949, almost 18,000 of the Japanese-American males located in the three western states worked in agriculture, with almost 10,000 of these being categorized as farm laborers. A bonus of focusing on farm laborers for repatriation was that on the average two-thirds were unmarried, and so did not have family obligations keeping them in the United States.[42] Based on analysis of the evacuees at Tule Lake, for example, the group that was most likely to want to return to Japan would be uneducated non-Christian single male farm laborers from the West Coast. In fact, in studies of the *Kibei*, second generation but Japanese-educated, males at Tule Lake, it was shown that fully 78.9 percent of this group chose segregation from the other Japanese-Americans who professed loyalty to the United States.[43] Many of these also requested repatriation back to Japan.

This subgroup alone—unmarried Japanese-American farm laborers living in the three western states—numbered around 7,000, and if 76 percent of them agreed to repatriate then these 5,000 volunteers alone might have been sufficient to be exchanged for every U.S. citizen being held by Japan. As a matter of fact, it has been reported that "80 percent of the *Kibei* and 60 percent of the Nisei, 17.5 years of age and over at Tule Lake (over 5,000 citizens), renounced their citizenship."[44] Clearly it was from this group that were to come most of the candidates that the U.S. government planned to offer to the Japanese government in exchange for U.S. citizens being detained in Japan.

Conclusions

The framework developed to exchange officials would largely dictate the exchange of non-officials. Within weeks of Pearl Harbor, the United States and Japan had negotiated a process for the exchange of official government employees and had begun the task of discussing the exchange of non-officials. Many of the conditions that applied quite logically to the exchange of officials did not, with hindsight, apply equally conveniently to non-officials. In particular, determining their numbers, their locations, and providing security proved to be daunting tasks. Once non-officials requesting repatriation were located, they then had to be made "reciprocal" with the Japanese exchangees in terms of numbers and social status.

Early in this process, Washington decided to utilize the war relocation centers to act as the administrative focus for housing, interviewing, and protecting those Japanese citizens and U.S. citizens of Japanese ancestry who requested repatriation. Once Japanese-Americans arrived at the relocation centers they were counted, registered, and interviewed to determine whether they wished to remain in the United States or return to Japan. A surprisingly high number—well over 20,000, or almost one-fifth of the Japanese-American population in the continental United States and almost 10 percent of the entire Japanese-American population in the U.S. counting Hawaii—would eventually request repatriation.

During the course of World War II, only about 3,000 Japanese were repatriated, but many of these came from other countries in the Western Hemisphere, and so the number of Japanese-Americans participating in the exchange was far fewer than expected. After the war ended, about 5,000 more Japanese aliens and U.S. citizens of Japanese ancestry returned to Japan. Of this total number of around 8,000, fully 4,724, or just over half, came from the war relocation centers. Of this number, 1,659 were Japanese citizens, 1,949 were American citizens, of whom "all but 100 were children under twenty years of age accompanying parents," while another 1,116 were adults who renounced their U.S. citizenship.[45] Thus, the war relocation centers played a crucial role in the U.S.–Japanese exchange program. Many of the administrative requirements demanded by Japan made the creation of the war relocation centers the only practicable way to comply. In particular, Tokyo's demand that Washington protect all Japanese-Americans seeking to return to Japan could not be acted upon efficiently without creating a security structure similar in many ways to the relocation centers.

As the next chapter will discuss in greater depth, the need for creating war relocation centers to provide security became more and more evident during early 1942 once non-officials were included in the U.S.–Japanese exchange program. Tensions arising from including non-officials in this program, if not resolved through diplomacy, threatened to undermine the official exchange as well. Only through intensive negotiations was the U.S.–Japanese exchange program able to pave the way for its first shipload of officials and non-officials.

2 Non-officials and the U.S.– Japanese exchange agreement

The previous chapter discussed U.S.–Japanese negotiations on exchanging officials and how the specific terms and phrases used impacted exchanges of non-officials. On 30 December 1941, the Japanese government issued Memorandum 42, which outlined its basic proposals for conducting future U.S.–Japanese exchanges of government officials.[1] For the first time, Tokyo also included among those groups its list of preferred categories of Japanese non-officials. One category was journalists. This was specifically mentioned in the 1929 Geneva Convention. But other categories included regular citizens, among them "treaty merchants," "scholars," and "students." The very nature of these categories in late 1941 meant that they would be mainly, if not completely, educated males, and probably from the samurai—or formerly noble—class. A high proportion of these would be qualified either to bear arms on behalf of Japan, or to work in the civilian sectors of the Japanese war effort. On the U.S. side, its top choices included teachers, missionaries, women, and children, with the latter two groups being given top priority for an earlier return; such people could have relatively little impact on the U.S war effort.

This Japanese memorandum appears to have crossed in the mail the American proposal dated 26 December 1941, discussed above, which subsequently seems to have become the basis of the exchange agreement. However, Tokyo's proposal to exchange selected groups of non-officials was quickly accepted by Washington, which had first brought up this possibility on 8 December 1941. When the American government responded to Memorandum 42 during early February 1942, it became clear that the exchange agreement negotiations had shifted in an entirely new direction: instead of discussing only the exchange of government officials, non-officials—presumably ordinary Japanese and American citizens who found themselves trapped in the other country by the outbreak of hostilities—would now be included in the exchanges.

Strictly speaking, the exchange of non-officials on a one-to-one basis was not covered by the Geneva Convention of 1929, which focused on military prisoners of war. Therefore, it was initially unclear to American and Japanese negotiators whether the treatment for officials and non-officials should be the same, or whether non-officials should be accorded fewer guarantees. This lack of clarity led to endless diplomatic conflicts concerning the exchange of non-officials.

The decision to include non-officials in the exchange

Memorandum 42, in addition to agreeing to the basic exchange plan of sending ships to Lourenço Marques, attached a detailed list of which Japanese citizens the Japanese government wished to be evacuated. When the U.S. responded to this memorandum on 9 February 1942, it stated that "in addition to the official personnel of the several Governments the United States Government is furthermore agreeable to the repatriation of all other nonofficial persons referred to in this portion of the basic proposal of the Japanese Government."[2] This positive exchange of memoranda opened the door for a much wider exchange than had been previously envisioned.

It may have simply been a coincidence, but just four days after this breakthrough, on 13 February 1942, J.L. DeWitt, who was in charge of security along the West Coast, wrote to the Secretary of War recommending that "(a) Japanese aliens, (b) Japanese American citizens, (c) Alien enemies other than Japanese aliens" be evacuated from the West Coast. Categories (a) and (c) would be interned under guard, while those in category (b) could join those in category (a) in the internment centers, or could leave the exclusion zones voluntarily and be "left to their own resources," or "be encouraged to accept resettlement outside of such military areas with such assistances as the State governments concerned or the Federal Security Agency may be by that time prepared to offer."[3]

While it is impossible to know for sure whether U.S. government officials made the association at this time, or whether this happened only later, as soon as the relocation centers were authorized and built they also became one of the prime means of locating Japanese citizens and U.S. citizens of Japanese ancestry who wished to return to Japan. If the war relocation centers had never been established, then something very similar to them would have been required to administer those Japanese-Americans who sought repatriation back to Japan.

In particular, the U.S. war relocation centers have been criticized for including women and children, instead of just male members of the Japanese-American community. However, on 30 December 1941, the Japanese government specifically stated that women and children had to be included in the unofficial exchange. Tokyo proposed that "temporary residents" and in particular "among permanent residents the women and children who desire to return to their country," as well as "those in special circumstances," be allowed to participate in the exchange. This meant that women and children could not be ignored, even though at this time the Japanese government estimated that there would be only a small number of non-officials—fewer than 300 in total—to be evacuated from "the United States, Hawaii and the Philippines."[4]

On 15 January 1942, a fuller explanation was telegraphed listing diplomatic personnel, their staff, and non-permanent and permanent residents. When explaining the difference between non-permanent residents and permanent residents, this Japanese document stated that non-permanent residents included quasi-officials, employees of public organizations, correspondents, employees of businesses and banks, missionaries, scholars, students, and "research fellows dispatched by respective governments." Meanwhile, from those listed as "permanent residents" only "women and children desiring to return home and persons who have special reasons" would be included in the exchange. In a slight change from the earlier message, this document explained: "Those belong[ing] to the above four categories are to be included in the exchange without regard to number or usefulness or otherwise in the prosecution of war."[5]

After receiving an additional American inquiry on the inclusion of non-permanent residents, the Japanese Foreign Ministry confirmed orally on 28 January 1942 to the Swiss Minister in Tokyo that the Japanese government was "particularly insistent that non-permanent residents ... be included among officials to be exchanged." Negotiators pointed out that in the United States even the thought of trying to locate the Japanese non-permanent residents, much less determine whether they wanted to be repatriated, was a daunting task because of the size of the country, the number of Japanese-Americans, and their wide dispersal. But the Japanese Foreign Ministry responded: "Inconveniences which American Government might foresee are same for Japan since proposal based on reciprocity."[6]

The Japanese government made its desires even more clear on 19 February 1942: "The Japanese Government understand that Japanese non-official persons belonging to the category mentioned in 1(b) [the so-called "treaty merchants"] of their Basic Proposal and residing in countries in the Americas including Canada which have broke relations with Japanese be embarked on the Exchange vessel. The Japanese Government, on their part, will embark such non-official nationals of those American countries residing in Japan, Manchukuo, China etcetera."[7]

In fact Japan was trying to exchange specific non-official Japanese citizens for non-specific non-official American citizens. This was not really reciprocal at all. Furthermore, the exchange was to include American citizens detained in the Japanese puppet state of Manchukuo, as well as in occupied China, while on America's side Washington was obliged to help repatriate Japanese from Canada, Central America, and South America, unoccupied sovereign countries. This was a much more difficult task, since each of these countries had sovereign governments that needed to agree to the exchange arrangements in advance, or else they would not participate.

On 7 February 1942, the U.S. government stated that it was "agreeable to the repatriation of all other non-official persons referred to in this portion of the basic proposal of the Japanese Government." However, this would be "subject to the capacity of the vessel to accommodate such persons after all official personnel has been accommodated." But the door was left open for future exchanges, since the State Department then offered: "Should the Japanese Government desire a further repatriation of persons who cannot be accommodated on the vessel to be used at this time, the United States Government will give consideration to the matter."[8]

But an entirely different problem soon arose: how to identify potential candidates for exchange. As early as 7 December 1941 the Japanese government ordered that in all territories controlled by Japan: "In addition to such police surveillance and protection as is necessary, individuals regarding whom there is ample ground for suspicion will be rounded up; and all military men, seamen, or aviation personnel as well as those qualified for these services, persons of special technical skill, persons suspected of being foreign spies, and all males between 18 and 45 will for the present be placed under arrest."[9]

Unlike in Japan, or in the other Asian countries where Japanese troops had invaded, and where Caucasian foreigners were easy to identify and where virtually all male American citizens were quickly rounded up and put into detention camps, in the United States the vast majority of Japanese non-permanent and permanent residents were not only unregistered, but their exact location was also unknown. In most cases, the U.S. government did not have any idea where the Japanese nationals mentioned in Memorandum 42 were living.

Also, unlike in Japan, China, and Manchukuo, where the maximum number of Americans was in the thousands, there were well over 200,000 persons of Japanese citizenry or U.S. citizens of Japanese descent living in the continental United States, in Hawaii, and in Alaska. Of these, many were *bona fide* American citizens by birth, while others were technically guest workers, illegal immigrants, or the above-mentioned "non-permanent residents" who were—in theory at least—only in the U.S. to study or work, but who might desire to remain permanently; meanwhile, within this vast group there was an uncounted and largely anonymous number of both Japanese citizens and American citizens of Japanese ancestry who wished to be repatriated to Japan.

The problems involved with locating and repatriating those loyal to Japan became especially clear in a telegram transmitted through Madrid dated 12 February 1942, in which the U.S. State Department stated that "to include in the exchange non official persons whose repatriation is desired by the Japanese Government the Spanish Embassy must inform the State Department as promptly as possible or [not] less than one week before eventual departure of vessel to be used for exchange of names and addresses of all Japanese national who want to return to Japan stating for each his classification and the terms of the exchange arrangement."[10] The Japanese government, however, did not have this information. Tokyo clearly expected the U.S. government to undertake the task of locating, interviewing, and transporting to a central location those loyal to Japan who wanted to be repatriated.

The February–April 1942 Japanese notes

Once both governments agreed to include non-officials, then the exchange program overnight became more complex; instead of a one-time exchange, multiple exchanges using multiple ships were now envisioned. On 19 February 1942, in a communication entitled "Further Observations of the Japanese Government," the Japanese government acknowledged "that the United States Government are agreeable to the inclusion in the exchange of all non-official persons referred to in 1 (b) of their Basic Proposal." The Japanese also asked that the U.S. government concur with the proposal that: "As regards repatriation of non-official persons, the Japanese Government consider it essential that both Governments should select vessels without delay to accommodate such persons who cannot be accommodated on the First Exchange vessels so that all the persons concerned would be repatriated within reasonably short space of time."[11]

Even while agreeing with the U.S. government to the exchange of non-official evacuees, and pushing for this repatriation within a reasonably short time, the Japanese government did not immediately respond to the State Department's request to provide names and addresses of all of its priority non-officials. It is extremely likely that the Japanese themselves did not have this information available, since the number of Japanese in the United States was large and very fluid; also, the vast majority of Japanese-Americans—in other words, the quantity—lived on the West Coast, while the majority of Japanese businessmen and students—the quality, in terms of social status—were located on the East Coast.

This problem was highlighted on 14 March 1942, in a telegram transferred through Madrid that concerned the repatriation of Japanese non-officials. Although unsigned, it would appear to be from the Japanese Ambassador assigned to Washington, who was in charge of the evacuation of Japanese officials. In this telegram he informed Tokyo that there did not seem to be "over 400" either "non permanent residents as well as those permanent residents who are desirous of returning to Japan for special reasons." Most of these belonged under the category "former treaty merchants."[12]

This telegram expressed the hope that they could all be repatriated at the same time, but acknowledged the difficulty of doing so: even though the Spanish Embassy was trying to compile a list based on the American sources, this telegram furthermore requested that the "Japanese Government will also make a list in consultation with the head officers of those firms concerned."[13] In other words, the Japanese Ambassador in the United States himself clearly did not have all of the necessary information and was hoping to receive the names and addresses from Japan.

To make matters worse, from December 1941 onward the Japanese government had a clearly defined hierarchy of who should be repatriated and in what order. First came officials, followed by journalists. Thereafter, on 2 April 1942, it reiterated its exact preferences for all other non-official Japanese. First on the list were "treaty merchants," and in particular those who worked for "banks" and "Japanese companies," and their families. Second on the list were the "other" treaty merchants not connected with banks and major companies, and their families. Third came Japanese travelers who had been passing through the

United States when the war broke out. Fourth came professors and their families. Fifth came Japanese students and their families. Sixth came religious representatives and their families. Seventh came permanent residents with a special reason to return and their families. Finally, in eighth place came "women and children" who were permanent residents, followed in last place by male permanent residents.[14] No specific mention was made of farmers and farm laborers, who otherwise might fit in the eighth and final category.

The Japanese government's top priority was clearly to regain its "treaty merchants" first. Such men were usually quite wealthy and enjoyed a high status in Japanese society—often as hereditary members of the former noble, or samurai, class—and they were also in a position to know more about the United States and its military capabilities than anyone else. According to a recent book that has reprinted MAGIC intercepts, some of these men may have even worked in factories linked to the defense industry.[15] Their unique knowledge would have been very helpful to the Japanese government during wartime, which would explain the high priority placed on their rapid repatriation. For this same reason, of course, the U.S. Justice Department was reluctant to part with these candidates for repatriation.

Understandably, the Japanese government's highest priority was to repatriate as many commercial representatives from major Japanese companies as possible. This was not as easy to do as it might first appear, since the U.S. government put the various treaty merchants into one of three categories. For example, the Japanese Ambassador reported that "legal proceedings for those now interned in camps will be finished soon," and that all non-official detainees would be classified into one of three groups: (1) unconditional release; (2) parole with or without bond; and (3) "detention for the duration of the war." As summarized by this telegram: "It seems very difficult to arrange repatriation of class (3)."[16]

The number of merchants put into category (3) was not small. Various U.S. government agencies objected to releasing "approximately 2,000" of "the approximately 6,000 persons designated by the Japanese Government for repatriation."[17] In the case of one employee of Mitsui & Co., located in Seattle, Washington, who had left the company after 20 years' service so as to avoid returning to Japan, he was still refused parole and was interned because he was "alleged by two former employees of Japanese Consulate at Seattle to be 'in effect an agent of a foreign principal.'"[18]

In many cases, it was exactly the individuals listed by the Japanese government that various groups in the U.S. government, including the Alien Enemy Control Unit of the Department of Justice, the Federal Bureau of Investigation, and the Military and Naval Intelligence, wanted to stop from returning. If it were practicable, substituting West Coast Japanese-Americans—who were largely farmers and farm laborers—would be preferable to sending back these well-placed candidates.

Tokyo time after time showed its eagerness to obtain the return of these highly ranked groups. The Japanese government officials in the United States even requested assistance from Tokyo on deciding which treaty merchants were considered most important. One communication explained that it would be best if a "separate ship be arranged for repatriation of diplomatic and consulate staffs and other Japanese nationals in South America," but if this was impossible then: "In case it turns out to be impossible to take back all of the former treaty merchants kindly advise us how the Japanese Government is going to decide who shall and who shall not be repatriated simultaneously with us."[19]

During mid-March 1942, the Japanese Ambassador to the U.S. urged on the Japanese government the "speedy conclusion of repatriation arrangements," because of the "increasingly depressing effect of the life of virtual imprisonment on the morale" of officials and non-officials alike, especially those "Japanese internees at camp Upton Fong Island including representatives of influential firms in New York [who] are subjected to military treatment." In concluding, the Ambassador wrote: "I therefore feel it incumbent upon me to arrange for the repatriation of every one of these merchants simultaneously with us [the diplomats] in spite of all technical and other difficulties."[20]

Tokyo's desire to repatriate as many treaty merchants as possible on the first exchange ship ran into several roadblocks. First, the Japanese Ambassador did not have complete information on who these merchants were, nor did he have their addresses. Second, the U.S. government realized the dangers inherent in letting well-informed merchants return to Japan and blocked the departure of many of them. Third, many of them declined to return to Japan. Finally, Tokyo's failure or perhaps its inability to provide specific details on which citizens it wanted repatriated put pressure on Washington to come up with its own solution to the problem.

Part of this solution clearly involved the Japanese-American war relocation centers, which were organized beginning in mid-March 1942, at approximately that same time. The centers were used to provide what was hoped would be suitable substitutes for those Japanese on Tokyo's lists who were not being allowed to return or had declined repatriation. This issue related to the differing priorities the U.S. and Japanese governments had on what type of non-officials they wanted to exchange.

The U.S. government's priorities for exchanging non-officials

The Japanese and the American governments hoped to attain different goals with the exchange of non-officials. As shown above, the Japanese government's hierarchical treatment of its own people, which gave higher priority to businessmen, those from well-known families, and those with an insider's knowledge of their enemy—such as professors and students—accounted for its prioritization. As for the U.S. government, it was extremely cautious to treat all non-official American evacuees equally, irrespective of personal wealth or social standing. This difference ultimately meant that Tokyo was much more picky than Washington about which evacuees it would accept.

In sharp contrast to Japan's priorities, which put merchants, scholars, and students near the top of the list, but women and children near the bottom, the U.S. government was more egalitarian. In fact, one document clearly stated that: "The United States Government does not desire to indicate any degree of priority for the repatriation of its nationals as between individuals." Once all U.S. officials, officials from other American republics and Canada, journalists and their families, and then Red Cross personnel and their families were exchanged, then the U.S. government made it clear that "women, children and the aged, and infirm should be given priority."[21]

When there were differences among these groups, top priority was accorded to American citizens not by rank but by circumstances. For example, the highest priority was given: "To those persons whose presence appears to be objectionable to the Japanese authorities as evidenced by their having been arrested or interned." The second highest should be given to people interned from Thailand, Indochina, and Hong Kong, who had to face some of the worst conditions in hot and over-crowded detentions camps. The third should be given to those interned far away from Shanghai and Tokyo, in places like Dairen, Harbin, Mukden, Hankow, Nanking, Hainan Island, Tsinan, Keijo, Tsingtao, Amoy, Swatow, and Chefoo. Finally, once American citizens interned in Shanghai and Tokyo were being considered, then it repeated again that top priority should go to "women and children dependents of nonpermanent residents."[22]

For American citizens who lived in China, there was also a U.S. group called "Quasi Officials." These included "Officers and employees of the Municipal Council of the Shanghai International settlement, officers and employees of the Chinese maritime customs, Chinese postal administration, Chinese salt gabelle, and advisors to the Chinese Government, and their dependents." Also, under this category were "Officers and employees of American organizations: commercial, religious, philanthropic, etc., sent out from the United States by such organizations."[23]

Finally, one U.S. government memorandum stated: "It is desired that the selection of persons to be repatriated under the categories set forth above shall be made by the Swiss representatives and it is expected that they will, in case of doubt, be afforded facilities for conferring with the officials of this Government." Additionally: "It is further expected that the Japanese Government will in every way facilitate communications between the Swiss representative and American nationals in order that the latter may be fully apprised of the opportunity for their repatriation and the conditions which have been laid down in the agreement for the exchange."[24]

A final consideration that did not usually affect the Japanese government was the number of American citizens married to non-Americans or those of alien origin. Gwen Terasaki, one of the few Caucasians to be the spouse of a Japanese diplomat who returned to Japan on the first exchange ship, commented on how she was frequently mistaken in Japan for a German, since it seemed inconceivable to many Japanese that she could be an American.[25] By contrast, many Americans were married to non-Americans. On 27 April 1942, Secretary of State Hull clarified that "alien spouses of European or oriental origin," all "alien minor children," "alien parents where presence of parent is essential to welfare of children," and finally even "alien nurse, companion or servant (except Orientals) accompanying American employer, provided presence certified by physician as necessary."[26]

As these communications show, the U.S. government was not attempting to secure the return of specific people from specific socio-economic groups. Instead, it first emphasized locality, by trying to repatriate detainees who were in tropical regions or were outside of major cities, and therefore had little or no access to modern medical facilities. However, once these groups had been taken care of, then its next highest priority was to try to repatriate as many women and children as possible.

During the first exchange, for example, the male members of the U.S. embassy and consular staff were reported to "have forgone the more desirable accommodations which in other circumstances would have been available to them, in order that as many as possible of the women and children and persons in poor physical condition might travel more comfortably."[27] This behavior was in sharp contrast to the Japanese attitude: Gwen Terasaki even commented on how staterooms were distributed on the Japanese exchange ship according to the status of the particular official, and how as a result she and her husband were provided with a superior room.[28] When traveling alone, Japanese women and children were accorded a particularly low status.

Problems with the Japanese lists

As early as December 1941, the Japanese government had informed the U.S. government where its priorities lay when it provided Washington with a list of types of candidates to be repatriated. As the June 1942 departure of the first exchange ship, *Gripsholm*, neared, last minute complications arose over the exact composition of its list, specifically over which Japanese were available for repatriation. According to a Japanese telegram dated 3 June 1942, by "omitting a large number of Japanese who are entitled to priority [the American list] fails to no small extent to conform with the policy set for by the Imperial Japanese Government." Threatening to delay the exchanges indefinitely, the Japanese suggested that the names be checked once again, and that in the meantime the two countries should "withhold the departure of the exchange vessel from both ends."[29]

A separate telegram from Tokyo listed the discrepancies that most concerned the Japanese. In some cases the American numbers were too large, and in others too small. For example, instead of only 51 non-officials from the U.S. there were 56, and instead of only 18 merchants and students there were 36. However, of the 10 Canadian merchants only one was listed, instead of 23 Japanese from Mexico there were none, instead of five from Panama and Costa Rica there were none, instead of 14 from Peru, Ecuador, and Bolivia there were only 10, and instead of five from Colombia there were none.[30]

This situation angered the Japanese. In a separate telegram, they expressed concern that *Gripsholm*'s limited capacity of 1,558 passengers might be inadequate to take both the New York City and Rio de Janeiro contingents. Therefore, with regard to 150 "former treaty merchants, students and others" who did not fit into the categories the Japanese had specified as priority evacuees, Tokyo concluded that "it is necessary to request that these one hundred and fifty persons be dropped." This telegram further criticized the U.S. government: "As is evident by discrepencies noted above, it is clear that the State Department list fails to no little extent to conform with policy of the Imperial Government, regarding the order of priority which they have transmitted to the United States Government."[31]

On 1 June 1942, the State Department sent to Karl Bendetsen, the head of the Wartime Civil Control Administration (WCCA), a list of 539 Japanese identified by the Japanese government as potential exchangees for the first sailing of *Gripsholm*. Previously, on 20 February, Secretary of War Henry L. Stimson had designated Lt. General John L. DeWitt as head of the Western Defense Command, and then on 11 March, DeWitt created the WCCA as a sub-unit of this Command and appointed Colonel Karl R. Bendetsen as its military director. Since the train trip to the East Coast would take five days, and the ship was scheduled to leave on 11 June, this left little time to locate and interview these people. While the WCCA determined that 176 were in their jurisdiction, they could talk with only 101 of these, and of this number 41 declined to be repatriated and another six were ineligible. On 6 June, therefore, a total of 54 of the 539 people listed by the Japanese were put on a train from California for New York.[32]

On 8 June 1942, the Japanese government threatened once again to postpone the exchange if the lists provided by the American government could not be made to conform to Japan's priorities:

> Until negotiations reach satisfactory results, it may be necessary to postpone the departure of the exchange vessel. However, as a practical problem, it is impossible for the Foreign Office to determine who would, and who should, not board the first exchange vessel, for it is evident that the Foreign Office does not know names of many of Japanese residents. It is therefore considered practical and advisable that determination of list be entrusted to joint consideration of Japanese representation at White Sulphur Springs and the Spanish Embassy.[33]

An explanation of these apparent differences appeared on 16 June 1942, when Washington informed Tokyo that: "139 names on the original Japanese list of April 9th are not on present sailing list because many persons had refused, [while] others could not be located. However, there had been placed aboard vessel 105 persons who most, if not all, had subsequent to April 9th, been requested by the Spanish Embassy to be placed aboard ship."[34]

The ship was held in port for over a week while this conflict was ironed out. According to a Japanese passenger on *Gripsholm*: "We found out later that the Japanese government had withheld the sailing of *Asama Maru* at Yokohama and *Conte Verde* at Shanghai until all the Japanese nationals were on *Gripsholm*. That took eight days of boiling hot sun in New York harbor with the boat filled to capacity." The trip to southern Africa was uneventful, albeit long and dull.[35] The Japanese government eventually backed down and accepted the American changes to its preferred list. A total of 1,500 passengers departed on the first voyage of *Gripsholm*. Of these, 1,083 embarked in New York and an additional 417 embarked at Rio de Janeiro; the only non-Japanese included 18 Thai nationals who boarded the ship in New York.

Conclusions

As the deadline for the first exchange neared, both the Japanese and U.S. governments tried to include additional priority evacuees on their lists, while withholding or threatening to withhold certain key persons from the other country's list. At times, Japanese and American names were traded, almost like baseball cards. In June 1942, several last minute controversies threatened to delay the exchanges indefinitely. These included the medical condition of Mrs. Sato and the status of three Americans, one named McKinnon and a married couple by the name of Lane, and three Japanese, the first named Ichiro Matsudaira and two other unnamed evacuees.

One of the final stumbling blocks between Washington and Tokyo prior to the first exchange was the case of Mrs. Satsu Sato, the wife of the former chancellor of the Japanese consulate in San Francisco. According to an American note dated 2 June 1942, Mrs. Sato suffered from tuberculosis. Her doctor's advice was quoted: "Mrs. Sato's tuberculosis is in a highly contagious state. She must be at all times under hospital isolation precautions." Therefore, according to a request by the U.S. State Department, if Mrs. Sato were to be moved to New York and evacuated on the first exchange ship, then the "Japanese Government will assume responsibility for any possible consequences of voyage by this invalid."[36] The Japanese government eventually backed down on its request that she be included.

However, the Japanese government first notified the U.S. government on 15 June 1942, immediately before the *Gripsholm* was to set sail, that three American citizens were not being evacuated on the first ship because they were accused of "grave crimes" against Japan, Manchukuo, or another Japanese territory.[37] On 16 June 1942, the State Department retaliated by making it clear that since Japan had "refused repatriation on the first vessel ... because [they] were suspected of criminal offense, the State Department intends to remove from 'Gripsholm' Ichiro Matsudaira and two other persons unless said three Americans are allowed to sail."[38] The Japanese responded with a fiery letter. They described as "unreasonable" the U.S. government threat to withhold one of their top priority repatriates and two others, and accused Washington of behaving "entirely against the code of international etiquette even between hostile nations." Specifically, Tokyo had been led to understand that Matsudaira's case had been settled, so the U.S. government decision was "in clear violation of their previous undertaking."[39]

Since the McKinnon and Lane cases were unconnected to Matsudaira, the Japanese government furthermore called this decision "unwarranted" and insisted that "the American Government will not deviate at this juncture from the previous undertaking by arbitrarily removing Matsudaira and two others, and that they will treat the question of release of Mckin[n]on and Lanes independently of those Japanese who they themselves have agreed to repatriate, leaving it as a pending question to be settled in connection with the second exchange. Otherwise, the Japanese Government will be constrained to hold the sailing of the Exchange vessels from this end."[40]

This case was eventually resolved, and McKinnon and the Lanes were included at the last minute in the exchange, but it was a simple fact that tensions between the Japanese and the American government were increasing exponentially over time. Although the U.S. government's top priority was to conduct the first exchange as expeditiously as possible so as to prepare the way for future exchanges, such tensions made future exchanges more and more difficult to organize. Similar problems were to plague negotiations leading to the second exchange, as well as contributing to a deadlock that eventually halted the third planned exchange altogether.

After all of the unexpected complications were resolved, and the exchange finally began, *Gripsholm* arrived at Lourenço Marques on 20 July, one day before the two Japanese ships. Once the passengers had changed ships, the Japanese ships departed on 26 July for Singapore and then on to Tokyo. Although the first exchange proved successful, there was constant friction caused by trying to match the Japanese lists with the actual candidates. The Japanese government would prove to be less willing to accept substitutes during the preliminary stages leading to the second exchange.

3 Exchanging journalists and non-officials from outside the U.S.

The U.S. offer to negotiate exchanges on behalf of Canada, Central America, and South American countries added yet another layer of complexity. This included exchanging Japanese officials, journalists, and non-officials located outside the United States for their Western Hemisphere counterparts living in the Far East. After departing New York, *Gripsholm* visited Rio de Janeiro, where just over 400 Japanese officials and non-officials boarded the ship for the journey to southern Africa.

Soon after negotiating its own exchange with Tokyo, Washington offered to include other countries. On 17 March 1942, the U.S. government specified what would happen to Japanese non-officials arriving from Latin America and Canada. Similar to government officials, the "non-official persons of Japanese nationality residing in those countries in the Americas which have broken relations with Japan will be entitled, to the extent that accommodations may permit and that they fall within the categories of the non-official persons to be exchanged, to embark upon the official exchange vessel."[1] Many of these persons were transported to the United States, for eventual embarkation on an exchange ship in New York City, or were sent to Rio de Janeiro, where the ship would make its only other stop before heading for the exchange port. Because they fell under the Alien Enemy Act of 1793, these Latin American exchangees were never part of the War Relocation Authority, but were administered separately by the Immigration and Naturalization Service (INS) at centers in Kenedy, Seagoville, and Crystal City, Texas.[2]

Many problems connected with this exchange were not easy to solve. The limited size of the exchange vessel was one example. Since only an estimated 500 berths were available on the first exchange ship for this category of non-officials, the U.S. government announced that the "views of the Japanese Government will be taken into consideration in allocating these berths." Also, "it is assumed that the Japanese Government will in expressing its views, take into consideration the fact that transportation facilities may not permit all Japanese non-official nationals from countries in the western hemisphere to reach the port of embarkation before the sailing of the official vessels."[3]

Although the task of locating, interviewing, and transporting these persons to the embarkation points was a difficult one, the U.S. government was eager to widen the exchange program so as to assist its neighbors to the north and south. Moreover, Washington wanted to repatriate all Japanese officials from the Western Hemisphere so as to cut off any chance that they might act as spies for the Japanese government. Finally, a higher number of Japanese evacuees might allow for the return of even more American citizens from China, Manchukuo, French Indochina, Thailand, etc. But there may have been other, more self-serving reasons as well. By broadening the scope of the exchange to include all of North and South America, there were many more "high value" Japanese citizens to exchange for Americans being held in Japan; while about a third of Japanese exchangees on the first exchange ship were not from the U.S., but were from Latin America, fully 90 percent of those coming from Japan were American citizens. This situation worked to the advantage of the United States.

It was also virtually certain that by widening the exchange a number of Japanese officials would miss the sailing date of the first exchange ship, thus making a second exchange necessary. Therefore, concluded one U.S. government message: "It may thus be necessary through no fault of this Government that a small number of Japanese nationals from certain countries await a later exchange vessel."[4] If the Japanese government had received back all of its officials on the first ship, there would have been no incentive to continue the program, which suggests that some delays may have been intentional. Washington's decision to include as many groups as possible thus helped guarantee the maximum number of returned American citizens as well as a higher number of total exchanges.

The exchange of journalists

In addition to diplomats and consular officials, a third major group to be exchanged by Japan and the United States included foreign journalists. This group was accepted as a separate category in principle during February 1942.[5] Since journalists were not government officials, the Japanese government specifically requested that they be treated like the other non-officials and that Tokyo be given the right to determine the priority of their departure: "The Japanese Government further propose that priority among non-official persons including press representatives for accommodation on the Exchange vessel should be decided upon by agreement between Governments concerned."[6]

The U.S. government appears to have accepted this proposal in the hopes of securing the return of all American journalists detained by Japan. Thereafter, on 1 May 1942, the Swiss Legation passed on a note from the U.S. government in which nine journalists in Japan, and a dozen in China, were listed as prime candidates for exchange on the first ship.[7] The Japanese government, however, appeared to be reluctant to allow certain journalists to leave the country, perhaps because of the type and quality of information they might have been able to pass on to American authorities. On 20 May 1942, the U.S. government urged Tokyo once again to include all eligible members of the American Press Corps from Japan and China on the first exchange ship.[8]

In return for Japan's cooperation, the U.S. government helped gather Japanese journalists from all over the Western Hemisphere for passage on the exchange ship. As for those journalists assigned to the United States proper, on 27 May 1942, Washington sent the following note through the Swiss Legation to Tokyo: "United States Government is able to place on first voyage of 'Gripsholm' 22 Japanese journalists with their five dependents making a total of 27 and comprising all Japanese journalists in United States who wish to be repatriated including those whose activity the United States Government has found objectionable and all those received from the other American Republics for repatriation."[9]

In return, Washington expected Tokyo to show a reciprocal consideration to the American journalists. It wrote: "the United States Government correspondingly expects Japanese Government to place on first sailing of repatriation vessels from Japan all American newspapermen including those whose activity the Japanese Government finds objectionable." A failure to reach agreement over this issue could be used as an excuse to delay the first exchange. Washington alluded to this eventuality in the final line of its communiqué when it stated: "State Department desire assurances to that effect before sailing of 'Gripsholm' now scheduled for about June 10th."[10]

In the end, what might have appeared to be a U.S. threat to hold back some of the Japanese journalists seems to have been largely unnecessary. In a manner similar to the category for government officials, almost all of the Japanese and American journalists were included on the first exchange ship. The return of American journalists to the United States proved to be an important source of information about Japan, since they had witnessed many aspects of the Japanese war effort both in Japan and on the Asian continent. Likewise, the Japanese journalists probably had information useful to Japan.

While such security considerations were largely ignored when it came to journalists, a category specifically mentioned in the Geneva Convention, they would become more important when considering whether to allow ordinary Japanese citizens—especially those with in-depth knowledge of the United States—to return to Japan. This would also affect decisions relating to the inclusion of Canadian and Latin American officials and non-officials involved in the exchange.

Exchange of Canadian and Latin American officials and non-officials

Adding Japanese from other Western Hemisphere countries to the U.S.–Japanese exchanges was made especially clear in a letter dated 17 April 1942, when Washington clarified that the use of the term "American" as versus "United States" in a Department of State communication of 25 March 1942 was "used in order that the condition of reciprocity referred to in the Department of States telegram of April 9th ... might be made available to all official personnel of the American Governments leaving Japan or territory under Japanese control."[11] The term "American" was used deliberately throughout U.S. communiqués in the hopes that the exchange agreement could be broadened to include other countries. Because of the confusion that this term caused, however, Washington needed to clarify to Tokyo on several occasions its offer to help organize the transport of Japanese officials and their effects from outside the United States. In return, in line with the principle of reciprocity, Washington requested: "The United States Government expects that Japanese Government, taking note of this assurance, will grant equal facilities for carriage of effects to all American officials of whatever nationality."[12]

The official government representatives and diplomats from a large number of South American and Central American countries were eager to take advantage of the U.S.–Japanese exchange agreement. One of the first to express this interest was the Minister of Peru, Ricardo Rivera Schreiber. On 10 January 1942, he wrote to Foreign Minister Shigenori Togo:

> I have the honour to inform Your Excellency, with reference to the official meeting I had the pleasure to entertain with Your Excellency on Wednesday last, that I have today received a cablegram from my Government to the effect that the Government of the United States has agreed to incorporate, on their side, myself and the other members of the Peruvian staffs in the evacuation arrangements now proceeding with Your Excellency's Imperial Government, regarding which Your Excellency was kind enough as to offer the necessary facilities.

A similar message was sent to the Swiss Minister in Tokyo who was in charge of arranging the exchange.[13] On 4 February 1942, the Venezuelan government made a similar request.[14]

On 30 January 1942, the Peruvian government promised to abide by the same terms as those agreed to by Washington in the U.S.–Japanese exchange.[15] Eventually, an estimated 1,800 Peruvian-Japanese were interned in the United States, which "represented 80 percent of all the Latin American Japanese interned in the United States."[16] The vast majority—some reports say as high as 80 percent—had volunteered to be repatriated to Japan, while for others the fear of anti-Japanese riots made leaving Peru a "prudent choice."[17] After the war, these stranded Peruvian-Japanese were urged to return to Japan, but many insisted instead on returning to Peru, which only allowed about 100 back in, usually if they were married to a Peruvian or had Peruvian citizenship. Unsure of what to do with them, during August 1946 the U.S. government decided to allow them to remain in the United States.[18] Finally, during June 1952, Public Law 414 made them eligible for U.S. citizenship.[19]

Japan's Foreign Minister Togo answered the letter from Peru rapidly, promising: "I shall be glad to see that the desired facilities are accorded if the necessary accommodation could be obtained on board the first ship which may be sent for the purpose of exchanging diplomats between Japan and the United States. But if no accommodation is available on such a ship, I shall have to ask Your Excellency to wait for the next or even further ship which may be dispatched."[20]

While attempting to cooperate with these governments, the Japanese government was clearly in less of a hurry to evacuate its own officials from the smaller American countries, from where it continued to receive information about U.S. war preparations. On 5 February 1942, the Swiss Minister passed on the following American communication to Foreign Minister Togo: "Please inform the Japanese Government that some of its officials in the Western Hemisphere have apparently not received instructions to comply with the Japanese Government's wishes … as they seem reluctant to avail themselves of the facilities offered."[21]

A few days later, another American note reiterated that Japanese officials in a number of other American countries were not adhering to the terms of the exchange:

> The United States Government notes *that certain* of the former Diplomatic and Consular Officials of Japan in other American Republics which have broken relations with, or declared war upon, Japan have apparently not received from their Government instructions to proceed to this country for the purpose of being included in the exchange now being negotiated and are unwilling to accept offers made to them of facilities for the journey here. The Japanese Government should inform its officials in the other American Republics of its desire that they take advantage of the facilities now being negotiated and of the need that these persons depart promptly for the United States in order to be present when the exchange vessel departs.

To assist these officials, the U.S. government also made the following offer: "The United States Government is willing that a separate block exchange of non American officials leaving Japan and Japanese officials leaving place outside the American [borders] shall take place at the same time and at the same port as the exchange of American and Japanese Officials."[22]

In late February 1942, the Japanese government responded. In particular:

> Regarding certain Japanese diplomats and consular officials formerly accredited to some Latin American countries who have declined to accept the offer of facilities for journey to the United States, the Japanese Government desire to make it clear to the United States Government that they have done so under instructions from the Japanese Government. Since agreement has

now been practically reached in the matter of the Exchanges they will be instructed to leave their former posts.[23]

Soon, there were reports that these Japanese representatives had arrived safely at the embarkation point in New York, including the legation staff from Mexico on 12 February, and the staff from Cuba on 14 February.[24] However, by mid-March, there were still Japanese officials who refused to leave their stations. In particular, the U.S. government stated "a separate communication have been made through Spanish channels with particular to the Japanese officials in Colombia."[25]

Other Asian countries affected by the exchange were Thailand and French Indochina (Vietnam). During February 1942, the U.S. government asked that Japan help facilitate the exchange of government officials from these countries. Meanwhile, Japan had asked for U.S. assistance in repatriating its officials in Iran and Samoa. To this, Washington had responded that it had no way to assist any officials in Iran and that perhaps Tokyo should "arrange for the repatriation of this personnel through Soviet territory." As for Samoa, Washington stated that "as far as concerns those parts of the Samoan Islands which are under the jurisdiction of the United States this Government is unaware of the presence there of any Japanese Official personnel."[26]

As a result of American offers, Japanese official representatives, as well as non-officials, were brought from all over North and South America to the embarkation point in New York City. By 20 May 1942, the United States government had gathered on the East Coast, within easy reach of New York City, a total of over 600 Japanese officials and non-officials ready for evacuation and repatriation to Japan. Of these, at least 46 were from South America, including Peru, Colombia, Bolivia, and Venezuela. Over 400 additional officials and non-officials were scheduled to be picked up by *Gripsholm* when it docked at Rio de Janeiro, the second evacuation terminus in the Western Hemisphere.

Meanwhile, approximately 10 percent of the officials and non-officials coming from Japan and other Far Eastern ports on the ship *Asama Maru* were non-U.S. citizens. These included the Ministers of Panama, Mexico, Peru, and Brazil, and a number of consuls from Peru, Chile, Mexico, Brazil, Paraguay, and Canada.[27] The *Conte Verde*, leased from an Italian firm, was carrying a mixture of U.S. and other officials and non-officials who had been based in China. Considering that a higher number of U.S. citizens were able to be included, the United States clearly benefited by including other countries from the Western Hemisphere in the exchange.

The American and the British exchanges

At the very beginning of negotiations, it was thought that perhaps the British and Americans would work together to arrange joint exchanges with Japan. However, by the end of February 1942, the British government had still not responded to the Japanese proposal.[28] For a time, it even appeared that the first U.S.–Japanese exchange might be delayed because of the slow pace of the British–Japanese negotiations. As a result, the U.S. government decided to conduct its negotiations with Tokyo separately. It was decided that all European officials and non-officials were to be included on the British exchange vessel, while all those nationals of countries in the Western Hemisphere were included on the U.S. vessel.

Therefore, even as the American diplomatic talks with Japan were progressing, the British were also arranging to exchange their official and non-official nationals with the Japanese. The two parallel efforts led to confusion. On 15 April 1942, the U.S. government had requested to learn from Japan "whether the American Japanese and the British Japanese exchanges are planned to move contemporaneously on more than one vessel and as two parts of the same movement."[29] On 27 April 1942, the Japanese Foreign Minister responded, suggesting that while more than one ship might be involved to transport the Americans and the British, in order to "ensure their security" it would be best if the "boats sailed together."[30]

However, on 7 April 1942, Washington had already protested Japanese plans for putting Belgian, Greek, and Dutch officials and non-officials on the ship reserved for the Americans. It stated: "This Government cannot agree to undertake to fix a formula for the inclusion in this exchange of Belgian, Greek and Netherlands nationals whose inclusion would reduce the number of Americans to be repatriated." It suggested that these groups should rightfully be included on the British ship. More to the point, Washington was concerned that problems with the British–Japanese exchange should not affect the U.S.–Japanese exchange: "United States Government must insist that although the two exchanges may be carried on simultaneously, they be considered as separate operations, and that the terms of one will not be used to restrict the scope of the other."[31]

It soon became clear that the British preparations were progressing much more slowly than the Americans'. During May 1942, the British requested that the exchange not take place until "August 15th at earliest." This did not sit well with the American authorities, who proposed on 26 May 1942 that: "United States Government on other hand is ready to proceed to exchange and now feels, in view of scanty facilities for shelter of passengers at Lourenço-Marques, that separation of exchanges may be helpful to all concerned. Accordingly United States Government intends to carry forward its plans to effect exchange by arrival of 'Gripsholm' at Lourenço-Marques about July sixth."[32]

While the U.S. government did prove willing to use pressure tactics and threaten to hold back certain Japanese to ensure that certain of its citizens were included in the first exchange, it was unwilling to delay the first exchange even by a few weeks so that the British could catch up. It proved equally unwilling to dilute its exchange program by allowing other Europeans aboard the first exchange ship, responding negatively on 7 April 1942 to a proposal that French citizens be included in the U.S.–Japanese exchange: "Seven women and children of French Embassy may not be accommodated on present exchange vessel as they would displace American citizens but they may be accommodated on another vessel later if no Americans are displaced."[33]

Washington was particularly concerned that the number of available slots for American citizens was fast being reduced by including these other European officials, especially considering the thousands of U.S. citizens being held by Japan. Unlike Britain, however, which had a limited number of Japanese officials and non-officials to exchange, the extremely large number of Japanese citizens and American citizens of Japanese ancestry who lived on the West Coast of the United States was an almost bottomless pool from which willing volunteers could be found to repatriate to Japan. The U.S. government clearly hoped to use this asset to negotiate the return of as many as possible, and perhaps even all, of its citizens from Japan.

Final preparations for the first exchange

By late May–early June, 1942, the number of Japanese and American officials and non-officials was gradually becoming more clear. According to Washington's list, there were 484 officials[34] and 681 non-officials[35] embarking at New York City, with another 319 officials and non-officials joining them at Rio de Janeiro to total 1,484. To make 1,500 exactly, 16 Thai nationals were added to *Gripsholm*'s passenger list.[36] On the Japanese side, *Asama-Maru* was scheduled to carry 890 passengers, while a second exchange vessel, *Conte Verde*, was to carry 625; of these, only 136 passengers aboard the *Asama-Maru* were classified under the category of government officials.[37]

As these numbers indicate, the Japanese government had a much larger number of government officials scheduled to be included in the first exchange than did the U.S. government. Not surprisingly, the number of Japanese non-officials on the first exchange ship was correspondingly fewer. This situation resulted in certain tensions, as the Japanese government insisted that the U.S. government work harder to include as many government officials on the first exchange ship as possible, to the detriment of the non-official passengers. To Japan, the first exchange vessel was arguably the most important, and might have been the *only* exchange ship had it secured the return of all of its officials at one time.

By contrast, the U.S. government was clearly more concerned with establishing a series of exchanges, so as to repatriate the largest number of citizens possible from Japan. For this reason, it did not put all of its hopes on the first exchange ship. It even appears that Washington might have tried to delay the return of some of the Japanese officials and so retain them for the second ship, perhaps as a guarantee that a second exchange would actually take place. As the deadline for *Gripsholm*'s departure neared, these conflicting goals produced tensions that at times flared into open acrimony.

Throughout the spring of 1942, Japanese officials from all over North and South America were transported and housed at various locations along the Eastern Seaboard of the United States. By and large, these officials were kept out of large cities, while being kept within easy reach by bus or train of New York City. Once they had all arrived safely, they would be transferred to New York City for embarkation on the exchange ships. Initially, 335 Japanese were housed at the Homestead Hotel in Virginia, described as a "vacation paradise with golf courses, tennis and badminton courts, bowling alleys, and ballrooms," until the Japanese ambassador, Kichisaburo Nomura, complained of overcrowding.[38] In response, the Japanese were moved to the Greenbriar Hotel, as confirmed by a 15 April 1942 letter to Tokyo written by the Japanese Ambassador, in which he announced that he and his group had been transferred from Hot Springs to White Sulphur Springs, West Virginia, arriving safely on 4 April 1942.

They were not alone. The Japanese officials joined an estimated 480 German citizens, who were also awaiting repatriation on the S.S. *Drottingholm*, scheduled to leave in May. According to what the Japanese Ambassador had heard, after the *Drottingholm* repatriated the "German, Italian, and other Axis officials and nationals," this same ship might then return to the United States to be used to transfer the Japanese to the agreed-upon point of exchange.[39]

The Japanese Ambassador expressed his concern that if they had to wait for the return of the *Drottingholm,* then this might delay the U.S.–Japanese exchange. Therefore, he recommended that "under present circumstances, I [am] inclined to view the American Government may be approached with a request for provision of separate vessel or vessels for us so that we may be able to repatriate simultaneously with those Germans and Italians, provided that various circumstances in Japan permit dispatch of Japanese repatriation vessel at about same time as departure of American ships from here." He also recommended that all evacuees be taken at the same time, suggesting that "the American Government will send simultaneously two or more vessels with enough capacity to accommodate Japanese officials and all Japanese nationals now under consideration for repatriation in North, Central and South American Countries."[40]

In Japan, similar preparations were being carried out in order to get the American officials ready for the exchange. There were also many last minute requests to add people to the evacuation list. For example, on behalf of the wife of the American Minister to Japan, Mrs. Grew, the Swiss Minister requested that her two personal servants, a British woman named Eleanor Cole and a German woman named Marie Langer, be allowed to join the evacuation as members of the U.S. diplomatic personnel.[41] This request appears to have been approved.

However, one of the biggest outstanding problems was the Japanese government's insistence that the U.S. government find and repatriate a large number of Japanese citizens who appeared on their high priority list. Simultaneous with negotiations detailing who was going to be allowed to depart on the first exchange were ongoing talks to prepare for a second exchange. In May 1942, the U.S. government informed the Spanish embassy that: "The list of about 1,500 permanent [Japanese] residents from the United States to be repatriated on the second voyage of exchange vessel is under preparation, and will be submitted to the Spanish Embassy within a few days."[42]

Although the lists for the first exchange included many Japanese government officials and Japanese non-officials living on the East Coast, this much longer list of 1,500 non-official Japanese evacuees included many persons from the West Coast. Without a doubt, most of these names were drawn from the lists of Japanese-Americans residing in the war relocation centers who had requested to be repatriated to Japan.

Conclusions

Starting with government officials, the exchange discussions next included non-officials, like journalists, and then finally officials and non-officials from other parts of the Western Hemisphere. Tokyo clearly put a high value on repatriating both officials and non-officials from outside the United States. It even requested that nationals from Panama, Costa Rica, Ecuador, and Peru be given "priority over other Japanese nationals."[43] As new—and ever higher—numbers arrived at the embarkation point in Rio de Janeiro, then the number of Japanese non-officials able to depart New York had to be correspondingly reduced. These constant changes were explained in a 29 May 1942 note from the State Department: "List of persons embarking at Rio de Janeiro is believed to be incomplete. Additions to that list must necessarily be compensated by deductions from list of Japanese non-officials to be embarked at New York as it is desirable to complete evacuation of Japanese from Brazil on the first voyage of the vessel."[44]

The Japanese were determined that the two sides exchange equal numbers of evacuees, even of non-officials, and they referred time and time again in their official documents to the need for "reciprocity." Whenever the number of evacuees changed too radically, Tokyo threatened to delay the exchange until more accurate lists could be procured. On 29 May 1942, just a few weeks before the first exchange, Washington complained that it was "somewhat disturbed that these reciprocal assurances appear necessary at this time when the exchange arrangements are so nearly completed."[45]

The problem of reciprocity would apply in particular to the lengthy lists of preferred evacuees that the Japanese government had early-on sent to the U.S. State Department. Many were either difficult to locate or had declined the opportunity to return to Japan. Other Japanese specified on the lists, as it would turn out, had specialized knowledge of the United States and were considered a security risk should they be allowed to return to Japan; U.S.–Japanese tensions over this category of exchangees were particularly acrimonious, especially when the State Department tried to substitute thousands of candidates from the relocation centers in their place.

4 Final U.S.–Japanese negotiations for the first exchange ship

The first three chapters have shown how the scope of the exchanges grew from including officials only, to officials and non-officials, and finally to the inclusion of exchangees from other countries outside of the United States. By April 1942, the U.S. government was working hard to transport all of the evacuees to New York City in preparation for embarkation on the first exchange ship. To bring all of these people and their possessions together by the embarkation date proved to be truly a monumental undertaking. Although successful, as indicated by the more or less on schedule departure, much of the information that is available about this period is from official documents protesting various infractions and perceived mistreatment. These included disputes over baggage limits, personal and baggage searches, and disagreement over how much currency each evacuee should be allowed to carry.

The information provided by these documents is far from complete, but they do provide an excellent vantage point for understanding what factors fueled tensions that eventually contributed to the cession of the exchange program. Most importantly, these protests highlight the inherent difficulties involved with exchanging simultaneously both officials and non-officials living in the U.S., not to mention Japanese from a large number of nations throughout the Americas. These problems would become even more difficult to resolve a year later during the second U.S.–Japanese exchange.

Disagreements over baggage limits

American citizens' baggage and their other personal possessions were considered highly important. However, there were deep-seated tensions between Washington and Tokyo over luggage limits. To begin with, the negotiated limits were very lenient. However, in practice it proved almost impossible to include unlimited baggage, especially because of the different capabilities of the exchange ships. Therefore, baggage was quite often left behind either because it arrived at the embarkation point too late, it was over-sized and proved to be too difficult to move in the time allotted, or it was divided into too many small pieces. At one point, the Japanese government even proposed that all bags be small enough so that each individual could carry their own. Although this sounded reasonable in theory, in practice it often meant that evacuees were limited to carrying only one large bag apiece, which clearly violated the intent of the negotiated agreement.

On 12 January 1942, the U.S. government stated its intention to allow Japanese "diplomatic and consular personnel" to transport as much personal luggage as they desired, with the sole exceptions being that their baggage should fall within the limits imposed by the evacuation vessel and that it be ready for embarkation at the time of the exchange.[1] Later, on 9 February 1942, the U.S. government repeated that the "officials to be exchanged and their dependents and their servants and their employees be permitted to bring with them all their personal effects including such things as silverware, linen and the like which can be packed in trunks, boxes with handles and handbaggage."[2]

On 19 February 1942, the Japanese government agreed "to the proposition of the United States Government concerning personal effects: vis. officials to be exchanged and their dependents, their servants and their employees shall be permitted to take with them all their personal effects including such things as silverware, linen and the like which can be packed in trunks, boxes with handles and handbaggage." Likewise, the Japanese agreed that there would not be "any limitations other than those imposed by availability of space on the vessel and the arrival of the effects at the port of embarkation in time to be laden aboard the vessel."[3]

However, in a new proposal, the Japanese government stated: "The Japanese Government feel that each trunk, box with handles or handbaggage should be of such size and weight as may be carried by a single person."[4] Although this proposal may have appeared reasonable on paper, and the use of the word "each" certainly implied that every evacuee would be allowed to ship multiple items, in practice Japanese officials conducting the exchanges would later interpret this provision to mean that each evacuee could transport only as much luggage as they themselves could carry, presumably at one time and not with multiple trips carrying one bag per trip. For obvious reasons, this less liberal interpretation was in direct conflict with the earlier decision that the exchangees could "take with them all their personal effects."

The Japanese government initially wanted all officials to fill out a written declaration listing the contents of each piece of luggage. Technically, this violated the international norms for consular jurisdiction, which included the privacy of diplomatic luggage. Therefore, by 17 March 1942, the Japanese government withdrew this requirement. Soon afterward, an American communication referred to this issue and stated: "It is noted that the views of the Japanese Government concerning the personal effects of the persons being exchanged coincide with the views of the United States Government and it is presumed that the Japanese Government has now withdrawn its stipulation that the official embarking on the exchange vessels shall make written declaration of the contents of their baggage."[5]

In line with this agreement, Japanese officials repatriated on the first exchange ship were permitted to take all of their personal effects. According to the regulations of the American Export Lines, however, each non-official was given 32 cubic feet of baggage free of charge with all excess baggage charged at commercial rates. Over time, this limitation was interpreted as three suitcases maximum to be stored in the passenger's cabin and then an additional 30 cubic feet of stored luggage. All baggage of both officials and non-officials was transported within the continental United States at government expense. Also, it would appear that none of the Japanese detainees were forced to carry their own luggage, since there were adequate porters to assist them.

In Japan and Japanese-occupied areas, however, a dispute soon arose over who should carry the evacuees' luggage. Although this may appear to have been a trivial matter, to the Japanese dockworkers carrying enemy luggage may have involved a "loss of face." This may be the origin of the Japanese note from 21 February 1942 recommending that all luggage be of a type capable of being carried by a single person. On 30 March 1942, Washington disputed this Japanese proposal. In contrast to Japan's decision, the "United States Government had not contemplated applying a limitation regarding the weight of the containers nor personal effects and will not apply such a limitation if it is assured that the Japanese Government will be guided similarly." It offered to allow Japanese officials the opportunity to ship back household effects, assuming that they were either already packed or "have been entrusted to responsible forwarding agents or storage companies capable of preparing them for shipment."[6]

In the end, the Japanese government largely ignored American offers of unlimited luggage. The first exchange often limited an individual's luggage to what they could carry themselves. As a result, in many instances during this exchange American officials "were not permitted to bring with them all personal effects to which they were entitled under the exchange agreement." The U.S. government repeatedly protested this infraction as going against the exchange agreement. Some of the many examples listed in the U.S. protests included trunks, cases, boxes, and brief cases.[7]

One such protest concluded with the U.S. government asking Tokyo for "assurance that the Japanese Government will ship such baggage … on the second exchange and will facilitate the work of the Swiss representative in preparing it for shipment." It also stated that: "The Department of State will continue to accord the same generous treatment to Japanese repatriated on the second exchange provided that satisfactory assurances are received that the Japanese Government will accord similar treatment to the baggage of all Americans returning from Japan and Japanese controlled territory."[8]

Discussions on baggage limits were never completed prior to the first exchange. As a result, there were many discrepancies between the two sides. As the war progressed, however, limits on baggage continued to be a major problem. During the second exchange, for example, it was decided that each American national could only bring three suitcases and two smaller carry-on items. Not until after they boarded the ship, however, did it become clear that all three suitcases were to be stored in a cargo hold below deck and would not be available throughout the entire voyage. Although merely annoying to some passengers, to others these luggage restrictions meant leaving behind valuable possessions and irreplacable family heirlooms.

On the American side, between the first and second exchanges the baggage limits were set at 30 cubic feet of "luggage packed in trunks and valises, or, if boxes are used, an endeavor should be made to have them of equal size with handles at either end to facilitate handling." Repatriates to Japan could no longer take most types of printed material, since the "Japanese Government initially prohibited the exportation by Americans being repatriated from Japan of books, printed matter, sketches, documents of any sort, gold objects, photographic apparatus and radios." However, they could still bring "clothing linen, silverware and other types of personal effects."[9]

These new restrictions caused the Japanese repatriates great concern. R. D. Fitch, a special agent for the Department of State, described the difficulties involved with enforcing the 30 cubic foot rule to T. F. Fitch, his father, and the chief special agent in charge of getting everyone ready for the exchanges:

> Mrs. Shigeko Furuya, one of the five late arrivals from Heart Mountain Relocation Center, asked to see me privately after I had explained the baggage limitations and tagging procedures to her group. I stepped into an adjoining room, listened to her tale of woe and told her we would do everything possible to have the group placed upon the *Gripsholm*. As I prepared to leave, she withdrew a handsome roll of bills from her bosom and insisted that I accept it as a token remembrance. I rebuked her sharply for the insult and told her that such tactics were not employed in this country. She was still quite insistent but finally decided that my refusal was final. The following day, for reasons which I cannot explain, Customs officials inspected and approved approximately fifty-two cubic feet of luggage for her. This had been placed in the baggage car and when discovered by me the following morning, I again informed her of the limitations and had the excess removed to Fort Missoula.[10]

Although the implications are unstated, this story would certainly suggest that some customs officials were less than thorough, or perhaps less than honest in abiding by the regulations.

However, in a new twist, while Japanese officials and "those persons forced to leave the United States" did not have to pay for transportation to the departing ship, it was decided at some point during 1943 that voluntary repatriates did have to pay. If they could not pay, they would "have to wait." This restriction would prove to be especially burdensome for those evacuees living in the relocation centers, since most of them were housed either in the center of the country or on the West Coast. The question of paying for domestic transportation of voluntary non-officials was an issue that was still under discussion between the U.S. and the Japanese as late as 1943. Due to the State Department's eagerness to promote additional exchanges, however, this restriction appears to have been largely ignored in the days and weeks immediately prior to the second exchange.[11]

Personal and baggage searches

In addition to safeguarding the persons and possessions of its citizens, the issue of personal and baggage searches was also of concern. This problem elicited at least two major Japanese protests after the first exchange was completed. According to international norms, all Japanese government officials were accorded diplomatic immunity, and so they and their bags were not searched. However, the status of non-officials was less clear. Disputes over differing interpretations of what kinds of searches were proper were to plague the entire exchange program.

The issue of searching officials was definitively decided on 12 January 1942, when the Swiss Minister to Japan wrote to Foreign Minister Shigenori Togo that the U.S. government had agreed to the "inviolability of the baggage" of the Japanese Ambassador, the consular officials, and their families.[12] However, non-officials were different. One U.S. document stated: "The persons of those to be exchanged will not be searched." But, as for their luggage, it cautiously stated: "The question of the examination of the effects of non-official persons to be included in any subsequent phases of the exchange movement which may be arranged will be dealt with at another time."[13] This rather vague proposal was apparently accepted by the Japanese government at this time, which stated in a 19 February 1942 communication: "As to personal effects to be brought away by non-official persons the views of the Japanese Government coincide with those of the United States Government."[14]

Later, the U.S. government further stated that "Such [personal] effects will not be subject to search, be subject to any tax or duty nor subject to any limitations other than those imposed by availability of space on the vessel and the arrival of the effects at the port of embarkation in time to be laden aboard the vessel."[15] The Japanese government completely concurred with this U.S. proposal, and furthermore proposed that: "The Japanese Government will demand neither individual declaration nor lists of contents."[16]

But these regulations did not apply across the board to non-officials: their status and the status of their luggage were left vague. According to a Japanese "Memorandum" from 16 July 1943: "At the first exchange the American authorities searched the persons of the non-official Japanese evacuees, stripping them, without a single exception, of their clothes, and examined their luggage in the most unsparing manner." Tokyo promised that during future exchanges it "will not search the persons of evacuees and [will] examine their luggage in a lenient manner," if "at the coming exchange both sides shall strictly comply with the terms of the agreement."[17]

The U.S. government responded to this protest in several different messages. One of these is undated, but clearly refers to the memorandum in question by repeating many of the salient sections. As for searching evacuees and their luggage, this note explained that: "At the time of the first exchange the United States Government found it necessary to search the persons of a few Japanese non-officials because it had good reason to believe that certain of those persons were attempting to take with them important amounts of currency in excess of the amounts permitted under the exchange agreement and other things which were prohibited in the interest of national defense. The results of the search justified the suspicion in these cases."[18]

Turning the tables on the Japanese protest, the American Memorandum then went on to report that: "The United States Government is furthermore informed that many non-official United States nationals had their persons searched prior to leaving Japanese occupied territory, and that even officials of the United States Government departing from Manchuria and Chosen (Korea) had their persons searched."[19] Assuming that this is true, then the American treatment of the Japanese evacuees—especially those Japanese nationals with official status—would appear in some ways to have been more lenient than Japan's.

Still, Washington agreed to halt most searches during future exchanges, applying them only "in a limited number of cases where considerations of national security are felt to exist," thus prompting officials "to exercise a normal search of the type customarily made in such cases." In cases where women evacuees were to be searched, this would be done "exclusively by female matrons." Irrespective of sex, it granted that "a representative of the protecting power of the same sex be afforded the opportunity to be present, if desired by the person to be searched."[20]

Later, in a Japanese protest dated 27 October 1942, the Japanese government provided additional examples of violations of U.S. government promises that all searches of the "luggage of non-official evacuees shall be 'lenient' and that their persons shall not be searched." In particular, according to the Japanese, from 7 to 10 June 1942 U.S. customs officials and the FBI had searched Japanese evacuees' possessions, and had made "no scruple to break or damage them in the course of the examination." In the process, they had seized "watches, cameras, fountain-pens, cigarette-lighters, clothing, etc.," as well as "every written or printed scrap of paper including note-books, address-books, etc."[21]

On 11 June 1942, personal searches were also conducted at the Pennsylvania Hotel in New York of both male and female evacuees. At this time, "even a plaster applied to a wound was stripped off," "evacuees had their hair searched," and "Women were also made naked by women examiners, and many of them were subjected to the most humiliating search." As a result, the Japanese government protested against "such deliberate and flagrant violations of the stipulations of the Exchange Agreement, especially against the unlawful seizure of the evacuees' belongings without giving them receipts therefore and the most insulting and inhuman search of the persons of the evacuees."[22]

The U.S. government responded on 12 December 1942, clarifying once again that the Japanese subjects were treated well, even being transported to New York in "pullman sleeping cars" and while there being housed in a "first class hotel." Of the total number: "Only a few suspect individuals among them were subjected to search." Most importantly, from the point of view of the official U.S.–Japanese exchange agreement, only non-officials who did not have diplomatic immunity were searched: "No Japanese subjects with official status were subjected to searches of any sort."[23]

Even though the U.S. government would appear on the whole to have adhered to the terms of the exchange agreement more closely than did the Japanese government, the Foreign Ministry in Tokyo took great offense at what it claimed were willful violations of the agreement. Similar problems concerning searches were to plague the arrangements leading up to the second exchange. Additional conflicts soon arose over currency limitations.

Disputes over currency issues

The amount of money an evacuee could carry was also a problem, since neither government wanted evacuees to take large sums. Originally, the U.S. government proposed that "the persons to be included in the exchange will be granted all necessary facilities of whatever description for taking with them a supply of funds which—without possibility of question, will be sufficient to meet all their needs on the ship and elsewhere until their arrival at the place of exchange."[24] No specific numbers were suggested at this time, but instead Washington proposed that "the necessary amounts may be subsequently determined on the basis of reciprocity."[25] Later, on 19 February 1942, Tokyo suggested that "up to 1000 (one thousand) yen or its equivalent be allowed to each adult person to meet the needs on the vessel until the arrival at the place of exchange."[26]

The U.S. government accepted this suggestion in a telegram dated 6 March 1942, suggesting that the U.S. dollar equivalent be $300. In addition, it asked that the "Japanese Government will similarly afford the American nationals departing from Japan the facility of taking with them such part of their funds as they may desire in U.S. currency." Finally, treating the U.S. representatives from Thailand and French Indochina as a parallel case with Japanese representatives from "other American countries," Washington requested "that the Japanese Government will authorize the exportation of all funds of whatever character which these persons may be bringing with them."[27] On 17 March 1942, Washington repeated again its decision "accepting in substance the proposal of the Japanese Government regarding funds."[28]

The currency question became more complicated after Executive Order 8389 was issued. It required that the Japanese file applications for licenses in order to "permit the sale of personal effect or property and permit the use of the proceeds together with the existing personal bank balances and personal cash resources for transactions incident to the repatriation of the diplomatic and consular officers and employees of the various missions of the Japanese Government."[29]

To comply with this order, the Spanish Embassy had to provide the State Department with a list of names of Japanese personnel who wished "to effect transactions," their banks' addresses, and bank balances. As the personal effects in question were sold, the resulting sums would be deposited into these bank accounts. Thereafter, the Spanish "Embassy will be permitted to use the funds deposited in such accounts in the manner and under the conditions referred to for the payment of personal expenses incident to the repatriation of the diplomatic and consular officers and employees of the Japanese missions in the U.S. and the liquidation of their personal affairs."[30]

On 16 July 1943, the Japanese proposed that in future exchanges the same limits should apply as with the first exchange (1,000 yen or $300) and that such funds were intended for "use on board the ship until arrival at the place of exchange." At that point, any excess would be bought by the respective governments. They would be entrusted to the Swiss, in Tokyo's case, and to the Spanish, in Washington's case, for deposit in a local bank to be used for the "representation of American [or Japanese] interests."[31]

To this, Washington replied that evacuees should be given a choice of currencies. For example, "persons leaving the Far East will be permitted to take with them 300 United States Dollars or 1000 Yen or proportionate amounts of both currencies, as for example 150 Dollars and 500 Yen, and that reciprocally a choice of such currencies would be available to Japanese leaving the Western hemisphere." Assuming that Tokyo were to agree to this proposal, then the U.S. government agreed to "make such facilities freely available to all departing Japanese."[32]

If the evacuees in question did not have yen, they would be allowed to carry the currencies of whichever Japanese-occupied territory they were coming from. However, the Japanese government made it clear that while it would allow evacuees to carry other currencies besides yen, "it is not the intention of the Japanese Government to permit American evacuees to carry any currency of the United States or any other foreign country."[33]

As before, any monies over this 1000 Yen/300 Dollar limit would be "appropriated to the representation of American interests," which presumably in this case meant the representatives of the Swiss Legation.[34] This was the American interpretation, at least, as stated in the following passage: "The United States Government agrees that United States currency purchased by the Spanish representative on the 'Gripsholm' shall be deposited in an appropriate account in a United States bank for use in the representation of Japanese interests, and that Japanese currency similarly purchased by the Swiss representative on the Japanese exchange vessel shall be deposited in a bank and be used for the representation of the interests of the United States."[35]

As for which evacuees should be allowed to carry these sums, for "humanitarian reasons" the U.S. Government proposed that children be included in some exceptional cases.[36] The Japanese authorities agreed, and on 21 August 1943 they responded favorably to the American proposal that "an unaccompanied child under 21 years old or the oldest child of an unaccompanied family group" should be allowed "to carry the full amount of money permitted to an adult."[37]

These figures were generally applied to the second exchange as well. Not only were such sums important on board ship, where evacuees could purchase a variety of items from the ship's stores, but they were necessary to pay for transportation once the exchange vessels successfully returned to port. Unfortunately, there were cases where ships' stewards—aware that the American nationals had money—demanded bribes for food and other items that should have been freely available. On the whole, however, such incidents proved to be minor inconveniences.

Conclusions

The first U.S.–Japanese exchange largely followed the terms negotiated in late 1941 and early 1942: it was conducted during the summer of 1942 using the Swedish ship, the m/s *Gripsholm*, for the first leg of the journey from North and South America, and the s/s *Asama Maru* and *Conte Verde* for the second leg onward to Japan. *Gripsholm* was to leave New York around 10 June and arrive at Lourenço Marques between 6 and 10 July 1942, at which point the Japanese ships would arrive and the evacuees would be exchanged before beginning their long journey home. In the end, both the American and Japanese ships remained on schedule and the exchanges were successfully carried out as planned.

The U.S. government sent officials to observe the exchanges and to take care of problems with luggage, searches, and currency. According to one account by an American spouse of a Japanese diplomat, the State Department representatives on *Gripsholm* were particularly "likable and fair." She commented: "It was a great source of satisfaction to me that, almost without exception, those Americans who were officially connected with the internment and repatriation of Japanese diplomats displayed such human understanding and ability that they were not only respected by the Japanese but often held in deep affection."[38]

One complicating problem was the Japanese insistence that the number of evacuees from the entire Western Hemisphere equal those from Japan, Manchukuo, and occupied China. Most troubling was the changing number of Japanese evacuees on the ships leaving New York City and Rio de Janeiro. As of 18 May 1942, the number of those being exchanged was almost 1,500 on each side, including about 500 officials and 700 non-official Japanese from the United States, and another 300 or so official and non-official Japanese from South America. On the Japanese ships, by contrast, most of the evacuees were non-officials; only about 150 out of the 1,500 were categorized as government officials; this helps to explain why Japan agreed so quickly to include non-officials in the exchange, since only their inclusion allowed for one-to-one reciprocity. Also, there was a higher percentage of women and children on the ships coming from Japan, Manchukuo, and occupied China. This largely conformed to the U.S. government desire to give priority to women and children.

Once the first official exchange was concluded, then virtually all Japanese and American government officials had been successfully repatriated to their home countries. As might be expected, Japan's interest in the exchange program diminished once it had regained its top officials. This was not the case with the United States, since there were still many more thousands of American non-officials detained in Japanese camps in Manchukuo, occupied China, and in the Japanese home islands. In order to trade for these American citizens, the U.S. government would have to locate thousands of Japanese-Americans willing to repatriate to Japan.

5 Creating the Japanese-American war relocation centers

Previously, the creation of war relocation centers has been ascribed to the angry American populace searching for any way to strike back at Japan,[1] as well as detaining Japanese-Americans "temporarily prior to relocation out of the center into civilian life."[2] For many years, even the suggestion that the Japanese-American community presented a real security threat to the United States was met with a wave of derision; one of the kinder books on this topic concluded that General DeWitt's evacuation order of 18 March 1942 based on "'military necessity' was unjustified—but that the dereliction was one of folly, not of knavery."[3] In fact, Japan's intelligence efforts among the Japanese-American population were extensive, as one recent author who has studied the MAGIC code-breaking and the resulting intelligence has concluded. He argues that the Japanese interned in the United States "were actually victims of the Japanese Empire and its prewar plans and activities."[4]

For these interned to return home, however, it would be necessary to find a solution to the Japanese insistence on reciprocity, both in terms of numbers and social status of the evacuees. In the euphoria following the first exchange, there were high hopes that a second exchange could take place immediately. On 3 August 1942, the Swiss Legation passed on the following message to Tokyo: "It is expected that 'Gripsholm' would leave New York about September 1st with 1500 Japanese nationals on board and proceed to Lourenço-Marques for second exchange. ... Vessel would reach Lourenço-Marques on or about September 24th. United States Government desires confirmation that Japanese Government is prepared to forward an approximately equivalent number of nationals of the United States, the other American Republics and Canada in adequate shipping to Lourenço-Marques in time to effect the second exchange at that port without undue delay of the 'Gripsholm' there."[5]

Unfortunately, it would be over a year before a second exchange was allowed to take place. All of the factors mentioned previously, including numbers, social status, and treatment, were to become enormously complicated while preparations were being made for the second exchange. Due to these delays, more and more of the responsibility for resolving these problems began to fall on the war relocation centers. Beginning after 1 July 1943, those Japanese-Americans who had requested repatriation, or who were considered to be loyal to Japan, were segregated from the rest and moved to the Tule Lake relocation center in northern California. Their number soon grew to 6,000 Japanese citizens and United States citizens of Japanese ancestry.

Why were there so many Japanese-Americans?

The history of Japanese immigration to the United States is complex. Here it is important to outline some of the diplomatic and legal constraints affecting both the U.S. government and the Japanese government. These included the 1907 U.S.–Japanese gentleman's agreement, the 1907 Presidential Executive Order, and the 1924 U.S. Immigration Act.

After 1884, Japanese were able to come to the United States to work, but could not become American citizens. In October 1906, the San Francisco School Board ordered all Japanese students to leave the regular public school and matriculate in the Chinese-run Oriental School. The Japanese government immediately protested this incident, arguing that this was a clear violation of the 1894 U.S.–Japanese treaty granting Japanese aliens the same rights and protections as Americans.[6]

To gloss over this problem, in 1907 President Theodore Roosevelt and representatives of the Japanese imperial government signed a gentleman's agreement, whereby "Japanese children under the age of sixteen would be admitted into the regular public schools in return for Japan's agreeing to prevent emigration of skilled and unskilled laborers by refusing them passports. Agriculturalists and certain other groups, and the families of those already here, were still to be allowed to emigrate." This agreement was soon afterward extended to Hawaii and Mexico, and Roosevelt enacted an executive order forbidding Japanese immigration into the United States from Hawaii, Mexico, and Canada. Any Japanese who did so after 1907 were legally considered "illegal aliens" similar to the "Mexican wetbacks of a later date."[7]

While Japanese laborers could no longer come to the United States after 1907, the ones who were already in residence there could remain, and their families in Japan could join them if they wished. This meant in practice that most of the Japanese-American males evacuated from the West Coast during World War II had arrived in the United States before 1907, and many of these in the 1890s. Between 1910 and 1924, Japanese brides could still come to the United States, so that the Japanese-American women tended to be younger than their husbands. As a result of this anomalous timing, most of the children resulting from these marriages—known as "second generation" Japanese or *Nisei*—were "born between 1910 and 1924," and so by 1942 "most of them were between eight and twenty-five—high school age for the most part at that time."[8]

Because the 1913 California Alien Land Act prohibited Japanese who were not U.S. citizens from owning land, what land they did farm was usually acquired in the form of leases. Because of these restrictions, only about 8 percent of the

390,635 acres under Japanese cultivation in 1918 were owned outright. Sometimes Japanese parents would buy land and hold it under the name of their American-born children.[9] But lease rates remained high during the interwar years, and many such leases were subsequently lost during the years of relocation: "A lot of people were too old by that time to go back and start over, and a lot of them who leased land couldn't get the leases back. ... Some of them got back in, but I'm talking about the bulk of them who didn't get back in because they didn't own land."[10] The long-held misunderstanding that the U.S. government somehow took away the Japanese-American's property was based on the intricate legal distinctions between owning land and leasing land.

Between 1908 and 1923, 120,317 Japanese arrived in the continental United States, but another 111,626 departed, so the net gain was only 8,681. In 1924, the U.S. Congress passed the Immigration Act, which as one part of a longer bill outlawed all further Japanese immigration to the United States. President Calvin Coolidge was opposed to this provision, and stated at the time that it was a "deplorable" method for securing an end to Japanese immigration: "If the exclusion provision stood alone, I should disapprove it without hesitation if sought in this way at this time."[11] In Japan, nationalist rallies opposed the passing of this bill, and protestors called for designating 1 July, the day the bill took effect, as a "National Humiliation Day."[12]

Beyond a last minute spurt of family members and new brides to beat the 1 July deadline, some illegal immigration continued, and—of course—the Japanese already living and working in the U.S. were allowed to stay, and any children that they had immediately became U.S. citizens by right of birth. By 1940, there were an estimated 126,947 Japanese-Americans in the continental United States (not counting Alaska or Hawaii), of whom approximately 70,000 were American citizens by birth. Because of the nature of the U.S. immigration laws, however, Japanese citizens could not become naturalized American citizens, no matter how long they had lived in the country.

This differed radically from immigration practices in Canada, where Japanese immigrants could become naturalized citizens after only three years' residence; when World War II broke out, of the 23,149 persons of Japanese ancestry living in Canada, 58 percent were native born, 26 percent were Japanese citizens, and 16 percent were naturalized Canadian citizens. While the U.S. population of Japanese-Americans did not include this third group of naturalized citizens, one positive difference for the U.S.-born children of Japanese citizens was that they were accorded full constitutional rights, including the right to vote, while the franchise was denied to all Japanese-Canadians, including their Canadian-born children, until the law was finally changed in 1948.[13] Still, the percentage of Japanese in both countries was extremely small, representing less than one-tenth of 1 percent in each country overall, constituting 2.7 percent of the population of British Columbia and only 1.2 percent of the U.S. population on the West Coast.[14]

U.S. guarantees to safeguard the security of Japanese nationals

During the U.S.–Japanese negotiations leading to the agreement to exchange officials, the issue of providing adequate personal security was a major consideration. What Japan initially meant by security was that its government officials in embassies and consulates had to be accorded either police or military protection to insure their safety. When this term was applied to non-officials, however, the term "security" meant that the U.S. government would have to figure out a way to locate those Japanese citizens and American citizens loyal to Japan who wanted to be repatriated to Japan, and it would have to determine how to guarantee their physical safety until they boarded the exchange vessels. The war relocation centers provided one viable means of keeping Japanese-Americans safe. As late as spring 1944, Stimson, the Secretary of War, opposed releasing Japanese-American from the relocation centers for fear that violence against them might provoke "reprisals in Japan against our own prisoners."[15]

In the midst of hostile public reaction following Pearl Harbor, many Japanese-Americans feared—quite rightly as it turned out in some cases—for their personal safety. That this fear was not an exaggeration was shown by a number of cases where Japanese-Americans were harassed and physically attacked. The Japanese government responded to such reports by protesting its displeasure to Washington. For example, a Japanese protest from April 1944 stated that "at least four cases involving six deaths have come to knowledge of and have been protested against by Japanese Government."[16]

Meanwhile, U.S. government concerns about Japanese-Americans' loyalty were real. Such doubts surfaced immediately after Pear Harbor, when several Japanese pilots from the attack crash-landed and received assistance from Japanese-Americans in Hawaii. It was feared that Japan might have already built an extensive spy network in Hawaii, with the Japanese-American community serving as either a willing or unwilling accomplice. Interestingly, a recent article by a Japanese Vice Admiral has admitted that Japan's leaders during World War II largely failed in both their intelligence efforts and sabotage within the United States to take advantage of pre-existing problems, "for example, nationwide historical racial issues, and the relationship with Mexico."[17] In the Russo-Japanese War, Japanese sabotage efforts had been quite successful. So why did Japan fail in World War II?

On 5 December 1941, the Japanese embassy in Washington reported that its operatives were actively involved "in propaganda work among the Negroes," and Mexico City was suggested as a "most important base for intelligence concerning the United States." In earlier messages, references were also made to using "second generation Japanese draftees" to collect intelligence on the U.S. Army, while a certain "second generation Japanese lawyer" was helping to find out about the anti-Jewish movement, presumably to increase tensions between Christians and Jews. A message dated 9 May 1941 even stated that the Japanese intelligence would "maintain connection with our second generations who are at present in the (U.S.) Army," and: "We also have connections with our second generations working in airplane plants for intelligence purposes."[18]

According to these MAGIC intercepts, Japan had created an extensive intelligence network among both the first and second generation Japanese on the West Coast of the United States. On 12 February 1942, General DeWitt, chief of the Western Defense Command, warned Roosevelt that the "very fact that no sabotage has taken place to date is a disturbing and confirming indication that such action will be taken." Prior to copies of these translated messages becoming available through the Freedom of Information Act, one prominent member of the Japanese-American community criticized the "general's logic, the fact that there had been no disloyal acts was proof there would be treachery in the future and that it was only prudent to crack down on an entire racial segment of the population before anything happened."[19] However, this argument may not appear so strange in the post 9-11 world. The decision to evacuate the Japanese-Americans from the West Coast completely destroyed any Japanese intelligence network there.

On 27 May 1942, Colonel E. F. Cress submitted an analysis of the threat posed by Japanese-educated Japanese-Americans known as *Kibei*, which was short for *Kibeinisei*, or "return to America second generation." His report focused on Kibei who had spent three years or more being educated in Japan, and who were 16 years or older when they re-entered the United States. Naval Intelligence was able to use ships' manifests to track 2,064 people—56 percent of them young men—who had entered West Coast ports between 1936 and 1942 and who fit this description. Estimates of the total number, however, ranged "between eight and nine thousand."[20]

Until proven to be loyal citizens, Colonel Cress suggested that these Japanese youth, plus their parents, be segregated from other Japanese-Americans. He stressed: "It seems logical to assume that any child of Japanese parents, who was returned to Japan at an early age, grew up there, studied in Japanese schools, possible [sic] did military service in the Japanese army or navy, and then as an adult returned to the United States, is at heart a loyal citizen of Japan, and may very probably have been deliberately planted by the Japanese government."[21] Even authors who have criticized the U.S. internment of the Japanese-Americans have conceded that "some" of the Kibei educated in Japan, "and many Issei as well, were undoubtedly rooting for Imperial Japan."[22]

In the aftermath of Pearl Harbor, a direct attack by Japan on the West Coast also seemed a very real possibility. With hindsight this may appear to be have been a small threat, but during February 1942, Japanese Submarine I-17 shelled an oil field near Santa Barbara, in June Submarine I-25 shelled a coastal fort in Oregon, and in September, that same submarine "launched a small float plane that dropped incendiary bombs, starting a few small forest fires." The perceived threat of a Japanese attack was heightened following Japanese "balloon" attacks in Oregon that killed six American citizens.[23] These were the first American civilians to be killed in the continental United States.

The fall of Singapore on 15 February 1942 also had an immediate impact along the entire West Coast, since this victory—in theory at least—now freed Japan to turn elsewhere to attack; it is perhaps no coincidence, therefore, that Order 9066 was signed by Roosevelt on 19 February, just as Canada signed a similar "Order in Council P.C. 1486" on 24 February ordering the removal of all male Japanese at least 100 miles inland from the coast. On 13 February 1942, the Wallgren Committee, composed of many Western congressmen, had already "recommended to the President that all Japanese, both aliens and citizens, be evacuated."[24]

Thus, when the U.S. government ordered the evacuation of the Western states, it was reacting both to legitimate citizen concerns that certain members of the Japanese-American community might support Japan, and to concerns that Japanese loyalists could impede the U.S. war effort. In both cases the issue of race was not an end but a means to isolate the most likely supporters of Japan. While it may have been racial profiling, it was not racism. U.S. government actions after 9-11 paralleled this earlier case.

Creating the war relocation centers

The war relocation program attempted to address all of these concerns. On 11 February 1942 President Franklin Roosevelt ordered the War Department to prepare a plan to evacuate Japanese-Americans from the West Coast. After he signed Executive Order 9066 on 19 February, the Headquarters of the Western Defense Command and Fourth Army announced Public Proclamation No. 1 on 2 March 1942. It required any "Japanese, German or Italian alien, or any person of Japanese Ancestry now resident in Military Area No. 1," which included the states of Washington, Oregon, California, and Arizona, to register a "change of residence notice" at their local post office at least a day before they moved.[25]

This is an extremely important document that is often overlooked by authors examining the war relocation program. First, it shows that the Japanese were not being singled out for special mistreatment. In fact, German and Italian aliens were also required to register any change of address. The one exception was that this proclamation included "any person of Japanese Ancestry." Arguably, this addition was made because so many Kibei who had become U.S. citizens automatically at birth had in fact spent most of their youth in Japan. Many of these young men later stated in interviews that their primary allegiance was to Japan. As one 23-year-old Kibei later explained it, he was simply unable to forswear allegiance to the Japanese emperor. This was "the tragedy of the Kibei," since if "parents had not sent their children to Japan this sort of tragedy would not have occurred."[26]

Early in this process, Japanese-Americans were urged to move inland voluntarily so that they would not be located near the Pacific Ocean. Those who left the coastal areas, estimated to be around 8.000 to 9,000, were not interned during the war and never became part of the relocation program. For those who did not leave voluntarily, later Public Proclamations increased the restrictions—including curfews and an order not to travel in Military Area No. 1—until the War Relocation Authority (WRA) was established by Presidential Executive Order 9012 on 18 March 1942. As soon as the relocation program began, however, then all Japanese-Americans—regardless of whether they were citizens or not—were excluded from the West Coast until 2 January 1945, when this ban was rescinded.[27] Even then, many did not return to the West Coast, either because they had nothing to return to or because they were fearful that they would not be accepted back by the local communities.[28]

Milton Eisenhower of the Department of Agriculture was made the first director of the WRA. The goal was not to lock up Japanese-Americans, as is often stated, but to assist Japanese aliens and American citizens of Japanese ancestry to move inland, away from the more sensitive coastal regions. Because it was thought that most of them would remain involved in agriculture, this program was under the tacit direction of the Department of Agriculture. The WRA was authorized to pay for all transportation and provide housing and security.

Even at this early stage in the process, the creation of the war relocation centers conformed to Tokyo's demand that Washington protect all of its Japanese citizens living in the United States. Later, these centers were also to serve as the most convenient means for locating Japanese citizens and American citizens of Japanese ancestry willing to be repatriated to Japan. The creation of the relocation centers followed by several months Japan's decision to intern American citizens in Japan, in occupied Manchuria, and throughout China. By June 1942, Japan had even rounded up 42 U.S. citizens living in the Aleutian Islands in Alaska and sent them to camps on Hokkaido, Japan's northern island. These were the first U.S. citizens to be captured on American territory. Sixteen died in the Japanese camp and the rest remained incarcerated for the duration of the war.

Many Japanese-American evacuees recognized the validity of the security issue. They felt safer in the war relocation centers. Even when those who were sent to war relocation centers were given an opportunity to leave the camps and work on the outside, many of them were "afraid" and refused to leave: "They'd heard all these stories out of the Hearst press and they'd heard about the shootings and they were scared." Faced with leaving this "protective environment," many of them decided to continue living at the centers instead.[29] For some Japanese-Americans, fear of what might happen to them if they were sent to live outside the war relocation centers might have also motivated their decision to request repatriation to Japan. For instance, according to one Japanese document, motivated by fear, "an increased number of them applied for repatriation, or expressed their desire to be transferred to Tule Lake."[30]

However, most of the more than 20,000 people who eventually requested repatriation to Japan did so not out of fear of retaliation, but because they really were loyal to Japan. Fully 39 percent of the 18,422 evacuees at Tule Lake from September 1943 through May 1944 had requested repatriation or expatriation, while another 26 percent refused to declare loyalty, for a total of 65 percent.[31]

Many of these, in fact the majority at almost 70 percent, were also American citizens by birth. The numbers at Tule Lake were much higher than the average of all of the centers, where 21 percent of the males refused to declare loyalty during the initial loyalty registration, while that number dropped to 16 percent after the second registration.[32] Beginning on 1 July 1944, with the passing of Public Law 405, anyone who professed loyalty to Japan could renounce their U.S. citizenship—such people were called "renunciants"—and eventually thousands did so.[33]

It was impossible to know whether a particular United States citizen of Japanese ancestry actually felt any personal loyalty to the United States. Japanese-American communities on the West Coast often sent their young children—usually boys—back to Japan to receive a Japanese education. Frequently, by the time these young men returned to the United States they had not only forgotten how to speak English but they had also lost any sense of loyalty to the United States, assuming they had ever built up such a loyalty in the first place.

Interviews conducted in the war relocation centers make this very clear. One respondent, named Kiyoto Nakao, explained that although he was born in the United States, and so was automatically a citizen, he returned to Japan at age three and remained there until age 18. When questioned, he explained that "He considers himself loyal to the emperor. Wants to join the Japanese Army." Another, named Shizuo "Ted" Yoshikawa, went to Japan when he was 7 and returned at age 22. When asked he said he was "loyal to Japan ... not loyal to the United States."[34]

In addition to protecting Japanese in the U.S. from possible attack, the war relocation centers also protected the United States from possible espionage. After 1 July 1943, when the segregation program was put into effect and those who had requested repatriation or proclaimed their loyalty to Japan were sent to Tule Lake, the relocation centers provided a necessary and important function, especially in wartime, of ensuring that these persons could not damage or in any other way work against the war effort. Even the head of the Japanese American Citizens League (JACL), Mike Masaoka, supported the segregation program: "If all those people who wanted to go to Japan were sorted out and allowed to go back, that would make things much better for the rest of the Nisei who wanted to stay here."[35]

Conclusions

The number 6,000 was considered important, since on 30 June 1944 the estimates for the number of American civilians held by Japan ranged from a low of 5,593 to a high of 6,112.[36] For a one-to-one exchange to occur with the Japanese government, 6,000 repatriates were needed. This represented a relatively small percentage of the total Japanese-American population, which was estimated to be 126,947 in the continental United States and 157,905 in Hawaii; out of 126,947 people, 111,887 lived on the West Coast, with about 93,000 in California, 14,000 in Washington, and just over 4,000 in Oregon. Of the total of 284,852 people, 200,194 were born in the United States—and so were American citizens—while another 84,658—or about 40,000 in the continental U.S.—were foreign-born aliens with no chance under the laws of that time of becoming naturalized American citizens.[37]

This would appear to be a large number to choose from. However, most of the Japanese specifically listed by the Japanese government for repatriation refused to return to Japan. In an early effort to find volunteers willing to repatriate, the Army sent out form letters signed by Colonel Karl R. Bendetsen, in charge of the WCCA, to a number of Japanese-Americans during the spring of 1942: "Certain Japanese persons are currently being considered for repatriation to Japan. You, and those members of your family listed above, are being so considered." Since many of the recipients of these letters considered themselves to be loyal Americans, the letters created "anger and deep indignation, for in effect American citizens were being 'invited' to agree to deportation from their own to an alien land."[38] However, 54 Japanese-Americans did respond positively to this letter and were included on the first exchange ship.

After June 1942, responsibility for finding eligible candidates for repatriation switched over from Colonel Bendetsen at the WCCA to the War Relocation Authority. At almost the same time the head of the WRA, Milton Eisenhower, resigned and was replaced by Dillon S. Myer, from the Department of Agriculture. Eisenhower cited as one reason for resigning that he "had lost a year's sleep in ninety days," and advised Myer to take the job only if "you can do the job and sleep at night." This administrative turmoil may have contributed to delays in interviewing evacuees to determine whether they wanted to be repatriated. Certainly Bendetsen later gave this change in leadership as the reason why "the relocation effort was largely unsuccessful."[39]

Still, even though there had been only four Japanese-Americans sent from the war relocation centers, all from the Colorado River camp, in the first exchange, it was hoped that many more would volunteer in time for the second exchange. On 27 March 1943, Myer, director of the WRA, in a "confidential" letter to Paul Taylor, director of the Jerome Relocation Center in Dermott, Arkansas, noted: "Another peculiar aspect of the whole situation is, that of all persons in relocation centers named by the Japanese Government on the lists submitted to us by the State Department, something less than ten percent have indicated a willingness to return to Japan."[40]

During the summer of 1943, Myer optimistically wrote to the war relocation center directors that during the upcoming second exchange, of the 1,500 repatriates coming from the United States "perhaps as many as 500 of these may come from relocation centers."[41] Later, this number was revised downward to 325.[42] By the time the exchange actually took place the final number was only 314.[43] Even though the Amache relocation center in Colorado sent the "fewest number of evacuees" to Tule Lake of "any WRA relocation center," of the 125 residents it transferred to Tule Lake by 16 September 1943, 35 people, or almost one-third, were "expatriated or repatriated to Japan."[44]

On 11 September 1943, Meyer reported that while 381 people had been sent to New Jersey, only 314 actually sailed, with 55 having to return to the relocation centers. Still, Meyer proudly noted that the War Relocation Authority "has had an important part of this work." In particular, he stated that "it is with considerable gratification that I am able to report that to the best of our knowledge every person in the hands of WRA on whom agreement was reached between the State Department and the Spanish Ambassador, was ready to be turned over to the State Department representative at the time the train left." Finally, Meyer congratulated his project directors: "Everyone who has had any part in getting this job done on time can justly feel that he has helped in a very real and positive way not only toward getting 1500 Americans out of the Far East, but also toward moving much needed Red Cross supplies to captured American soldiers in great need, and toward laying the groundwork for future exchanges to get back several thousand additional Americans still believed to be in the Far East."[45]

6 Life in the war relocation centers

The Japanese-American war relocation centers served a variety of functions. They gave physical security; they provided a decent standard of living; and they supplied a venue to question Japanese-Americans to determine whether or not they wanted to return to Japan. A Spanish report dated September 1943 makes it absolutely clear that the West Coast war relocation centers were considered to be a main source of Japanese nationals wishing to be repatriated to Japan from late 1942 onward. After the second exchange, few East Coast Japanese-Americans wishing to be repatriated remained. Meanwhile, most of the Japanese-Americans in Hawaii who wished to repatriate were too far away to be easily transported to the East Coast of the continental United States, in addition to the fact that travel across the Pacific during wartime was considered highly dangerous.

Many of the Japanese-American evacuees frequently changed their minds on whether to repatriate to Japan. There are several reasons for this, including fear for their personal safety if released back into American society, or a change of heart after hearing reports of Japanese defeats in the Pacific theater. After the U.S. victory at Midway, in particular, there seemed to be a newfound reluctance on the part of the Japanese-Americans to return to a Japan on the brink of losing the war.

According to at least one report, many Japanese-Americans appeared to be making their decision on repatriation based more on which country they thought might ultimately win the war, rather than on national loyalty alone. During negotiations for the second exchange, one American note that was protested by Japan reportedly stated that the major outstanding problem was that "many Japanese subjects several times changed their minds as to whether they should be repatriated or not."[1]

Life in the war relocation centers

Contrary to popular myths equating the war relocation centers with German concentration camps, the centers were not prison facilities stuck out in the middle of a desert, let alone Nazi death camps. For example, the site of the Tule Lake Relocation Center was one of the most fertile in northern California. It was very flatteringly described in one Spanish government document as "a former lake bottom reclaimed after World War I by the U.S. Bureau of Reclamation and settled mainly by veterans of the war." Although far from other populated areas, this site was described as "extremely fertile although of a sandy, lava formation."[2] Not only was it prime real estate, but there was adequate water for irrigation, making it an extremely good agricultural area.

The Tule Lake war relocation center was especially large and was divided into about 60 blocks of barracks. Altogether, these blocks were divided into 1,920 rooms that were 20' x 25' in size, 840 rooms that were 20' x 20', and then 1,488 rooms that were 20' x 16' 8". The estimated floor space per person was 110 to 130 sq. ft. Although this might appear small at first glance, this average included children and even babies. Even though a book published in 1969 stated that in "the 1960s such quarters would have been condemned as below the poverty level,"[3] most dormitory rooms in modern-day U.S. universities and colleges have similar dimensions; for example, the typical Stanford University dormitory room allotment during the mid-1990s was almost exactly that same size.[4] Each room at Tule Lake was outfitted with windows, screens, light sockets, electrical sockets, and a coal stove. Washing facilities and lavatories were divided by gender. They had hot and cold water, as did the mess halls and the laundry rooms. In some blocks, the evacuees had even managed to construct deep-bottomed Japanese-style baths.[5]

The challenges of caring for some 18,000 people were enormous. Regular food was cooked in one large kitchen staffed by 739 employees on the cooking staff supported by 384 dishwashers, while a second "special kitchen has been set up for the preparation of Japanese dishes and meals which are then sent out to the various mess halls." In 1943, there was a "modern up-to-date slaughter house," a "new pickling house is under construction," and together "with canning operations it will serve to preserve much of the vegetable crop for use throughout the winter." Food was distributed to 62 mess halls, staffed by 389 waiters, waitresses, and laundresses.[6]

In addition to a mess hall, each block had its own recreation hall, which was either devoted to sports or was used for "special activities and administrative work." In 1943, some "35,000 board feet of lumber has been purchased and made into benches, tables and other equipment for the recreation halls throughout the Project." Also, a "Little Theater organization" was founded and it "gives new groups of plays each month." Outdoor sports included baseball, basketball, volley ball, and "sumo or wrestling pits," and groups like the Boy Scouts, Camp Fire Girls, and YWCA were active. There was one library with 22,000 books, and three motion picture projectors for showing films in the mess halls, where: "Films are largely fairly recent Hollywood releases." In order to purchase a more modern film projector, $4,000 was expended by the Tule Lake Cooperative Enterprise and "plans are underway to have regular shows in the high school auditorium."[7]

For school-aged children there were several nursery schools, an elementary school, and a new high school that contained 40 classrooms, including two science laboratories, one room for cooking classes, and one sewing room. The high school also had a 1,200-person auditorium and a stage that could be turned into a 60' by 90' basketball court. Unfortunately, during the segregation phase for Tule Lake, tensions ran so high that many teachers quit. This meant that "public schooling was no longer compulsory at Tule Lake."[8]

For older students, there was adult education in "English, floral arrangement, sewing, commercial subjects, etc." Finally, religious literature and services were available for the 50 Catholics, 1,200 Protestants, approximately 4,500 Buddhists, and then an indeterminate number who followed various Shinto sects; at the center were several Protestant ministers and six Buddhist priests.[9] The sole exception to this guarantee of religious freedom was State Shintoism, since "State Shinto is not regarded by the Japanese Government as being a religion."[10]

Throughout their stay at the relocation centers, the evacuees were allowed to vote in national, state, and local elections. On 4 August 1942, the Wartime Civil Control Administration wrote to all managers of the relocation centers explaining how this procedure would work. Each evacuee had to conform to the laws of the state that they came from. If that state allowed absentee ballots then: "Qualified citizen evacuees occupy the same position in regard to the exercise of their right of franchise by absentee voting as does any other citizen who for any reason is absent from his voting precinct, or is physically unable to go to his polling place on the day of election." So as not to interfere with the evacuee's ability to vote, "No restrictions will be placed on the discussion of politics and candidates for political office by the evacuees," and political candidates were even permitted to visit evacuees in the visitors' area "to talk to individual evacuees concerning the political campaign."[11]

Interaction with the outside world was not only possible, but was even encouraged. Visitors were not limited by number and could visit from 8:00 am-8:00 pm daily; they could even spend the night if given permission by the center administrators. Mail both leaving and arriving at the center was unlimited, and books and newspapers mailed directly from publishers were not examined. Other packages, however, were examined for contraband, which included "liquor, firearms, cameras, short wave radios." Except for parcel post packages, all other mail was uncensored and there was no restriction on the people to whom or the places to which the evacuees could write. The use of telephone and telegraph was also unlimited, although payment was required.[12]

There has long been a misunderstanding that the evacuees lost all of their possessions. This is simply not true. All commercial properties, defined as "property other than household and personal effects," were not shipped to the projects but were kept at government expense in warehouses. In addition, "evacuee property stored in Japanese churches, halls, and other similar places of private storage" was gathered and put in warehouses. These items, as well as household and personal property, could be shipped to the project, but "only upon acknowledgment by the Project Directors of their ability to receive and dispose of this property." This condition was due mainly to the limited storage space at the relocation centers. The one exception was: "Property now in private storage may be shipped direct to the project if evacuees desire so to do at *their own* expense."[13]

All evacuee medical care was provided gratis. One hospital with 225 beds serviced the entire center, and it had four Japanese doctors and one intern working full time. There was also a pharmacy that distributed all "necessary medicines," and there was dental care. All evacuees were given medical examinations when they first arrived and when they left. Examinations were also provided as necessary in cases of illness. If the local hospital staff was not adequate, then the Chief Medical Officer could authorize using outside facilities. As such times, "the patient is sent to nearest facility offering such care."[14]

Family life at the Tule Lake Relocation Center

Everyone at the Tule Lake Relocation Center was treated exactly the same by the administration even though the Japanese-American community could be divided into a number of distinct groups, including the four basic groups (1) Japanese citizens who felt loyalty to the United States, (2) Japanese citizens who felt loyalty to Japan, (3) American citizens who felt loyalty to the United States, and finally (4) American citizens who felt loyalty to Japan. This situation became particularly difficult when a husband and wife, or perhaps a parent and child, had conflicting loyalties; such disagreements led to family turmoil, and sometimes even to the splitting of a family, as some elected to return to Japan while others elected to remain in the United States.

To complicate this situation even further, there were divisions between the older first generation, *Issei*, and the younger second generation, *Nisei*. Most Issei were not American citizens, because the gentlemen's agreement forbade it, while most Nisei were, because they had been born in the United States. Among the older male Issei, many had never married because of the shortage of Japanese women. Called by a variety of names, including "fruit tramps," because they were largely engaged in fruit farming, these older unmarried Issei were described as "hard-living fellows with a reputation for spending their earnings on drink, gambling and women." Many of them were also troublemakers: "Having no stake in America in the form of children, property or established business, they were inclined to be resistant and obstructive, even though they had lost far less through evacuation than many of those who had families."[15]

Finally, there were the *Kibei*, young Japanese-American children, most of them U.S. citizens by birth, who had studied in Japan during their teens, and then returned to the United States when they were from 15 to 18 years of age. The Kibei represented a special problem since they were mostly American citizens, but because of their educational background in Japan were often the most outspokenly loyal to the Japanese Emperor. Also, as noted by one sociologist, "the Kibei were under severe cross pressures within the West Coast Japanese community, being accepted neither by the Issei elders nor by their fellow Nisei citizens. As a consequence they were very insecure individuals. A few of them seized the opportunity afforded by the confusion that prevailed in the center during the early months to ... foment anti-administration sentiments among the residents."[16] In 1944, a high school dance held at Tule Lake was interrupted by "Kibei vigilantes" who told the more Americanized Nisei "Your're going back to Japan."[17]

During the fall of 1943, Japanese of Japanese nationality and Japanese of American nationality were mixed together at the Tule Lake Relocation Center, irrespective of their national loyalties. Conflicting loyalties led to disagreements over many fundamental issues, such as whether young men should register for the draft, which family members should repatriate to Japan, and how best to keep the family together. As the war heated up, so did conflicts in the relocation centers. These became particularly sharp between those young men who expressed loyalty to the United States and so signed up to join the U.S. military and those who were loyal to the emperor and so refused to register. Personal conflicts of this type eventually led to demands by the evacuees themselves to be segregated into various groups. A segregation program was introduced at the Tule Lake Relocation Center beginning in the fall and winter of 1943.

The number of evacuees at the Tule Lake Relocation Center was constantly changing, due to births, deaths, entrance to colleges and universities, and permission to live and work outside of the camps. As of September 1943 there were just over 13,250 evacuees at the center. Of these, the number of men (7,011) was slightly greater than women (6,242). Although the exact number of evacuees who were Japanese citizens and of those who were American citizens was not known for sure—in part perhaps because of the difficulty in obtaining proper documentation such as birth certificates—it was estimated as of September 1943 that of this number some 4,607 (2,734 men and 1,873 women) were Japanese citizens, while the much larger number of 8,846 (4,277 men and 4,569 women) were Americans by birth.[18]

An unusually large proportion of the evacuees at the Tule Lake Relocation Center who requested repatriation were Kibei, those considered potentially most dangerous because of their recent experiences as students in Japan. When a segregation program was instituted beginning during the summer of 1943, therefore, the Tule Lake Relocation Center became the most logical choice for concentrating those who wanted to return to Japan, since fewer evacuees would have to be shifted from one relocation center to another. Therefore, the Tule Lake relocation center also became the focus for administering all Japanese citizens and American citizens of Japanese ancestry who were to be included in the exchange program with Japan.

The problem with labor and discipline

According to the Geneva Convention, the Japanese-American evacuees could not legally be forced to work. However, at the Tule Lake Relocation Center, approximately 6,000 of the 15,000 detainees elected to work voluntarily as members of a cooperative. Employment of all kinds, both within and outside of the center, could be found through the placement office. Most of the 6,000 laborers who elected to work within the center were members of the Tule Lake Cooperative, which ran a variety of businesses, including a thriving fish market that opened in July 1943.

To help organize the evacuees at Tule Lake, the Cooperative League of America was asked by the U.S. government "to find and hire people who could organize consumer-owned and operated, non-profit stores." Don Elberson was sent to Tule Lake during 1942, and his daughter recounts that he worked hard there to build the cooperative on "non-racist, democratic principles."[19] By the following year—1943—the Tule Lake Cooperative paid a "nine per cent patronage dividend" which was "payable half in cash orders and half in certificates of indebtedness which represents the return of approximately $100,000 in earnings." Monthly wages were $12 for apprentices, $16 for unskilled labor, and $19 for skilled labor and professionals.[20] Initially payments were not always made on time and not always accurate, but this was not so much the fault of "specific individuals" as due to "the complications of administrative procedure, confusion, rapid growth, limited personnel and equipment, ignorance of policy, and lack of communication from the Washington offices down to the foreman."[21]

The Tule Lake Relocation Center grew its own vegetables. Unlike with the general American public, vegetables were not rationed at Tule Lake. But, like all other American citizens at the time, for other types of foods the evacuees were required to follow the National Food Rationing regulations. They were given 48 points per month for processed foods, 16 points per month for meat, and 2 pounds of sugar per person per month. Extra food could be purchased at the Coop stores, which stocked a variety of fish and poultry, fruits and vegetables, and soft drinks. It also sold tobacco products of all types, toiletries, hardware, dry goods, and clothing.[22]

According to a report from 1943, 44 percent more land was under active cultivation then than just a year before. This corresponded to a 1,200 acre increase, which meant that a total of 3,900 acres were under cultivation. The members of the Tule Lake Cooperative were also raising some 30,000 chickens and 1,000 hogs and: "The products of all farming operations are going completely for the use of the Tule Lake Project and other relocation centers."[23] As a result of these farming operations, the basic diet for evacuees at the Tule Lake Relocation Center was actually better than for the general public living outside the center.

In addition to any money earned working, the administrators of the relocation center were responsible for providing stipends for basic necessities, such as clothing. A monthly clothing allowance of $3.75 was provided for those 16 years or older, $3.25 for ages 8-16, and $2.25 for children under 8. This allowance was paid to any adult and their dependents once they had been "employed 15 days or more per month," as well as to "all people who are in need." However, for those who for some reason could not work, and so were particularly in need, additional monthly stipends were paid to "destitute Japanese" of $4.75 for male adults and $4.25 for female adults, with $2.50 for children ages 13–17, and $1.50 for children under 13.[24]

As might be expected with a community of this size, there were occasional deaths due to illness or old age. The main causes were listed as tuberculosis, diabetes, and peptic ulcers; there was only one case of suicide listed, identified as a 45-year-old man named Mitsuye Kashi who had died of "Strangulation due to rope around neck." The families of the deceased decided if they should be buried in the community cemetery or cremated; in line with Japanese traditions, most chose cremation. Wills were prepared free of charge "for anyone wishing," and in cases of intestate deaths the State Bar of California had helped "getting over two thousand California lawyers to agree to take the cases of evacuees at a reduced fee schedule."[25]

The center administrators were also in charge of law enforcement. They could punish misdemeanors by depriving evacuees of "pay, clothing allowance, unemployment compensation and/or public assistance grants up to a limit of 90 days." Evacuees could also be jailed for up to 90 days in the Klamath County Jail, Klamath Falls, Oregon, but while there: "Such prisoners are considered prisoners of the WRA and not of Klamath County." For felony cases, the evacuees were turned over to the Modoc County police and they were tried according to the Laws of the State of California. From January to September 1943, a total of 350 arrests were made. Most of these were for "traffic offenses, persons out of bounds and arrests incident to registration resistance." The mere fact that traffic offenses were one of the major law enforcement problems shows that many evacuees had access to cars or other motorized vehicles. Ten of those under arrest were awaiting trial at the time of the Spanish report, and they were given legal advice by a Project Attorney and his assistant.[26]

This short description of the Tule Lake Relocation Center shows that life there was in no way comparable to survival in a concentration camp. However, it was wartime, and since they were cut off from regular American society most of the evacuees "had no way of knowing that much of the deprivation they were suffering was a common lot with the rest of the nation." As one critic of the centers admitted: "The camp hotheads, justified as they were in the vociferous protests, were unwittingly contrasting the plight of the *nihonjin* [Japanese] with a fat and prosperous America they had known before the war—not with an America terribly deprived and shackled by the demands of an all-out and world-wide struggle."[27]

Military registration and loyalty oaths

In addition to providing a good livelihood for the Japanese-American evacuees, however, the relocation centers carried out other necessary functions, including military registration and requests for repatriation to Japan. During most of 1942, the Wartime Civil Control Administration (WCCA) was in charge of the exchanges. However, as of 15 November 1942, the War Relocation Authority was solely responsible for handling Japanese citizens and American citizens of Japanese ancestry who had applied for repatriation.[28]

After the attack on Pearl Harbor, the WCCA was established and retained control until the first exchange was completed. Its job was to set up temporary assembly centers to prepare Japanese citizens for repatriation to Japan and to get them ready to move into the war relocation centers. Because of delays organizing the second exchange, however, "practically all of the potential repatriates have now been transferred from assembly centers to the relocation centers administered by War Relocation Authority." Given this fact, on 9 October 1942, John J. McCloy, Assistant Secretary of War, informed Dillon Myer, Director of the WRA, that "it has seemed the only sensible thing for War Relocation Authority to assume the responsibilities previously assumed by Wartime Civil Control Administration in making the necessary transportation arrangements and taking care of all other related details." For the time being, however, the WCCA continued to "canvas" those individuals mentioned on the Japanese priority lists "to ascertain their desires concerning repatriation." This information would then be forwarded to the State Department.[29]

Once this change took effect, then the WRA suddenly became the single largest organization involved in the U.S.–Japanese exchanges. It ran ten relocation centers: Colorado River in Parker, Arizona, Manzanar in Manzanar, California, Gila River in Casa Grande, Arizona, Tule Lake in Stanley, California, Central Utah in Delta, Utah, Minidoka in Eden, Idaho, Heart Mountain in Vocation, Wyoming, Granada in Granada, Colorado, Rohwer in Rohwer, Arkansas, and Jerome in Jerome, Arkansas. By contrast there were only three Immigration Detention Camps in Camp Kenedy in Kenedy, Texas, Camp Seagoville in Seagoville, Texas, and Ellis Island, New York; four U.S. Army Internment Camps at Camp Livingston in Simms, Louisiana, Camp Lordsburg in Lordsburg, New Mexico, Ft. Meade in Ft. Meade, Maryland, and Camp Forrest in Tullahoma, Tennessee. Finally the U.S. State Department kept some Japanese officials at the Assembly Inn in Montreat, North Carolina.[30]

The WRA was in charge of registration and repatriation questions within all of the relocation centers. In early January 1943 the Army lifted its Selective Service rule that barred Americans of Japanese ancestry from serving in the Army. Registering for the military was required by law for all young men older than 18. Eventually, a total of 25,778 Japanese-Americans served in the Army, with 13,528 of these from the continental United States and another 12,240 from Hawaii. Because of their skill in translating Japanese codes, including the Z Plan that made the Marianas invasion a success, MacArthur's chief of intelligence reportedly credited the Nisei with saving over a million U.S. lives.[31] When a draft call went out on 20 January 1944 that included eligible Nisei, most of those who had registered from the relocation centers joined up, but "300 refused to be inducted."[32]

Just because they were eligible to serve did not mean Japanese-Americans were automatically inducted into the army, since many were not able to pass the physical examinations, or were excluded for other reasons. For example, at the camp at Topaz, Utah, 113 men volunteered to join the army, but only 59—just slightly over half—were accepted. Sometimes those who volunteered were subjected to mistreatment: "Those who did volunteer found themselves and their families threatened by Nikkei [Japanese] who had become violently anti-American as a result of the controversy."[33] Perhaps as a result of internal pressure not to volunteer, all ten relocation centers together only provided 805 volunteers, which was far below the administration's optimistic 3,600 estimate, based on roughly 350 volunteers from each center.[34]

Many of the young men of Japanese ancestry were suspicious of joining the army, looking at registration for the draft as a virtual death sentence: "We are taught that if you go out to war you should go with the idea that you are never coming back ... the men go out prepared to die. If they live through it, that's their good luck."[35] But the fact that so many young Japanese-American women volunteered for the Women's Auxiliary Army Corps (WAAC, later called just the WAC) put pressure on the men to volunteer: "The young women also held parties for the male volunteers, and suddenly enlisting became exciting and fun."[36]

In the war relocation centers, before volunteers for the army would be considered for induction they had first to declare loyalty to the United States. Beginning in January 1943, questionnaires were distributed "to determine those individuals in whom the United States can place full trust and confidence." Before being given the questionnaire an address was read. It explained "there are some individuals in this center whose ties with the Japanese Empire are such as to disqualify them for positions of trust in this country. This does not mean that they will not be treated humanely, but it does mean that it would be unwise for this government in this time of crisis to give them an opportunity to endanger the national security." Those who registered and then were inducted would be formed into their own combat teams within the U.S. Army to be a "symbol of something greater than your individual selves" and a "living reproach to those who have been prejudiced against you because of your Japanese blood."[37]

The Army and the WRA used two slightly different questionnaires. The Army questionnaire asked young men who were American citizens: "27. Are you willing to serve in the armed forces of the United States, wherever ordered?" Meanwhile, the WRA asked women and aliens the following question: "27. If the opportunity presents itself and you are found qualified, would you be willing to volunteer for the Army Nurse Corps or the WAAC?" As for loyalty, the Army asked: "28. Will you swear unqualified allegiance to the United States of America and faithfully defend the United States from any all attack by foreign or domestic forces, and foreswear any form of allegiance of obedience to the Japanese Emperor, or any other foreign government, power, or organization?" On this question, the WRA asked: "28. Will you swear unqualified allegiance to the United States of America and foreswear any form of allegiance or obedience to the Japanese Emperor, or any other foreign government, power, or organization?"[38]

Morgan Yamanaka, who lived at Tule Lake, answered "no-no" to questions 27 and 28. He was not alone, but was one of 18,700—or about 16 percent of all evacuees—who either answered "no-no," or who after answering "yes" then refused to register and "who were ultimately labeled 'disloyal' and segregated at Tule Lake."[39] In his case, the fact that his brother, cousins, and uncles in Japan were probably already in the army led Mr. Yamanaka to decide "I would not want to fight our brother." Meanwhile, John Kanda, also at Tule Lake, answered "yes-yes" and was eventually drafted as a replacement for the 442nd Regimental Combat Team, serving in the U.S. Army with distinction in France and Italy.[40] According to one account, however, many Japanese-Americans answered "no-no" out of "familial duty," since they were afraid of either being forced to leave the centers or of being inducted into the army, thus splitting up their families; according to this view, only about 5 percent of the evacuees answered "no-no" out of a "strong conviction" or as "a protest against their imprisonment."[41]

For the Issei, the loyalty question was particularly troublesome. Many of them "unquestionably sympathized with the forces of the enemy."[42] Even if they did not, if they declared their loyalty to the United States by denouncing the Japanese emperor this was tantamount to renouncing their Japanese citizenship. Yet, because of the particular rules under which they had come to the United States, they were also prevented from becoming U.S. citizens. What this meant in practice was that the Issei were being asked to "voluntarily assume a stateless status," where they were no longer citizens of Japan and yet were also not American citizens.[43] For many Issei, being stateless may have been considered a worse fate than declaring false loyalty to Japan.

There was a very good reason why the Japanese men were eligible to be inducted into the Army, but not into the Navy. On 17 April 1944, Frank Knox, Secretary of the Navy, wrote to Harold Ickes, Secretary of the Interior, to explain why the Navy would not accept these otherwise highly qualified candidates. By this time the Navy's limited ranks were full, so any new recruits would be inducted for general service and sent overseas to work at a U.S. naval base. According to Knox: "While they might be wholly loyal, it would be quite possible for disloyal Japanese to impersonate these naval personnel with highly damaging results. Furthermore, one disloyal person could do tremendous damage aboard a naval ship, while his capacity for sabotage in an Army unit, with the type of organization and employment in that service, would be very limited indeed."[44]

However, many Japanese were asked to teach Navy officers at the Navy's language school at the University of Colorado, Boulder. There was pressure among the older generation not to accept such offers, since "many Japanese accused these Issei instructors of betraying Japan. It has been contended that teaching the naval officers who would use the benefits of the instruction for destruction of Japan is not a proper act for any Issei who is loyal to Japan. Some of the extremists have argued that their act is that of traitors." While many of the

Issei agreed to teach at the school, they could not help but wonder if they would be treated as traitors after the war: "Some of them were worried what would happen to them after the war when they return to Japan."[45]

After the registration process was over, one-on-one interviews were conducted with the young men who had refused to register. As a group, most of them had lived in Japan and had received most of their elementary schooling in Japan. They usually felt primary loyalty to Japan, therefore, rather than to the United States. According to representative answers listed on interview forms, Sumito Sumida, age 24, "is loyal to the emperor. Will not register." Fujio Uchiyama, 27, "says he is loyal to Japan. Refuses to register." Shigeru "Sam" Nagao, 26, "will not register under any condition." Don Oshita, 22, "wants to go back to Japan. Will not register." [46]

Registration was made more difficult by active opposition among the Kibei. In the war relocation centers, many young men organized protests against the registration process, trying their best to dissuade Japanese-Americans loyal to the United States from registering for the draft. According to interview data, many of these young men proudly asserted their opposition to registration. For example, Kazuo Miyaki, 21, "participated in a mob and definitely obstructed registration." Eiichi Yamamoto, 27, "was in the mob this morning to obstruct registration."[47]

Registering for repatriation

In addition to processing registration for the draft, accepting and processing requests for repatriation was another primary task of the War Relocation Authority. While the Washington office was theoretically in charge of the entire effort, because of its close links to the State Department, most of the work took place on the West Coast. Therefore, the San Francisco office of the WRA "will locate evacuees under consideration for repatriation, will circularize lists to determine whether evacuees will accept or decline repatriation if offered, and will tabulate, summarize, and analyze replies as may be required." Meanwhile, Project Directors at each relocation center "will be responsible for accomplishing or expediting all phases of repatriation at the Relocation Centers."[48]

Repatriation was entirely voluntary. The U.S. government did not force Japanese nationals to return to Japan, nor did the Japanese government order them to return. In fact, early in the negotiations for the U.S.–Japanese exchanges it became clear that many candidates identified by the Japanese government for repatriation did not intend to return to Japan. Therefore, the U.S. government decided that: "Every person whose name appears on official lists must be given the opportunity to indicate privately on the basis of his own choice and determination whether he wishes to go to Japan."[49]

Those Japanese who were named by the Japanese government were sent a form letter. If they accepted repatriation, they were required to fill out four copies of the form "Individual Request for Repatriation," Form R-100. If they declined it they had to sign a form entitled "Declaration of Declination." This form stated:

"I, —— declare that I have been informed that I am under consideration for exchange to the Empire of Japan by reason of the request of the Japanese Government. I further declare that I desire to remain in the United States and that I do not desire to go to the Empire of Japan, nor otherwise to be repatriated to Japan."[50]

For those who appeared on one of the lists developed by the Japanese government for repatriation, they could either accept and fill out the proper forms or sign a declaration refusing to repatriate. Sometimes this decision was very traumatic, so that people would change their minds several times before making a firm decision. For example, on 8 March 1943, George Hiroshi Sawamura wrote to the administrator of the Central Utah Relocation Project, in Topaz, Utah, to say that he had changed his mind about repatriation:

> When I put in for repatriation, I wanted to be with my parents. Although my parents were born in Japan and they want to return to their homeland, I, upon more thorough reflection, realize that I have nothing in Japan, spiritually or materially, which I can call my own. Everything I value is in this country. The flurry and excitement during the registration for persons between 17 and 38 years of age caused me to hastily put in for repatriation. I now know that I was mistaken.[51]

What especially discouraged those in the relocation centers was the mystery that surrounded the repatriation process. As one person living in the Poston, Arizona, relocation center later commented:

> When we were put here we thought that we'd be here just a few weeks and then would be allowed to go out. When we found out that that wasn't so and that we were all going to be treated like enemy aliens, we thought we would be allowed to stay here in peace as neutrals during the war. We didn't expect all this haggling with the government. We didn't expect that the people would be split and bothered by one request and proposition after another. We didn't expect fights over self-government, registration, volunteering, relocation, and now segregation. Haven't these people been tortured enough?[52]

Of course, much of this apparent mystery had to do with the strict legal requirements for the U.S.–Japanese exchanges, which stipulated that administrators ensure that repatriation was voluntary. Many who claimed repatriation changed their minds later. For this reason, the Japanese-Americans in the war relocation centers were required to meet with administrators for formal interviews and were asked to fill out copious forms.

In most cases children under 18, even though full American citizens by birth, were required to do whatever their parents thought best. Therefore, even though the children might be born-and-raised American citizens, speak English, and perhaps never have even visited or lived in Japan, they might be forced by their parents to choose repatriation. Sometimes the parents relented and let the children remain. For example, on 8 March 1943, Kaoru Yoshifuji wrote that he wanted to cancel his repatriation request, explaining that at first his whole family had requested repatriation together but "the young members of our family have now agreed and decided to stay here with the consent of our parents."[53] Although children often "convinced" parents not to return to Japan, parents could "decide" on behalf of any child under 18, so there were probably many cases of young Japanese being forced to request repatriation. As one Japanese-American later related: "To many an internee it was a sad thing to watch friends and cousins fling away their citizenship. It seemed stark tragedy to watch family-oriented Niseis surrender completely to the plans and dictates of their embittered fathers."[54]

In an effort to help these young Japanese-Americans, sometimes the directors of the relocation centers would bend the rules slightly and allow minors above the age of 16 to make up their own minds about repatriation. In other cases, when the youths celebrated their eighteenth birthday they could immediately decide whether to withdraw their repatriation request. However, most times they had no choice but to do whatever their parents decided was best for the entire family; this situation had many parallels with the modern-day case of Elian Gonzales, who in 2000 was forcibly returned to Cuba when the U.S. courts ordered the government to hand over the six-year-old boy to his father, even though his mother had died in the process of getting her son out of the country.[55]

The same kinds of problems occurred between husbands and wives, since traditionally men had made decisions on behalf of their spouse and most of the Japanese husbands were older than their wives. Sometimes an Americanized wife could change her husband's mind: on 5 March 1943, Shigeo Sakamoto wrote to explain "My wife Sadako and my three children refuse to join me to return to Japan. ... Since they refuse to return with me I wish to remain here." Other times it might be an older child who changed the parents' minds. On 8 March 1943, Yutaka Okita wrote: "My daughter, Aiko, who is 26 years old, has received education in the United States. She has changed our minds and has impressed us as to our advantage in staying in this democratic United States."[56]

It was hard to keep track of the number of people requesting repatriation, since it was not uncommon for them to change their minds ... sometimes more than once. By 27 March 1945, however, the Special War Problems Division, Department of State, was able to provide "a list of 20,161 individuals of the Japanese race who accept repatriation."[57] Although accurate through May 1944, there was constant change to this list as children reached their eighteenth year and could decide for themselves. The instructions to Project Directors emphasized that all Japanese seeking repatriation to Japan had to be treated well. They were reminded to conduct all "inspections and examinations ... with proper dignity and without embarrassment to the repatriates." This was for a good reason: "It should be borne in mind that repatriation is a reciprocal arrangement, that the United States expects similar correct treatment to be accorded to American nationals being returned to the United States, and that breach of faith on this occasion may complicate the return of Americans from the Orient on future exchanges."[58]

The length and detailed instructions of this document show that by the end of 1942 one primary responsibility of the war relocation centers was facilitating the U.S.–Japanese exchanges. A supplemental instruction reminded the Project Directors that if "any of the Japanese named on your list for repatriation fail to leave for any reason, wire immediately to Mr. Fitch in Washington the name of the Japanese and the reason for failure to leave. This is important as we have to substitute (sic) for them at the last moment and we must notify the Japanese Government."[59] This reminder suggests that many of the rules and regulations adopted by the war relocation centers were in place to satisfy the Japanese demand for reciprocity.

Conclusions

The vast majority of Japanese citizens and American citizens of Japanese ancestry identified by the Japanese government for probable repatriation— reportedly as many as 90 percent of the total—declined the opportunity to be repatriated and thereby return to Japan. Instead, thousands of other Japanese citizens and American citizens of Japanese ancestry not on the list declared their desire to return to Japan. It would appear from the general tenor of the official protests that the Japanese government was surprised and not altogether pleased by these results. In fact, it accused the U.S. government of putting pressure on the Japanese-American evacuees not to agree to be repatriated.

The most probable reason for the Japanese government's disappointment was that many of the individuals mentioned by name on its list were highly valued merchants, teachers, and students—all potentially of great importance to Tokyo's on-going war effort. Meanwhile, those individuals who voluntarily agreed to return to Japan included large numbers of elderly and the infirm, and many young and unskilled Kibei; some of the Kibei could barely speak the Japanese language or read Japanese characters, so they were not necessarily even trusted by their fellow Japanese. This meant that these candidates were not considered to be of high importance by the Japanese government.

In sharp contrast to the Japanese government's pressing desire to obtain skilled people knowledgeable about their enemy, the U.S. government had altogether different priorities. From the American perspective, by late 1943 and early 1944 the conduct of the war was going quite well. Therefore, Washington's highest goal was to repatriate its citizens, especially women and children, in order to ensure the health and well-being of the largest number possible. Unfortunately, negotiations leading up to the second exchange proved particularly difficult.

7   Tokyo protests mistreatment of officials and its impact on the second exchange

Japan was not pleased with the first exchange. On 27 October 1942, the Japanese government sent a lengthy protest through the Spanish Embassy accusing the U.S. government of mistreating many of the Japanese officials involved in the exchanges. The Japanese government stated that it was "astonished at the most inhuman cruelty and insult inflicted upon them" during the "course of their arrest, examination, internment and transport." In particular, the Japanese protest noted that the "United States Government have thereby violated their solemn declaration to apply, as far as possible, to interned non-combatants the provisions of the Convention relating to the Treatment of Prisoners of War signed in Geneva in July, 1929."[1]

On 12 December 1942, the U.S. State Department sent the first of several memoranda answering this Japanese protest. It assured the Japanese government that it had "instructed all of its officers concerned with the handling of Japanese subjects to exercise the most scrupulous care that their actions with relation to Japanese under their control shall be governed by the humanitarian principles of the Geneva Prisoners of War Convention and the generally recognized principle of international law with a view to the maintenance of the highest possible standards of humanitarian treatment." Therefore, as in the past when it had investigated all complaints of "alleged mistreatment," the "American Government is now making a thorough investigation of every complaint … with a view to removing the causes of the legitimate complaints and taking appropriate disciplinary action with regard to them."[2]

As for the detention, transport, and treatment of all evacuees, Washington noted that "upon the outbreak of hostilities the American Government proceeded to the construction at expense of detention and internment camps prepared in accordance with the provisions of the Geneva Prisoners of war convention." All evacuees were transferred "with the utmost rapidity possible," using "standard trains," and with the "greatest possible comfort." Contrary to Tokyo's criticism, evacuees were not like convicts, but were "placed in special detention stations and camps." Even clothing was provided "in most cases" from "American army stores" in "accordance with the provisions of the Geneva Convention for the supplying of needed clothing to prisoners of war."[3]

Numerous Japanese protests and U.S. government attempts to respond to them ultimately delayed the second exchange. The divergence of views between the Japanese and U.S. governments over the future of the exchange program was large, and growing. The Japanese government, in particular, appeared eager to seize every opportunity to criticize the U.S. for not fulfilling the terms of the 1929 Geneva Convention, even though Japan had never ratified that particular agreement. Meanwhile, in Japan's own detention camps, thousands of American citizens were being denied even the most basic food allotments, proper clothing, and medical care.

Alleged mistreatment of Japanese officials, family, and staff

After the first exchange, the Japanese government sent a lengthy protest to the U.S. government that accused the American authorities of "cruel and inhuman" treatment of Japanese officials, their families, and members of their staff. It stated that "grave insult was inflicted upon the Japanese officials in utter disregard of well-established international usage concerning the treatment of Consular officials," and expressed its astonishment at such "outrageous measures indulged in by the American authorities."[4] Before the second exchange of officials and non-officials could be arranged, these protests had to be addressed.

The bulk of the information provided by the Japanese government in its protest concerned the Japanese consulate-general in Honolulu, since the consul-general of that office was included on the first exchange ship. This protest was divided into six main sections that followed in chronological order the raid on the consulate-general in Honolulu and the internment of its personnel, the U.S. searches of that office and the residences, "unreasonable" restrictions put on the consular officials during their internment, their voyage to the continental U.S., their stay at the Arizona Plateau internment camp, and finally unwarranted delays related to their embarkation onto the first exchange ship.[5]

According to the Japanese account, approximately ten Hawaiian policemen began to guard the Japanese consulate-general in Honolulu at 9:30 am on 7 December 1941. At about noon, a group of about ten officials, including "Benjamin Van Kuren, Captain of Detectives of the Honolulu Police Station, his men, and members of the F.B.I.," stormed the back door, and gathered the consul-general and others into a room where they examined their clothing and forced them to undress. The Japanese protested that they "even committed such an act of affront as to force the consul-general to take off his under-pants" so that they could be searched. From that day through until 22 January 1942, the consul-general, his wife, and six other members of the staff were kept under constant guard in the Consulate-General building, and during this period, they "were not permitted to converse with their respective families who were allowed to have a walk in the compound at the same time, nor to return to their homes situated within the compound."[6]

The Japanese government also protested U.S. authorities searching the consulate-general and the official residences nearby. According to the Japanese account, the "police searched freely every part of the office, without obtaining the permission of the consul-general or asking him to be present thereat." The searches led to the destruction of the door to the "cable room" as well as of several steel cabinets. In the residences, U.S. authorities "wantonly opened trunks and chests, searching and seizing articles," which included "radios, cameras and money." While most of the money was later deposited with the Bishop National Bank, a total of "sixty dollars, two baseball gloves, two rolls of bleached cotton" were stolen from Mr. Tsukigawa, a chancellor, while "twenty-one dollars and one set of Sheaffer fountain pen and sharp pencil" were stolen from a Mr. Seki, another chancellor. According to this protest: "The police authorities admitted the probability of this theft on the part of the policemen."[7]

In addition to their detention and the searches, the members of the Japanese consulate-general in Honolulu, their families, and the staff were forced to live under many restrictions. From 7 December 1941 through 18 June 1942, when these officials actually embarked on the exchange ship, they were not allowed to read any newspapers. Without money, they could not buy many daily necessities, and when they were sent to the continental U.S. they asked and were denied permission to "purchase overcoats, sweaters, socks, underwear, etc., for their families, (these articles had not been necessary in such a mild climate as in Honolulu) but Captain Van Kuren allowed them to buy only tooth-paste, tooth-brushes and one other article." Finally, prior to their departure all luggage was searched, and "photographs, memos and all other papers" were seized "at random."[8]

The searches reportedly continued at sea. For example, on 8 January 1942, the Japanese officials and their families boarded a steamer bound for the United States. Before departure, they and their luggage were searched. The personal searches were thorough and the "consul-general and his staff were forced to become almost naked." The women, in particular, were forced to disrobe until the wife of the one of the consular officials was wearing only a "chemise", at which point even her underwear was inspected from behind. The womens' hair was also "ransacked" so as to "ascertain whether nothing was hidden there." When the luggage was once again searched, "several hundred articles" were seized, which included "books, note-books, toys, cakes, toilet articles, soap, knives, lighters, cards, albums, etc." The searchers were so thorough that they evidently "even tore off the eyes of Teddy bears and cut the body open to examine inside."[9]

After arriving in the continental U.S., the Japanese party of 23 were put on a train and on 19 February 1942 arrived at a camp at Arizona Plateau. Later, they found out that they were at the "Triangle T. Ranch near Dragoon," where they were housed in "four bungalows suitable only for temporary shelter." During April, an F.B.I. agent named Tillman came from Honolulu to interview them. From 17 to 22 April 1942, he subjected the consular officials and their families to "very severe cross-examinations," which included subjecting "Mr. Okuda, Vice-Consul, to a cross-examination lasting many hours using threatening language."[10]

Finally, the sixth and last section of this lengthy Japanese protest detailed delays in embarkation. According to the Japanese government, the consul-general and his staff left Arizona on 8 June 1942, and arrived in New York City three days later. Even though other Japanese officials had already boarded the exchange vessel, the group from Honolulu were kept "imprisoned" in the Pennsylvania Hotel for a week, and were allowed to embark just on 18 June, only three hours before the ship departed. During this time, no information was given to the Japanese ambassador, Admiral K. Nomura, even though he made "repeated inquiries" as to their whereabouts. In concluding, the Japanese government stated: "These measures towards the members of the Japanese consulate-general at Honolulu were, it must be admitted, unnecessarily strict and severe, contrary to international usage, and utterly incomprehensible."[11]

The Japanese government insisted that the United States government answer these charges prior to a second exchange. This attitude was generally in line with Tokyo's insistence on "reciprocity" pertaining to all matters related to the exchange. The American side, by contrast, took the view that such alleged mistreatment was a separate matter, and so should not impact the continuation of the U.S.–Japanese exchanges.

The U.S. response to Japan's protests

The U.S. government responded carefully to the lengthy Japanese protest. The State Department emphasized that "comments of Japanese Government do not take into consideration proximity of former Japanese Consulate General to military and naval installations and fact that after Japanese attack on island of Oahu certain precautions were immediately necessary in view of probable further hostilities in that area." Therefore, the policemen were sent to "protect the Japanese Consulate General," and the consul-general acknowledged at the time that it was "under protective custody in view of outbreak of hostilities." According to this note: "Mr. Kita Consul General was for his part full aware of these circumstances and later expressed his appreciation for considerate treatment he and his staff had received."[12]

Soon after the attack on Pearl Harbor, the governor of the territory of Hawaii had issued orders "prohibiting any alien Japanese from possessing any weapons, cameras, radios, codes ciphers, sketches of information regarding military and naval installation." As a result, the consul-general was "requested to turn over to authorities any of these articles which he and his staff might have." According to the State Department, these were requests and once articles were collected receipts for them were willingly provided. Therefore: "It has been ascertained that no threats or force were used in any case."[13]

As for the possible misuse of confiscated funds, the consul-general initially put this money into his own safe, the "combination of which was known only to members of the Consulate General." Later, it was deposited in the Bishop National Bank, but the consul-general was allowed "to withdraw up to dollars 1200 a month from blocked account in his name for living expenses of members of Consulate General and their families." Damages to the premises were done with the consul-general's permission, since the necessary keys had been lost or mislaid and in one case: "Mr. Kita himself broke mirror over chest of drawers in his bedroom." While the missing money, pens, and baseball gloves were never found, the State Department official in charge of the investigation did conclude: "However it has been determined that none of above mentioned articles were taken by police authorities."[14]

In its response to Tokyo, the State Department denied that the consul-general, his family, or the staff of the consulate had been mistreated in any way. In fact, the precautions they were asked to follow were "in view of probable air attacks" and these same precautions were the same as being "followed by almost everyone on island." Instead, they were able to live "almost normal life" and even enjoyed "on first day of hostilities" meals that included some of the "best food available on island." Prior to being moved to the continental United States, the Japanese nationals were able to purchase whatever they needed. However, contrary to Japan's protest, they were not given permission to buy the heavy clothing described for the simple reason that it was "impossible to buy heavy winter clothing since none of the clothing stores in territory of Hawaii carried that type of clothing."[15]

While acknowledging that searches of the Japanese officials were conducted on the ship before leaving port, these were the same for all passengers: "In view of fact that ship was travelling in war area Mr. Kita [the consul-general] was also informed that search would have to [be] made [of] everyone boarding ship as well as their baggage." Such a search was made at the order not of the U.S. government but of the ship's captain, who deemed it "to be necessary in interest of safety of vessel and its passengers," and it "was conducted with due regard to modesty of individuals and female nurse was requested to search female passengers."[16]

Once on board ship, the Japanese officials were under the authority of the captain of the ship. Granted, while at sea the Japanese nationals were under armed guard, but this was for their own security so as to prevent "other passengers" or members of the "crew" from molesting them. Their windows were covered in line with "military requirements." Finally, as a sign of goodwill the Japanese nationals were given the necessary equipment and raw materials to prepare their own food "in their own style and this method was found to be most satisfactory."[17]

As soon as the Japanese nationals arrived in the continental U.S., concern for their safety and well-being once again became paramount. Accordingly, for the "protection of these Japanese nationals it was considered necessary to keep secret any information regarding their movements." National security concerns dictated that they not be "given indication of their destination." Finally, the delays in embarkation occurred because a "definite sailing date had not been agreed upon by interested Governments," and it was considered best not to move "them from their quarters until sailing date was definitely known." Therefore, rather than being "subjected to any threatening language or treatment," all of the Japanese nationals "were given courteous treatment and every attempt was made to make their stay in Arizona and New York as agreeable as possible."[18]

The State Department took issue with the Japanese protest, stating that "this Government cannot agree that treatment was unnecessarily strict and severe."[19] The U.S. government argued that such issues should not impair negotiations for a second exchange. However, these negotiations were to drag on throughout the rest of 1942 and much of 1943 before a second exchange was arranged.

U.S.–Japanese negotiations for a second exchange

As outlined in a 16 December 1942 report to President Roosevelt: "The first exchange was facilitated by reason of the fact that it was largely composed of officials of the two Governments concerning whose exchange there was no question."[20] The same could not be said for the second exchange, which was tainted from the start by Japanese accusations—many of them later proved to be either exaggerated or untrue—about the poor treatment of their officials. The real issue under dispute was the Japanese government's insistence that it had the sole authority to determine which Japanese citizens and American citizens of Japanese ancestry should be allowed on the second exchange. Rather than accept any person in these two categories who wished to return to Japan, the Japanese government wanted to force certain persons to return and to exclude others.

Even though the first exchange was a success, it was almost derailed at the last minute by a series of diplomatic protests. When the Japanese government had insisted upon the inclusion of "certain non-official nationals" several of these "could not be produced." In the end, it was decided that "rather than hold up the departure of the vessel [these individuals] were promised for the next exchange."[21] Almost as soon as *Gripsholm* had left port, the U.S. State Department began the complicated task of trying to compile a list for a second group of 1,500 Japanese that would be acceptable to officials in Tokyo.

Throughout July 1942, the State Department collected names for a provisional passenger list. These included the "few Japanese nationals promised for the second exchange" who had not been able to board the first ship, as well as the "remainder of those until then designated by the Japanese Government for repatriation." However, the vast majority of the list comprised "Japanese nationals not so designated who had voluntarily expressed their desire to be repatriated."[22] Many of these names were taken from the lists compiled at the war relocation centers of those who had requested repatriation.

Immediately before this list was to be delivered to Tokyo in early August 1942, the State Department was informed by Tokyo that "the Japanese Government wished included in the second exchange only those Japanese nationals designated by it." The State Department immediately altered its list to include all of "those designated by the Japanese Government then ready for departure," which totaled 580 people. The bulk, however, some 900 people, were once again "made up of Japanese nationals seeking repatriation but not named by the Japanese Government." When the final revised list was delivered to the Japanese government on 1 September 1942, it was explained that these people could be delivered "immediately" and that the second exchange could proceed without delay, but that to "repatriate in the second exchange only those named by the Japanese Government would indefinitely delay the sailing of the exchange vessel."[23]

Negotiations on the nature of the second exchange were intense. In a note dated 6 July 1942, "B.L."—the initials of Breckinridge Long, the Assistant Secretary of State—explained to a subordinate at "SD" or "Special Division," probably Joseph Green: "I do not want us to be placed in the position of being asked by the Japanese to exchange a particular individual and then find ourselves unable to do so. For that reason I specifically do not want to ask the Japanese to furnish any particular list." To resolve this security dilemma, Long advised: "You already have a number of names left over from the last vessel and various others in custody who can be repatriated. I suggest that you make up a list as far as you can and submit it to the Japanese." Undoubtedly, some of the candidates that Long had in mind were the Japanese nationals being held at the war relocation centers.[24]

But the Japanese did provide several additional lists during July 1942. By 6 August 1942, the State Department informed Japan that it had received eight separate lists, including one dated 17 May, two dated 7 June, two dated 27 June, one dated 30 June, and one dated 1 July. Altogether, they included 2,023 names. Of these, 580 had been located, agreed to repatriation, and could be in the second exchange. Another 331 Japanese from Peru could also be included, which would make 911. However, of the remaining 1,453 people, 15 had already departed on the first exchange ship, five were in Hawaii, 22 were not at the address listed, and 80 had refused repatriation. The vast majority—some 1,331—could not be located, because the Japanese lists did not include current addresses.[25]

Faced with difficulties finding these people, the State Department said: "Every effort is now being made to locate them and to ascertain their wishes as regards [re]patriation, but it is inevitable that this will require considerable time, perhaps several weeks, and there is no assurance that any substantial number of them will accept offer of repatriation." Therefore, to avoid delay in the second exchange, the State Department wished to offer Japan a "list of 466 (four six six) additional persons in United States whose present addresses and family status are known and who have asked to be repatriated."[26]

Although the numbers given in various documents did not match exactly, according to the State Department's suggestion, once the 580 persons from the Japanese lists had been added to 331 from Peru to total 911, this would leave approximately 590 to 640 available berths on *Gripsholm*. Therefore, if Japan accepted these 466 additional names the second "vessel could be filled to capacity promptly, and otherwise inevitable delay avoided."[27]

In closing, this U.S. memorandum urged the Japanese to act quickly for the good of both countries' citizens:

> In these circumstances, it is believed to be evident that as between one group of persons whose present addresses are unknown [and] for whom no family data are available, and who have given no indication of a desire to be repatriated and another group of persons whose present location and family status are known who have specifically asked to be repatriated and for whom tentative arrangements have already been made to sail on the "Gripsholm," it would be preferable to draw ... passengers needed to fill boat for forthcoming sailing from latter group.[28]

On 10 August 1942, the State Department sent a second memorandum through the Spanish embassy to Japan. In this document were listed all of those Japanese evacuees seeking repatriation being held at the Lordsburg Internment Camp in New Mexico, Camp Livingston in Louisiana, Camp McCoy in Wisconsin, and Fort George G. Meade in Maryland. The numbers were 183, 571, 19, and 22, respectively, for a total of 795 persons.[29] These additional lists gave the Japanese government even more names to choose from.

The Japanese ultimatum

By now the Japanese government's notes and memorandum clearly showed increasing suspicions concerning U.S. goodwill. The response to this U.S. suggestion was immediate and unequivocal. On 5 September 1942, Tokyo stated that it was "utterly surprised" that only 580 people from its eight lists, which included a total of 3,963 names, had been located. These low numbers were even more surprising given that the "United States Government is placing whole Japanese residents under its control and supervision by way of registration, restriction of movement, detention or internment of alien enemy, or compulsory removal affected along Pacific coasts."[30] This was a direct reference to the role played by the Japanese-American war relocation centers in the exchange process.

Although Tokyo proved willing to accept the 331 Japanese nationals from Peru, the rest had to come exclusively from its own lists. The Japanese government made it absolutely clear that "it insists that Japanese residents to be repatriated by second exchange should be determined upon locating those persons named in above-mentioned lists submitted by Japanese representative." It concluded that the U.S. government is "expected to make every effort to locate Japanese in the lists." As for conducting the second exchange rapidly, Tokyo concluded: "Japanese Government will have no objection to delay ... departure of exchange vessel."[31]

The Japanese government's position was firm. According to "secret sources," the U.S. State Department was told that the Japanese government "on September 4 [1942] had determined not to make a second exchange for the time being and to postpone it for two or three months, but that the American Government was not to be advised."[32] Because Japan would only accept people who appeared on its own internally-generated lists, this meant that it refused to accept those candidates offered by the U.S. government, which included hundreds, and eventually thousands, of Japanese citizens and American citizens of Japanese ancestry who were being housed in the war relocation centers.

Part of the delay was caused by the fact that a total of 538 Japanese nationals, plus 1,630 dependents for a total of 2,168, were considered by various U.S. security agencies to be a serious security threat to the United States. On 16 December 1942, Laurence E. Salisbury, a career foreign service officer in the State Department, wrote a memorandum critical of this decision. Based on Japan's replies "the Japanese Government insists upon the persons it has named as a *sine qua non* of the exchange of the American nationals." Salisbury warned that "the American Government will either have to surrender to Japan persons whom the investigative agencies have stricken off the list or make up its mind to leave its citizens in the Far East for the duration."[33]

The resulting deadlock reached by negotiators in Washington and Tokyo threatened to delay a second exchange, perhaps indefinitely. To break the deadlock, the U.S. government—and arguably President Franklin D. Roosevelt himself—had to make a crucial decision whether or not to include every Japanese listed by the Japanese Foreign Ministry, including those who were thought to endanger American security. Although the U.S. State Department had claimed in its negotiations with Japan that the people could not be located, many of them were actually being detained by the U.S. government, or were on special government lists as representing a danger to national security. If Washington agreed to let them return to Japan, it had to be willing to accept the corresponding risk that their return might alter the course of the war. Only the president could make that decision.

Final determination of the lists for the second exchange

Throughout late 1941 and early 1942, the United States government had conducted extensive investigations of many of the 6,000 Japanese nationals mentioned in Tokyo's numerous lists. On the advice of the Alien Enemy Control Unit of the Department of Justice, the Federal Bureau of Investigation, and the various branches of both the Military and Naval Intelligence services, 538 Japanese nationals plus 1,630 family members had been classified as security risks. Of these, 46 people plus 90 family members were from "the first and second categories, those being the principal persons desired by the Japanese Government."[34]

The United States government faced a weighty decision near the end of 1942. Based on interviews of the remaining people on Japan's lists, between 75 and 80 percent declined to be repatriated, leaving fewer than 1,000 willing candidates, or far too few to fill the second exchange ship, even including additional exchangees from Canada, Central America, and South America. Meanwhile, thousands of Japanese citizens and American citizens of Japanese ancestry being held in the war relocation centers had requested repatriation. Washington offered these applicants as substitutes. However, the Japanese government refused to consider these candidates as equal to their own top choices.

A variety of reasons were given for denying the repatriation of 538 persons from Japan's lists, including being suspected "Japanese agents," "Japanese sympathizers," or having "technical qualifications or associations of possible or probable value to the Japanese war effort, such as fishermen, seamen, newspaper editors and publishers, priests, members of secret societies," and in particular "Army and Navy reserve officers." For these reasons, U.S. security agencies concluded that "repatriation of those objected to would be inimical to the national safety" of the United States.[35]

The only problem with this solution was that while an exchange agreement had been signed with Germany that specifically stated that "each party thereto might withhold from the exchange anyone whose repatriation might be considered inimical to the national interests," no comparable agreement had been signed with Japan. This was because it was determined by the State Department that: "An all-out exchange without this exception was considered to be necessary with respect to Japan because of the uncivilized treatment to which American nationals left in Japan and Japanese-occupied areas might be expected to be exposed as the intensity of the war would increase."[36]

By late 1942, the State Department was in a quandary. Either the U.S. government had to agree to repatriate everyone from Japan's list who was willing to return, or the Japanese government might respond by withholding selected American officials or by canceling the second exchange altogether. People withheld might include American foreign service officers being held in Manila, a number of U.S. professors from Yenching University and Peking Union Medical College in China, Americans with "important technical qualifications and knowledge of the Japanese war machine which would be useful to this country's war effort," or a number of American businessmen who had sent their families back to the United States but had remained in Asia on the advice of the "Department of Far Eastern policy."[37]

On 6 July 1942, Joseph C. Green, head of the Special Division that was organizing the exchanges, wrote to Breckinridge Long explaining that "the preparation of a passenger list of Japanese is a much less complicated problem than the preparation of a passenger list of Germans and Italians." Green told Long that during two meetings on 10 June and 30 June representatives from the security agencies "disclaimed any intention of pressing any objections to the repatriation of any Japanese to whose repatriation we were obligated by [in] the terms of our Exchange Agreement with Japan, and agreed to leave the compilation of passenger lists entirely to the discretion of the Department of State." Green furthermore warned Long that: "There is no indication that they will reverse this position unless they are again invited to make objection to the repatriation of Japanese."[38]

Long apparently ignored this advice and asked the security services to list their objections. This delayed for many months negotiations for a second exchange. On 3 November 1942, the State Department offered the Japanese government a list of 1,800 persons who were willing to repatriate, and were all mentioned on the Japanese lists, but not on the U.S. list of 538 security risks plus family members. On 16 December 1942, the Japanese government responded that it "does not think it possible to come to an agreement for the second exchange unless the United States 'clarifies its attitude'."[39]

This situation was presented to President Roosevelt during December 1942 for his consideration. The U.S. government had to decide whether to "surrender to Japan persons whom the investigative agencies have stricken off the list or make up its mind to leave its citizens in the Far East for the duration."[40] Faced with this dilemma, Roosevelt appears to have personally authorized the State Department to make a new proposal to the Japanese government. On 4 February 1943, Washington "upped the ante" by now proposing that Tokyo agree to exchange 4,500 persons from each side in three exchanges to take place on 1 April, 15 June, and 30 August 1943. The real purpose behind this offer, however, was to "eliminate our explaining to the Japanese that we cannot send back some of their requests because the agencies have objected to them."[41]

The State Department was hoping that Tokyo would be attracted by quantity over quality. Japan would get back its prime candidates, but only in exchange for a higher number of Americans. As part of this three-part exchange, each government would "endeavor as far as possible to follow the desires of the other Governments and the wishes of the individuals." Finally, even after these three exchanges were completed, the United States had "several thousand Japanese" who were "not yet named for exchange by the Japanese Government who have expressed a desire to return to Japan and whom the United States Government is willing to exchange."[42] This last group, of course, were almost all of the Japanese citizens and American citizens of Japanese ancestry being held at various war relocation centers.

By making this proposal the U.S. government was tacitly admitting that it had withheld certain Japanese-Americans who had appeared on Tokyo's lists. In return for giving them up, Washington hoped Tokyo would agree up front to three exchanges that would include a total of 4,500 people. This proposal, although workable in practice, may have been generated more to appease Congress, which was even then asking questions about the stalled exchanges, and the various U.S. security organizations, which wanted to know what to do with the detained Japanese aliens. This plan, if it had been enacted, would have appeared to show that the United States was securing the return of the maximum number of citizens for its concession in giving up certain "high value" Japanese.

The Japanese response

The Japanese reply to this new U.S. proposal put a damper on all hopes of arranging three exchanges at once. It arrived only in May 1943, long after the first of the three newly proposed exchanges should have taken place. The Japanese government stated that it was "glad to note from above-said memorandum that United States Government are ready to comply with Japanese requirements" that the U.S. list be satisfactory to the Japanese government. But, Tokyo would not commit to three exchanges, stating instead that it hoped for a "speedy agreement" on the second exchange, while leaving to "future negotiations question of enlarging scope of exchange." Due to changing wartime circumstances, Tokyo furthermore requested that the third exchange take place at Marmagao, in Portuguese Goa on the western coast of India.[43]

In effect, the American attempt to leverage the return of the 2,168 security risks for a guaranteed block of three exchanges including 4,500 Americans was refused, even while its offer to return any willing Japanese from Tokyo's lists was accepted. Japan was standing firm on its understanding of the original exchange agreement. Washington now had a clear choice: it could either accept the Japanese "list for the second exchange" or accept "the breakdown of the whole repatriation project, or at least suspension for a very long time." Faced with these limited options, Maxwell Hamilton, the Chief of the Division of Far Eastern Affairs, advised that the U.S. government accept Japan's offer. In a 7 May 1943 letter to Assistant Secretary of State Long, Hamilton argued that Tokyo had perhaps made "commitments to repatriate designated Japanese" to either their "families" or "employers," and as a result perhaps had "a feeling that national honor is now involved in the issue."[44]

Hamilton recommended that the U.S. proceed based on the Japanese conditions. He hoped that this would "facilitate the negotiation of further exchanges looking to the repatriation of the greater part of our people in the Far East."[45] The Secretary of State appears to have agreed to Maxwell Hamilton's solution, and he gave the order for the exchange to proceed.

Soon afterward, on 25 May 1943, the "security agencies withdrew objection to inclusion in the second exchange of a sufficient number of Japanese designated for exchange by the Japanese Government to render more likely than previously successful consummation of the second exchange." Thereafter, "On July 3, 1943 the Acting Secretary of the Navy informed the Department that the War and Navy Departments withdrew the objections which they had made in regard to the repatriation of Japanese for subsequent exchanges. Shortly thereafter the Attorney General informed the Department similarly in regard to FBI and AEC."[46]

One reason for this 180-degree reversal of policy was that by July 1943 the U.S. was on the offensive in the Pacific, and the specific knowledge of the internees was two years out of date, so they represented less of a security risk than before. Another reason for this change of heart may have been the release, on 5 June 1943, of the "Resolution Concerning Detention and Expulsion of Dangerous Axis Nationals" based on the results of the Third Meeting of the Ministers of Foreign Affairs of the American Republics. This resolution had been approved on 21 May 1943, just days before the security agencies withdrew their objections. This document set certain hemisphere-wide standards for repatriation for all of the member countries in the Western Hemisphere, including the United States. With hindsight, it seems clear that Assistant Secretary of State Long was waiting for this body to set policy before he released the Japanese nationals who were suspected of being a security threat.

In this resolution, the member states resolved that "a general policy of repatriation of nationals of member states of the Tripartite Pact and states subservient thereto is contrary to the interests of Hemisphere security, because it would provide the Axis governments with well-informed and well-trained agents and other useful personnel of great value to the Axis in the further conduct of their military and political warfare both within and without this Hemisphere." While repatriation was opposed as a general rule, the sole exception was to obtain one's own citizens in return. Therefore, repatriation was allowed "as it may be necessary to repatriate in exchange for nationals of the American republics, detained in Axis or Axis-dominated territory, whose return to this Hemisphere is believed desirable in the interests of its security or for like social and compelling reasons."[47]

This document validated the U.S.–Japanese exchange program and was crucial for convincing the U.S. security agencies to allow a second exchange to proceed. From late May through early September, the State Department and the Japanese Foreign Ministry worked out the particular persons to be exchanged. In addition to Japanese from the United States, there were about ten Japanese merchants from Peru and Bolivia, approximately 75 Japanese diplomats from Chile, 25 Japanese from Mexico, and about 60 Japanese nationals from Canada.

In return, the U.S. government hoped to receive about 25 U.S. officials detained in the Philippines, approximately 40 Chilean officials, and then over 1,400 non-officials from Canada, a number of American republics, and from the United States. Divided by region, there would be 67 American civilians from Japan and Manchuria, 130 from Guam, 18 from Indochina, one from Thailand, 10 from Hong Kong, 160 from Manila, and 850 from occupied China, or about 1,250 total.[48] Washington's priorities were to release first those under arrest, followed by women and children, and then men who were seriously ill. Washington also made it clear that it expected Tokyo to agree to include John Leighton Stuart, President of Yenching University, and Henry S. Houghton and Trevor Bowen of Peking Union Medical College.

In line with Washington's decision to agree to Tokyo's demands, on 24 June 1943 it presented Tokyo a list of 1,248 Japanese to be repatriated from the United States. Including 254 from other parts of the Western Hemisphere, the total was 1,502. If this new list was found to be acceptable, then the *Gripsholm* would leave New York on or about 1 August, would stop in Rio de Janeiro to pick up additional passengers, and would arrive at Marmagao on or about 15 September 1943.[49] On 4 August 1943, the Japanese government indicated its readiness to proceed with the second U.S.–Japanese official and non-official exchange based on these proposed terms.[50]

The success of the second exchange

On 2 September 1943, *Gripsholm* departed Jersey City with just over 1,330 Japanese nationals for a six-week voyage to Marmagao, the main port in the Portuguese colony of Goa on the west coast of India.[51] Of these, 61 were from Canada and 31 from Mexico.[52] On the way, it would stop at Rio de Janeiro and Montevideo, Uruguay, to pick up another 173 Japanese nationals. According to one source, a total of 55 percent of the passenger list were Latin-American Japanese.[53] In return, the Japanese ship *Teia Maru* would leave Japan in mid-September with approximately 1,250 American citizens, as well as 250 nationals from Canada and other American republics. The exchange was scheduled to take place on 15 October 1943, and actually took place only one day later.

Meanwhile, *Gripsholm* was also carrying a number of relief supplies for U.S. civilians and P.O.W.s, including medicine, food, vitamins, and blood plasma for the remaining civilian detainees. According to a bill of lading, there were 28,130 cases of supplies, weighing 730 tons. These supplies included food parcels, medical supplies, clothing, shoes, sanitary supplies, cigarettes, and donated supplies from the YMCA and Catholic Welfare organizations. Mail and parcels were also included, and made up 1,740 bags including about 16,000 next-of-kin parcels, for another 43 tons of weight, making the entire shipment of supplies over 770 tons. A breakdown shows that this included some 78,000 13lb food parcels, over 5 million vitamin pills, over 14,000 pairs of shoes, as well as many books, recreational materials, and religious materials. Since these supplies were to be off-loaded in Manila, it can be assumed that most of them were for those American civilians and military personnel interned in the Philippines.[54]

Almost as soon as *Gripsholm* left the United States on the first leg of the exchange, the U.S.–Japanese negotiations hit a snag. At the last moment, the Japanese government indicated that it would not allow to participate in the exchange a total of 11 U.S. citizens accused of espionage—including Stuart, Bowen, and Houghton—three Americans "under suspicion of having carried on political activities," as well as Ernest Leroy Healey, who had been convicted of trying to escape a detention camp.[55]

Secretary of State Hull was irate at the news, especially since so much time had been spent convincing the U.S. security agencies to drop their objections to the Japanese security risks. In a 4 September 1943 letter to the Japanese Foreign Ministry he pointed out that on the "motorship *Gripsholm* which has just sailed from the United States are various individuals who might have been successfully prosecuted for espionage had the United States Government wished to withhold them from the exchange contrary to the exchange agreement." There were also several who were "defendants in criminal prosecutions" who were released onto the ship. Therefore, Hull requested an explanation from the Japanese not only as to why these American citizens were removed from the repatriation list but also as to their "actual inclusion in the present exchange."[56]

On 8 September 1943, the Japanese Foreign Ministry indicated that it was not aware that the U.S. had released Japanese nationals onto *Gripsholm* who might have been prosecuted for espionage or other crimes. This Japanese "tongue-in-cheek" response was a subtle criticism of the U.S. delay in getting all of the Japanese candidates cleared and ready for repatriation. But in a series of notes exchanged during 24-27 September 1943, the real reason for withholding these particular Americans became clear: Foreign Minister Shigemitsu did not believe American claims that as many as 80 or even 90 percent of the Japanese nationals on Tokyo's lists had declined repatriation. In fact, these numbers were accurate, and on 30 November 1943 the Special Divisions branch produced a list of 3,961 Japanese who had refused repatriation.[57]

By now, however, Japanese trust in U.S. intentions was at a low point. On 1 October 1943, Shigemitsu accused the United States government of stating that some Japanese residents had "refused to be repatriated," when "there are number of person who as matter of fact desire to come home." Specifically, he referred to a 14 September 1943 message delivered by President Roosevelt to the U.S. Senate as proof that the "United States Government intend to accord unduly discriminate treatment to Japanese nationals who have expressed desire to evacuate." From this, Shigemitsu concluded that: "It is presumed from this that undue pressure was brought to bear upon them when they were questioned as to their intention of evacuation or not."[58]

The President's statement, in fact, discussed the reasons for segregating Japanese-Americans at the Tule Lake relocation center, not why certain names on Japan's priority list were not included in the exchange. Thus, the cascading misunderstandings connected with the U.S.–Japanese exchanges appear to have come full circle: one major reason for segregating the Japanese-Americans was because Japan refused to repatriate them quickly enough, while Shigemitsu's refusal to release Americans accused of espionage was linked to the U.S. decision to segregate Japanese-Americans. This was a vicious circle that could only exacerbate the increasingly poor diplomatic relations.

Shigemitsu's argument elicited a second sharply worded memorandum from the Department of State. This memorandum clarified that, in fact, the "proportion of refusals of repatriation among those of the Japanese at liberty whose repatriation has been requested by the Japanese Government is even higher than among the Japanese who are interned or who are in the Relocation Centers."

Since these refusals were determined "exclusively by letter" there was no "possibility that pressure could have been exercised upon them." As a result, the U.S. government "rejects as baseless and without any foundation in fact or logic the assumption of the Japanese Government that any pressure or discrimination existed to influence the decision of any Japanese regarding repatriation."[59]

According to the State Department's information on the rate of acceptance of repatriation, therefore, the Japanese-Americans being kept in the relocation centers were arguably even more "loyal" to Japan than those Japanese nationals whom Tokyo had specifically requested be returned. Yet, the Japanese Foreign Ministry continued to refuse to accept large numbers of candidates from the war relocation centers for repatriation. The State Department recommended that the "Japanese Government may wish to take note that many hundreds of persons being transferred to the segregation center to await repatriation to Japan are persons who have expressed an urgent desire to be repatriated but who have not been designated by the Japanese Government for repatriation."[60]

Only days before the arrival of the ships and the beginning of the second exchange at Marmagao, the State Department accused the Japanese Foreign Ministry of not conducting the exchanges according to the original terms. Against the warning of many security organizations, the U.S. government had complied with Japan's demand that only those Japanese who appeared on its lists be included in the exchanges, irrespective of their status to the ongoing prosecution of the war. Tokyo's insistence on 8 September that it was not aware that some of the Japanese on board *Gripsholm* "could have been prosecuted for espionage" was therefore simply not understandable to the State Department. As a result, Washington suggested that "in the interest of the successful prosecution of further exchanges of nationals" all "such exchanges can best be carried on if both parties thereto will guide their conduct in accordance with the original statement which provided that there should be no exceptions on the grounds of the importance of the individuals to the prosecution of the war effort."[61]

Conclusions

Although the United States government secured the return of thousands of American citizens—and so the exchange program as a whole was a success—it was clearly Tokyo, not Washington, that was calling the shots. In particular, the Japanese Foreign Ministry not only forced the State Department to agree to use the Japanese priority lists, but Tokyo never agreed to accept for repatriation the much larger number of Japanese citizens and American citizens of Japanese ancestry especially segregated at the Tule Lake Segregation Center awaiting their chance to be part of the exchange program.

The numerous U.S. State Department communiqués trying to explain the exact circumstances that undermined the validity of the Japanese protests over the mistreatment of Japanese officials and non-officials clearly did not satisfy the Japanese Foreign Ministry. Diplomatic talks on a third exchange quickly reached an impasse. The Japanese government even accused the U.S. government of corruption. For example, on 21 January 1944, Tokyo responded to one American document by suggesting that perhaps it "may be either that the American officials who were in charge of the group did not report the full facts to the Government or that they made a wilful misrepresentation in order to conceal their misbehaviour."[62]

Accusations of this type did not sit well in Washington. When the U.S. government finally answered this second protest on 21 July 1944, it stated that after giving each of these points "careful consideration," there was "nothing to be added" to its previous messages. Japanese-American diplomatic negotiations had become so acrimonious that there appeared to be little chance of reaching any kind of understanding on these issues any time soon. Perhaps reflecting this sense of hopelessness, the final sentence of this U.S. communiqué rather bluntly stated that all Japanese allegations regarding mistreatment of Japanese nationals on Hawaii were untrue, and so: "The protest must accordingly be rejected."[63]

8　Rising tensions at the Tule Lake Segregation Center

On 30 September 1943, the Tule Lake Relocation Center officially closed and then reopened a month later on 1 November as the Tule Lake Segregation Center.[1] Those not desiring to return to Japan were sent to other relocation centers. It was thought that this move would be temporary, and that the Japanese citizens and U.S. citizens of Japanese ancestry would remain at Tule Lake only until a third U.S.–Japanese exchange could be arranged. This third exchange never took place.

Many of those who requested repatriation to Japan were not older Japanese, but were young men who were U.S. citizens by birth but had received either all or part of their formal education while living with relatives in Japan. This would make providing proper security even more difficult for the administrators of the Tule Lake Relocation Center. During October 1943, right as the segregation policy was being instituted, a protest erupted into what was described at the time as a "mutiny." According to a report from the Spanish embassy, the root cause appears to have been that "employees of Relocation Centre were blamed for negligence in relation to provisions for evacuees and funds for purchasing them."[2]

Demands quickly escalated to include a determination of the status of those residents segregated for repatriation. The protestors wanted "to have all internees returned to join their respective families."[3] When 14 representatives chosen by the evacuees tried to reach a settlement, they were declared "mutineers" by the camp authorities. U.S. troops were then dispatched armed with "tanks and machine-guns." They "arrested more than two hundred evacuees whom they considered responsible" for fomenting the disturbance.[4] These events undermined negotiations for a third exchange.

The segregation program

Japanese citizens, and those of "Japanese origin who were American citizens" as Tokyo put it, who refused to declare loyalty to the United States, were scheduled to be moved to a "Special Relocation Center" at Tule Lake. During the segregation process an estimated 20,000 evacuees were moved from one relocation center to another: "After long and serious deliberation, the decision has been made that the responsibility of the War Relocation Authority can best be fulfilled if a separation is made between those who wish to follow the American way of life, and those whose interests are not in harmony with those of the United States." Dillon S. Myer reassured the evacuees, however, that segregation was not in any way a "punishment" and that the War Relocation Authority "recognizes the integrity of those persons of Japanese ancestry who frankly have declared their sympathy for Japan or their lack of allegiance to the United States."[5]

These constant changes disrupted everyday life at Tule Lake as there was "a large displacement of population to other Centers." In addition, many Japanese who expressed a desire to be repatriated to Japan were shipped to the Tule Lake Segregation Center from other relocation centers.[6] According to the forms handed out to evacuees explaining the segregation program: "This position has been taken in order to promote the general welfare and to provide a place of protection for those evacuees who are known to favor the cause of Japan."[7] As described by a Japanese-American minister who was at Tule Lake at the time, for "those transferred in from other centers, Tule Lake was the first stop on the journey back to Japan."[8] Even when it became possible for residents to leave Tule Lake and resettle along the West Coast, the diehard loyalists, known as "resegregationists" because they wanted to be housed separately from those who had expressed loyalty to the United States, signed petitions expressing their determination "to remain in camp until they were repatriated."[9]

The initial idea behind segregating the Japanese-Americans appeared during winter 1942–1943 and may have even been suggested by the evacuees themselves. For example, in a 19 February 1943 interview with Juichi Nimura, aged 58, Mr. Nimura explained how he, his wife, and their six children had all applied to be repatriated to Japan. He stated that his allegiance was to Japan, that he was eager to return, and "that the Emperor of Japan was his ruler and that if asked he would fight for Japan but not for the United States." Even though Mr. Nimura had been chosen block manager of Block 45 by the evacuees, he stated that he felt uncomfortable being in charge of Japanese who wanted to remain in the United States. When asked, Kimura stated: "He does not think that repatriates should hold official positions in the Tule Lake Relocation Center."[10]

Tensions were high between loyal Japanese-Americans and those who wished to be repatriated. During September 1943, the Spanish representative overseeing the Japanese-American evacuees, named Antonio R-Martin, completed a detailed report of the Tule Lake Relocation Center. In it, he warned that by 1 November 1943, Tule Lake was to be segregated into different groups, in part to reduce tensions between those loyal to the U.S. and those loyal to Japan. This segregation was to a large degree based on the evacuees' answer to Question 28 of the basic registration form, which stated "Will you swear unqualified allegiance to the United States of America and foreswear any form of allegiance or obedience to the Japanese emperor, or any other foreign government, power, or organization?"[11]

According to regulations, "Issei [first generation Japanese] were required to answer on their willingness to abide by the laws of the United States." Those who answered in the negative were considered a security risk, and were to be placed in separate housing from the rest.[12] Critics of this process have pointed out that "German Americans and Italian Americans were not required to forswear allegiance."[13] Unlike the Japanese, however, very few of the German- or Italian-Americans with U.S. citizenship had received their primary education outside of the United States, like the Kibei did.

Because of the many diverse groups within the Japanese-American community, the segregation process was not based solely on citizenship. Instead, it was based on each individual's answer to Question 28 during the registration process. Thus: "In recognition of the fact that many alien-born evacuees are prevented from being loyal American citizens by legal technicalities, and that some individuals who legally are American citizens actually are sympathetic to Japan in the present war, the process of segregation will be conducted without regard for citizenship." In particular, those who signed a request for repatriation to Japan would be segregated: "This policy of having each person, regardless of age and sex, sign his own application for repatriation or expatriation is in keeping with the WRA principle that those people going to the Tule Lake Center are going by virtue of their own acts or statements which show they are not loyal to the United States or sympathetic to the war aims of this country."[14]

The segregation program was intended to divide the evacuees into different groups according to their expressed loyalty either to Japan or to the United States. Directors of the War Relocation Centers were told to explain the program to the evacuees. In particular, they "emphasized that segregation is for the benefit of the evacuees. Certainly the government has nothing to gain from it. ... Segregation is not to be interpreted as a discriminatory measure; rather it is simply a putting together of people who wish to live as Japanese rather than as Americans."[15] The segregation plan was difficult to implement, since as noted above there were multiple reasons why evacuees might decide to declare their loyalty to Japan, including fears for their personal safety or duty to their family. Tensions often erupted into fist-fights, especially among young men who had received the bulk of their education in Japan as opposed to those educated in the United States. During this registration process, the Spanish representative reported that "the residents of the Tule Lake Center were subjected to the embarrassment of armed soldiers entering the camp." In particular, these troops were brought in to "pick up a group of young men who were termed recalcitrants."[16]

Because the Japanese-Americans being sent to Tule Lake Relocation Center were considered untrustworthy, it was reported that this center "would be placed under military supervision" and that the "treatment accorded there would be more stringent than other centers." Evidently, even the hint that one might be transferred to Tule Lake could be used as a threat at the other relocation centers. According to one report, "Mr. Merritt, Commandant of Manzanar Relocation Centre ... made it clear that transfer to Tule Lake was a punishment meted out to

Japanese subjects and United States citizens of Japanese origin who failed to swear allegiance to United States."[17]

One reason this program was instituted was for the benefit and well-being of those Japanese-Americans who declared their loyalty to the United States, since many of them felt uncomfortable being housed together with fellow Japanese-Americans loyal to Japan. But this could work both ways. According to a 10 April 1944 report, one 40-year-old man "applied for repatriation after he had become involved in some difficulty with other persons in this [Topaz, Utah] center, and it became quite necessary for him to transfer away from here. He preferred applying for repatriation and going to Tule Lake to transferring to any other center."[18] When a test sample of 47 were asked about their future plans, 32 requested immediate repatriation, six wished to return to Japan after the war, and nine were undecided.[19]

Reasons for requesting repatriation differed. For example, Takeji Fujiki said "I am worried about my parents in Japan," while Blossom Fujita said: "I am filing this application to go to Japan because I desire to join my fiance who is a Japanese subject, residing in Japan and who is now sending for me." Hidetoshi Furuzawa cited business reasons, stating that "since his evacuation, he has lost thousands of dollars in business and feels that even after release from this camp, he would have to start from the bottom." Ben Tsutomu Sato simply stated "Believes that he will get a better deal in Japan." Others, like Tadashi Sakuma, held a grudge: "Discharged from the Army last February because of the change in the Army policy. Indignant."[20]

Still, it is undeniable that many Japanese felt excluded by Americans. Noboru Yamamoto stated that "he owed quite a bit to this country, but in spite of that, he never felt that he was an American, and was told by many people that he was not an American because his country was fighting Japan." A large number, perhaps as high as 10 percent, claimed that they were requesting repatriation because their civil rights were being denied. For example, Shigezo Eimoto said: "Do not desire present status as part-time United States Citizen. Feels he isn't given full civil rights as an American citizen and therefore wishes to return to Japan and serve her."[21]

Many who wished to return to Japan immediately were upset by the delays and blamed them on the U.S. government. As late in the war as 3 March 1945, Mojiro Ono, Vice President of a group entitled *Sokuji Kikoku Hoshi Dan*, wrote a letter to the State Department requesting that his group members be "re-segregated" and allowed to live only with other Japanese loyalists. In his letter he stated: "Our sole loyalty lies with Japan, and as loyal service to our mother country, we, the petitioners, are willing to give up everything, both materially and in manpower to devote all of our efforts and be of any assistance to our country, Japan. We have no intention of helping with the national effort of America."[22]

Positive effects of the segregation program

For those who expressed loyalty to the United States, segregation made it easier to be considered for the center's work-release programs. In many cases, evacuees could leave the center during the days to work, or in some cases were allowed to find permanent outside employment and housing. For example, during the week ending on 14 August 1943, it was reported that 18,676 evacuees were on leave from the 11 relocation centers for seasonal, short-term, or indefinite employment, leaving 93,748 evacuees remaining in the centers; at Tule Lake, 2,239 were on leave while 13,232 remained. In other words, at any one time as many as 20 percent of the evacuees in any particular center were not even living at the relocation centers, but were outside working at a large variety of jobs.[23]

Others, especially Japanese-Americans of college age, were given permission to leave the relocation centers permanently to attend college or university; departure lists show that dozens of young men and women left the centers to attend college, including Hisayo and Yoshie Morinaga to Oberlin College on 30 September 1942, George Inouye to Swarthmore College on 19 October 1942, Tom Toshio Hayashi to Columbia University on 5 February 1943, and Isaac Igarashi to Temple University on 11 February 1943.[24] In June 1943, the National Japanese American Student Relocation Council published a pamphlet containing the names of thousands of "American Students of Japanese Ancestry" and where they were studying; several names taken at random would include Bernice Abe at Swarthmore, Yoji George Azuma at Brigham Young, Cornelius Yasushi Chiamori at Cornell, and Nobuo Eshima at the University of Denver.[25]

Not only did the U.S. government help these young people apply to colleges and universities, in most cases it covered all of their travel and tuition costs and fees. Some students, like Kiyoaki Murata, had only been in the United States for five months prior to Pearl Harbor. Yet, he was helped to attend Carleton College, Northfield, Minnesota, where he "found Carleton truly like a big family. ... Although the students expressed interest in my situation and background, not one of them made reference to the fact that my country was at war with theirs." He was also invited to lecture at the Army Specialized Training Program (ASTP) at the University of Minnesota, and later completed his master's degree at the University of Chicago.[26]

This program gave an enormous educational advantage to Japanese-Americans—in particular when compared to other Asian-American groups that were not included in this program, such as Chinese-Americans—after the war ended. By 30 June 1946, a special scholarship fund of some $270,170 had been "distributed in 1,419 grants to 966 individuals."[27] According to one study, after the war: "For the first time, Japanese Americans had real options with respect to the kinds of careers they wanted to pursue. ... Not only could they train to become teachers, engineers, and managers, but they could be hired as such."[28]

Most of these educated Japanese-Americans accepted their good fortune and understood, or at least learned to live with, the underlying conditions that had led to the creation of the war relocation centers. Others, however, like Murata, used his largely free education paid for by the U.S. government and from public donations to criticize the United States. In 1991, Murata published in Tokyo his memoirs entitled *An Enemy Among Friends*.

Relocation centers as "concentration camps"

The perception that the relocation centers were somehow comparable to the Nazi concentration camps, where millions were killed, can perhaps be traced back to the 1943 judicial opinion by Mr. Justice Murphy, a judge on the Supreme Court of the United States. When the evacuation orders were challenged by Gordon Kiyoshi Hirabayashi, the case went all the way to the Supreme Court where Judge Murphy directly compared the two kinds of camps in his judicial opinion.

On 21 June 1943, the final decision on the legality of the war relocation centers was made that "circumstances within the knowledge of those charged with the responsibility for maintaining the national defense afforded a rational basis for the decision which they made." However, in his attached opinion, Murphy stated: "Under the curfew order here challenged no less than 70,000 American citizens have been placed under a special ban and deprived of their liberty because of their particular racial inheritance. In this sense it bears a melancholy resemblance to the treatment accorded to members of the Jewish race in Germany and in other parts of Europe."[29] It should be noted that by the summer of 1943, the most horrifying revelations about the Nazi concentration camps—including the gas chambers, medical experimentation, and mass graves—had yet to be discovered or reported; therefore, Murphy's comment acquired a completely different meaning after the war ended.

Concern about the abuse of the Japanese-Americans' constitutional rights was especially acute in the three West Coast states. On 27 November 1943, all of the congressmen from these states were invited to a meeting at the New House Office Building in Washington to meet with representatives from the Special War Problems Division, the War Department, the Justice Department, and the War Relocation Authority. Attorney General Biddle explained the government's view of the situation to "a number of congressmen [who] showed themselves to be greatly disturbed regarding the whole question of Japanese aliens and Japanese-American citizens in the United States and displayed a disposition to ask Mr. Biddle oratorical and hypothetical questions that were not always polite."[30]

The U.S. Attorney General especially reminded these congressmen of the "international aspects of the problem" and in particular focused on U.S. efforts to abide by the Geneva Convention. He then turned the meeting over to Mr. Benninghoff and Mr. Gufler from the State Department, who explained "this Government's undertaking with regard to the application of the Geneva Convention to civilians and pointed out the Department of State's primary concern to protect American citizens in Japanese hands and the role played by reciprocity in this connection."[31]

After lunch, the discussion continued, and the State Department representatives made it clear that their primary concern with the Japanese subjects in the United States was that "treatment of these persons should be such as to afford a basis for demands for good reciprocal treatment for Americans in Japanese hands," and that these U.S. "demands for good reciprocal treatment would have the support of the Spanish authorities acting as protecting Power for Japanese subjects held by the United States." These State Department officials also pointed out the "desire of the State Department to continue exchanges with a view to obtaining the repatriation of American citizens in Japanese hands." Following this discussion the congressmen present at the meeting "showed understanding for an agreement with the position of the Department."[32] The congressmen at this meeting also discussed the segregation program at the Tule Lake Relocation Center, which was taking place at this time.

American citizens of Japanese ancestry who were loyal to the U.S. sometimes felt threatened by those who had expressed their desire to be repatriated to Japan. When one young man at Tule Lake decided to move his whole family out of the center, his pro-Japan neighbors warned him "under no circumstance should you cooperate with the United State government," and thereafter "made their life miserable, and even showed signs of being ready to attack and harm the young man."[33]

According to a Japanese government protest, dated 18 April 1944, the segregation program also had U.S. security in mind:

> United States Government intend to release evacuees not necessarily but as far as possible; but they cannot release any who are dangerous to United States; and any who wish to return to Japan are deemed most dangerous to United States; therefore those persons at relocation centres who have repudiated allegiance to United States and those who do not cooperate with authorities there, as well as those who desire to return to Japan, will be transferred to Special Relocation Centre at Tule Lake.

In order to determine who was dangerous and who was not the "United States authorities, at various times from February to August inclusive 1943 put to Japanese subjects and United States citizens of Japanese origin interned at relocation centres [the] question whether or not they would swear allegiance to United States."[34]

During these interviews, U.S. officials were concerned that they not make any mistakes, since putting an evacuee into the wrong category could mean the difference between releasing or holding them. Therefore, those evacuees who were Japanese citizens were asked at different times about their loyalty to the United States. When they refused to respond to initial questioning, more lenient loyalty oaths were suggested. For example they were first asked "whether they would renounce allegiance to sovereign [Emperor] of Japan and swear unconditional allegiance to United States." Second, they were asked "whether they would cooperate in defense of United States in event of that country being attacked by enemy." Finally, on the third occasion they were asked "whether they would swear to abide by United States law and refrain from all such actions as would interfere with prosecution of war."[35]

Those Japanese-Americans who were American citizens by birth were asked different questions. For example, to determine which second generation Japanese—who were American citizens by birth—felt loyalty to Japan, they were asked "whether they would swear unconditional allegiance to United States and renounce allegiance to any foreign country." If they agreed, then the men and women were asked additional questions. Men were asked whether they "would voluntarily enlist in United States Army." Women were asked whether they "would volunteer for enlistment in women's Auxiliary Army Corps."[36] In fact, many Japanese-American men and women did volunteer to serve in the armed forces, and their record during the war was exemplary.

Many of the Japanese citizens who were asked these questions were "indignant at gross insolence of first and second questions" and so "abstained from or refused any answer." Even the third question, which was more neutral, did not achieve an affirmative response.[37] Apparantly, these evacuees continued to feel loyalty to the Japanese emperor and to the Japanese nation, while not feeling particularly loyal to the United States. In the course of these interviews, many Japanese citizens even expressed their hope that Japan would win the war.

As for those of Japanese origin who were American citizens: "Most ... [at the Tule Lake Relocation Center] answered above-mentioned questions in negative." In other words, even those Japanese-Americans who were American citizens by birth refused to swear their allegiance to the United States or to volunteer to join the armed services. According to Japanese protests, the U.S. authorities attempted to "force them to alter their negative answers to affirmative answers, and summoned some of them on as many as five occasions in order to extract desired answers from them," but with no success.[38]

The Tule Lake Segregation Center "mutiny"

On 4 November 1943, a disturbance that was later referred to as a "mutiny" broke out at the Tule Lake Segregation Center. The major underlying cause appears to have been the disruption of normal life due to the implementation of the segregation plan. The immediate cause, however, seems to have been the failure on the part of several of the Tule Lake personnel to carry out normal procedures, especially related to the equal distribution of food. When tensions reached boiling point, several of the personnel were attacked and government troops were called in to restore order.

One Japanese-American minister who was present immediately prior to this incident reported increasing tensions, especially among the Kibei: "One was the sudden increase of vandalism—a totally senseless kind of vandalism. One night a group of Kibei young men who had just arrived from another center piled up chairs from the school building and made a bonfire of them." Another time, a group of Kibei youth made fun of new arrivals by "making remarks in Japanese to the Nisei and Caucasian staff." Finally, in clear defiance of the center's administration, "a group of men put up a sign in Japanese to publicize a 'training school' for youths wishing to become fighters for the achievement of the 'Great East Asia Co-Prosperity,' under the aggressive military leadership of imperial Japan." The young minister in question had left Tule Lake by the time of the incident, in part because he was warned "that if I stayed on, my life would be in danger because resentment and hostility were so intense among the people that one never knew what might happen to those who were, rightly or wrongly, identified as pro-American."[39]

Near the end of October 1943, several community leaders, led by Mike Kunitani, complained to the center administrators about overcrowding, poor sanitation, and disruptions in food supplies. In particular, however, they demanded that segregation be speeded up so that those who had requested repatriation be separated physically from those who intended to remain in the United States. Furthermore, they demanded that all of the residents at Tule Lake be accorded prisoner of war status under the Geneva Convention. Finally, and most importantly, they organized a ten-day work stoppage, right as the fall harvest was due in, so as "to bring matters to a crisis stage."[40]

In response, the Army was called in to administer Tule Lake beginning on 4 November. This was in direct response to efforts by the striking farm workers to halt food deliveries to workers harvesting the vegetable crop, because they were volunteer farm workers brought in from the other relocation centers to bring in the harvest. The Tule Lake workers, however, saw them as strikebreakers. According to Myer, this incident took the administrators by surprise: "The fight was over moving food out to these outlanders, you see, who were brought in to harvest the crops which they [the residents of the Tule Lake center] wouldn't harvest."[41]

As a result of this incident, some 200-evacuees, plus 14 supposedly elected representatives of Tule Lake Segregation Center, were detained by the U.S. authorities. On 6 January 1944, after a six-day hunger protest, a note was sent to the Spanish embassy that included the following letter to be transmitted to Foreign Minister Shigemitsu in Japan:

To: Foreign Minister Shigemitsu
Tokyo, Japan

207 Japanese leaders, including all representatives, of Japanese residents at Tule Lake Segregation Camp held in Army prison have been on hunger strike from January 1, 1944 stop without food for a week, they are now weak and many of them cannot stand up stop these Japanese are leaders of Japanese loyal to Japan in the incident which

BEGAN NOVEMBER 4, 1943 STOP PLEASE MEDIATE IMMEDIATELY IN BEHALF OF
JAPANESE IN TULE LAKE INCIDENT BEFORE MANY JAPANESE LEADERS DIE OF
HUNGER STRIKE.
TEMPORARY TULE LAKE JAPANESE COMMITTEE[42]

In the aftermath of the November incident, and perhaps after receiving this letter,
the Japanese government demanded that a Spanish representative be given an
opportunity to confirm that the "treatment accorded to evacuees in Tule Lake
does not differ from treatment accorded to those at other centres." In particular,
the Japanese wanted to confirm that in the aftermath of this incident the evacuees
at Tule Lake were not being forced to conduct "compulsory labour."[43]

Meanwhile, with regard to the reported incident itself, the Japanese
government made the following three demands:

(1) Withdrawal of troops from Tule Lake and restoration of control of that
    relocation centre to non-military authorities;
(2) Recognition of legitimacy of committee of 14;
(3) Release of 14 committee-men and over 200 persons arrested in connection
    with the incident.

Only by conforming to these three demands, argued the Japanese government
protest, could the two governments "relieve state of anxiety prevailing at Tule
Lake" Segregation Center.[44]

The U.S. government answered this protest with its own version of the events
during the spring and summer of 1944. After the State Department's
communication clarified the purpose of the segregation policy, this document
turned to the actual points presented in the April 1944 Japanese protest. First, it
explained that the incident took place "shortly after the completion of the first
major segregation movement." For obvious reasons, this was a period of
transition, when many Japanese-American evacuees were unsure of what exactly
was happening to them and when they might be able to return to Japan. In this
context, the 14 representatives of the evacuees "met with officials of the war
relocation authority including the national director and presented a series of
demands." The national director made it clear that "the war relocation authority
would not accede to any demands," but that he was willing to "consider requests
or complaints made on behalf of the evacuees at any time."[45]

In a letter to Secretary-of-State Hull, dated 27 January 1944, John H. Provinse,
acting director, discussed the 1 November 1943 meeting: "One point of complaint
involved food, and the Director indicated that the facts would be ascertained and
that correctional action would be taken if justified by the facts. No other promises
were made." After careful investigation, problems were discovered with the
system of food allotment and distribution. The problem was not, as suggested by
the Spanish embassy, that food that was intended for the evacuees was instead
being used to "feed persons employed outside the project in harvesting crops,"

but that foodstuffs "were subsequently discovered stored in Japanese houses in greater quantities than would normally be expected." According to Provinse:

> This Authority has now made an investigation of the situation regarding the handling of foods, and finds that foods were properly allotted to the mess halls but that some of the evacuee chefs did not serve the full allotment. The action of these chefs constitutes misconduct on their part as employees of the Authority, and it was improper from the standpoint of their responsibilities to the evacuees who were dependent in part upon them for food preparation. The nature and extent of administrative action that may be appropriate in such cases has not yet been determined.

Provinse did pointedly conclude, however, "that the efforts of the committee in this respect might well be addressed to the members of the evacuee group who are guilty of such misconduct."[46] The assurances of the acting director proved to be inadequate. Three days later, a group of malcontents "armed with clubs entered the area where employee[s] of the war relocation authority reside and made attacks upon some of the personnel."[47]

Henry L. Stimson, in a letter to the Secretary-of-State Cordell Hull, described what happened next: "On the evening of November 4, 1943, a group of approximately 400 evacuees, many armed with clubs, entered the administrative and motor pool areas. The residence of the Project Director was surrounded, and it became plain that the security of the administrative staff was threatened. At this point the Project Director called upon the military to enter the Center and restore order."[48]

In response to these threats, U.S. troops stationed outside the relocation center "were summoned inside to restore order."[49] This involved several injuries: "In restoring order, three persons who resisted (one a Japanese national) were injured, none of them seriously." In addition, "Six individuals who resisted the authorities at the time of the initial disorder were placed under temporary arrest, from which they were shortly released."[50] After order was restored, however, "the center was placed under army jurisdiction for a period of several weeks while conditions were being gradually restored to normal."[51]

To the administrators of the Tule Lake Segregation Center, the incident appeared to be a direct result of organized resistance to the U.S. authorities by those who had already professed their loyalty to Japan. If nothing else, this outbreak appeared to confirm U.S. government fears that those who professed themselves loyal to Japan did represent a threat to the rest of the Japanese-American community who claimed to be loyal to the United States. Only when it became absolutely necessary was the Tule Lake Segregation Center put under military control. This period of military control lasted through early 1944.

In the end, most of the problems that had sparked the incident at Tule Lake were resolved. According to Myer: "Of the 70,000 people left in centers in 1944, probably at least half had never had it so good."[52] However, the long-term "international implications" of the Tule Lake incident proved to be quite serious.[53] In sharp contrast to the demands of the protesters for immediate repatriation to Japan, the Tule Lake mutiny in fact further helped to undermine all chances for a third wartime exchange.

The aftermath of the Tule Lake mutiny

The period of military control at the Tule Lake Relocation Center ended on 15 January 1944, at which point "the center was returned to full civil administration." As one U.S. government communiqué to the Japanese government promised: "The war relocation authority is now responsible for all phases of internal administration at the center and has been for the past few months. As long as the residents of the center continue to maintain a peaceful and well ordered community, it is not contemplated that there will be any further occasion for summoning troops or placing the center under military control."[54]

The Tule Lake "mutiny" was short-lived and with hindsight proved to be a relatively minor event. In fact, soon after the mutiny was quelled and the mutineers segregated from the other interns, the situation at Tule Lake reportedly returned to normal:

> It is true that certain members of the committee and approximately two hundred other evacuees were temporarily confined immediately following the riot at the center, because they were suspected of complicity in its instigation. The majority of those confined, however, have now been released and those found guilty of inciting the riot will ultimately be transferred to other quarters. Their treatment will comply fully with the applicable provisions of the Geneva Convention of 1929, but they will not be in a position to foment unrest among the other residents of Tule Lake, the majority of whom desire to live quietly and peaceably.

The U.S. government attitude toward the evacuees would not change, even in the face of complaints from the protestors. In particular, according to Secretary of War Stimson: "The sense of the complaint made by the segregated residents is that they were not allowed to remain where they could continue to threaten the authorities and intimidate their fellow-evacuees."[55]

The question at Tule Lake was not whether the residents of the center will be "treated according to the principles and provisions of the Geneva Convention or whether the administration is prepared to cooperate with the evacuees in reaching a solution of common problems," but whether "a small group is to be permitted through methods of violence to force their leadership on the remainder of the community in such a manner as to cause a recurrence of a riot such as that of November 4."[56]

Based on this consideration, it was the judgment of the officials in charge of the relocation authority that in "the interests of the great majority of the evacuees at Tule Lake" Segregation Center, these "troublesome individuals be housed in separate accommodations where their propensity for creation [of] discord cannot contribute to the discomfort of the large number of law abiding residents of the camp."[57] Thus, although a Spanish protest from 11 January 1944 had specifically advocated that "the segregated elements of the community be permitted to mingle with the others," Stimson concluded: "The policy of segregating unruly elements is designed to create an atmosphere in which the peaceful and cooperative elements of the community may return to normal pursuits and to the enjoyment of the benefits deriving there from."[58]

To protest their being segregated from the rest, several hundred evacuees organized a hunger strike. According to Stimson:

> In connection with the hunger strike of about 200 adults in the separate area which began December 31 and came to an end January 6, I would like to point out that this action was wholly voluntary on the part of the evacuees. Nevertheless, food in sufficient quantities was made available at all times, perishable stocks being replenished each day, and care was taken by this Government to provide daily medical examination by competent physicians.

Of special interest was the fact, according to Stimson, "that of the segregated group, only about 25 per cent are nationals of Japan."[59] This statistic was confirmed in a Spanish note from 27 January 1944, which stated that "three quarter parts of those interned are American residents and one quarter part nationals of Japan."[60]

Even though the Spanish embassy admitted that the majority of those confined were U.S. citizens, and so "are outside the protection of the Spanish Embassy," it did entreat "the Department of State, with the utmost urgency, to use its good office with the corresponding authorities that they may exert their usual benevolence and humanitarian spirit, to avert major disorders which threaten for the near future, and release not only the Japanese proper, but the Japanese American citizens." The U.S. response was immediate, as the Secretary of State warned Stimson of the "vital nature of this problem arising from the desire of this government to keep open negotiations with the Japanese Government, looking toward future exchange operations through which Americans in Japanese hands may be repatriated and to do its utmost for the relief and protection of Americans under Japanese control."[61]

These documents show that the vast majority of those being segregated were not Japanese citizens at all, but were American citizens of Japanese ancestry who were under American jurisdiction. Given the practices of the Japanese-American community this, in turn, suggests that a large number of them were young men— Kibei—who had received their primary education in Japan before returning to the United States to work. During this unsettled period, both military personnel and the relocation center's main authorities tried to treat the evacuees leniently. The period of military control over the center lasted only about ten weeks. However, the U.S. government's position on the "committee of fourteen" was very different. Instead of being lenient, it stated that "the war relocation authority is not prepared to recognize this particular group since there is considerable evidence that it represents no more than a small minority of the total Tule Lake population."[62]

Acting Director Provinse even questioned the authority of the so-called "Kuratomi committee," stating his personal view that it was "neither responsible nor representative." Furthermore: "Not only was there a resort to violence before adequate opportunity was had to examine and consider their requests, but there is also reason to doubt that the committee accurately reported to the evacuees generally the nature of the commitments made to the committee." Depending on whether one took it at face value or some ascribed underlying meaning, Kuratomi could have even been threatening a mutiny when he stated to relocation center authorities on 1 November 1943: "We do not want to commit any riots or conduct ourselves in a disorderly manner."[63]

In fact, the committee of 14 participated in the riot, and it "is evident that rioters cannot expect the lawful authorities to accept them as competent negotiators, or as representing a peaceful and well-disposed majority."[64] Therefore, according to Acting Director Provinse:

> At no time did the Kuratomi committee present to the War Relocation Authority evidence that it was selected by a representative process or that it was authorized to speak for the population. We have, in fact, good reason to believe that its member had used "strong arm" pressure tactics to establish their position as leaders of the evacuees community. In fact, certain leaders of the evacuee community have insisted that the leaders of the "strong arm" group be retained in a separate compound so that a truly representative committee could be established without fear of reprisal against peaceful members of the community and their families.[65]

As a result, during a vote on 11 January 1944, which was "participated in by about 8,000 persons eighteen years or age or over, comprising approximately 90 percent of the adult residents of the Center," the committee of 14 was rejected as "unrepresentative" and a new group was elected.[66]

In the wake of the Tule Lake "mutiny," the Japanese government protested that undue pressure was put on the Japanese-Americans, accusing the U.S. authorities of trying to force those loyal to Japan to pledge their allegiance to the United States. This protest was a one-sided account of what turned out to be, in fact, a very complicated factional dispute. Still, diplomatic tensions sparked by the Tule Lake "mutiny" were destined to have both a long-term and a highly negative impact on the exchange program.

The April 1944 Japanese protest and U.S. response

The Tule Lake "mutiny" was without a doubt the most serious single incident to occur at any of the American relocation centers during World War II. Several months later, during April 1944, the Japanese government officially protested this incident, calling the U.S. authorities' actions against the Japanese nationals and American citizens of Japanese ancestry "unjust and inhuman." Somewhat illogically, considering Japan's own emphasis on absolute loyalty among its citizens to the Emperor and to the Japanese nation, this protest also accused the U.S. government of using the segregation plan as a "pretext" for forcing "Japanese subjects to renounce allegiance to Japan."[67]

Therefore, instead of recognizing the direct link between renouncing allegiance to Japan and expressing loyalty to the United States, this Japanese communication quixotically denounced Washington for regarding "those who expressed desire to be repatriated as disloyal to United States." In addition, Tokyo's protest accused the U.S. government of using the series of questions about allegiance to Japan and loyalty to the United States as "threats" and "compulsion" directed at "United States citizens of Japanese origin in their attempt to force them to alter their answers whether they would swear allegiance to United States or not."[68]

This accusation suggests that, to the Japanese government at least, the "United States citizens of Japanese origin" should be treated as a special group, perhaps on a par with the handful of British-Americans who enjoyed dual citizenship. According to the Japanese view, therefore, those who belonged to the category "United States citizens of Japanese origin" should be allowed to retain their chosen loyalty to Japan while still retaining full rights of American citizenship. Basing their protest on this ethnic view as compared to a legalistic view, the Japanese government stated that it "most emphatically protest against such measure[s], and demand its immediate discontinuance."[69]

Clearly, the U.S. government did not agree that this type of dual citizenship was possible, especially between two belligerent nations at war. With this rationale in mind, the U.S. government answered this Japanese protest four months later, on 10 August 1944. Instead of using the phrase "United States citizens of Japanese origin," it preferred the phrase "American citizens of Japanese ancestry" so as to clarify that many Japanese-Americans had never been to Japan. This document also went to great lengths to distinguish the difference between legal nationality—citizenship—versus ethnic nationality—bloodlines. For example, this U.S. document clearly stated that "the Japanese Government has a legitimate concern for Japanese nationals only," and cannot claim jurisdiction over "American citizens of Japanese ancestry."[70] This cut to the very heart of the Japanese protest, which presupposed the superiority of ethnicity over citizenship, and by doing so presupposed that the Japanese government had the right to protest on behalf of all Japanese-Americans who were also American citizens.

Before responding to the specific points in the Japanese protest, the U.S. government document first attempted to explain again the purpose of the registration process and questions concerning swearing allegiance to the U.S. government. According to the American view, this process took part "at all relocation centers in the early part of 1943" in order to "acquire information of the background and attitudes of (1) male American citizens of Japanese ancestry with a view to possible desire to serve in the army of the United States; (2) Japanese nationals and other persons at relocation centers with a view to restoring them to normal life outside the centers."[71]

Although this memorandum did admit that some Japanese nationals had been asked several times to affirm their loyalty to the United States, it claimed that this was a mistake. In fact, the question in dispute—number 28—was the only one referred to by the Japanese government in its April 1944 protest out of the many questions that the registrants had been asked:

> This question was originally drawn up primarily with American citizens of Japanese ancestry in mind. Through an inadvertance however it was phrased in identical form both for American citizens and for Japanese nationals. However as soon as it was realized that this wording was not applicable to Japanese nationals, substitute question was presented to them. In the period between presentation of the original question and development [of] the substitute a third type of question was used at the Manzanar relocation center. When the substitute question was presented to the Japanese nationals residing at the Manzanar center the answers to the interim question were disregarded. Consequently although at first Japanese nationals were asked to answer the same question as were United States citizens no attempt was made to force them to renounce their allegiance to Japan and with the change in question they were finally asked merely whether they would promise to abide by the laws of the United States and to refrain from interfering with the war effort.

This explanation would appear to conform perfectly with the Japanese protest, and would suggest that one of the main goals of the registration process was not merely to determine national loyalty but to also determine which evacuees might pose a danger to the U.S. national security during wartime.[72]

As for the Japanese claims that coercion was used to force respondents to change their answers and claim a loyalty that they did not feel, this memorandum explained in great detail:

> Throughout the entire registration program every person was free to answer all questions including the question referred to in the Japanese Government's memorandum according to the dictates of his judgement and conscience. At no time did any official use restraint or duress to force anyone to change an answer previously given. Since the entire purpose of the registration was to

obtain honest answers regarding the background and attitudes of the registrants it seems obvious that any attempt to use compulsion in influencing the replies would be self defeating.

However, this note did acknowledge that when there was evidence that certain respondents had perhaps been influenced by "threats from other evacuees," "undue emotional strain," or a general "lack of understanding when they gave their original answer," they were given an "opportunity to reconsider their answers." This was done to "assure each person the fullest possible opportunity to make his own answer on the basis of his own individual choice," and if they "preferred to let their original answers stand after reconsideration were freely permitted to do so."[73]

As for the Japanese government's claim that the "majority" of the so-called "American citizens of Japanese origin" answered the "question under reference in the negative," the U.S. government assured Japan that this assertion simply was not true. In fact, as the U.S. government communiqué makes clear "the answers to the question were such that it was necessary to transfer only a small minority of the American citizens of Japanese ancestry as well as only a small minority of the Japanese nationals to the Tule Lake center."[74]

Furthermore, transfer to the Tule Lake Relocation Center was not intended as a "form of punishment" of any kind, but to segregate those evacuees "whose loyalties and sympathies lie with Japan" from those who were either loyal to the United States or were "law-abiding aliens." Contrary to the explanation given in the Japanese protest, after the relocation centers had been operating for about a year, it had become apparent that "there was at all centers prior to the segregation program a considerable amount of tension between these two groups," and to many "it became clear that peaceful orderly communities could probably not be maintained as people of sharply diverging loyalties were living in such close proximity." Therefore, the segregation plan was undertaken not so much at the desire of the American government but at the suggestion of many "evacuees including [a] number that have openly professed their intention of returning to Japan," who "urged that a separation be made between those two groups."[75]

It was after due consideration of this plan, therefore, that the U.S. government decided "to consolidate in the one center at Tule Lake all those who had expressed a desire to move to Japan or who had indicated by word or action that their loyalties are not with the United States." The three main differences were:

(1) that those segregated at Tule Lake are not eligible to leave the center except through an appeals board procedure,
(2) that they are not permitted the same degree of latitude in establishing their own community government, and
(3) that additional precautions have been taken to insure maintenance of law and order.

But, in all other ways, the U.S. government assured its Japanese counterpart, the Tule Lake Segregation Center was similar to the other relocation centers. In particular, the "living conditions and facilities ... are in accordance with the standard set for all war relocation authority centers."[76]

Conclusions

Based on the available evidence, one of the main factors behind the so-called "mutiny" at the Tule Lake Segregation Center would appear to be that the U.S. authorities had begun actively to segregate the evacuees who professed loyalty to the United States from those who were loyal to Japan. The segregation program was thought necessary because of constant delays in carrying out the third Japanese-American exchange and the resulting increase in tension between those who professed loyalty to the U.S. and those who professed loyalty to Japan. Interestingly, if this and other exchanges had been carried out as quickly as expected, then these individuals would have already been repatriated to Japan and the so-called "mutiny" might never have taken place. Viewed in this way, the Tule Lake incident resulted from the Japanese government's decision to delay the exchange program, not from the U.S. policies.

According to the various American viewpoints forwarded by the U.S. State Department at the time, the problems experienced at the Tule Lake Segregation Center were mainly between different groups of evacuees, with the most radical of the American citizens of Japanese ancestry joining with Japanese nationals in opposition to those Japanese nationals and American citizens who were loyal to the United States. Based on these divisions, Acting Director Provinse even urged the Spanish embassy to reconsider its view of the incident as being either directed at or instigated by the administration of the relocation center: "I am sure that the Spanish Embassy, in its capacity of representing Japanese interests in the United States, does not wish to become involved in a factional dispute between groups of evacuees and for that reason, we would hope that the Embassy might wish to reexamine the situation locally."[77]

The evidence presented above, when added to U.S. government offers for the Spanish representative to investigate the situation at Tule Lake, appears to confirm that the source of the problem at the relocation center really was "factional" in nature. Due primarily to delays in repatriating the residents of Tule Lake, tensions rapidly increased between those Japanese-Americans who were loyal to the United States and those who were loyal to Japan. Japan could have defused these tensions by quickly agreeing to a third exchange. Tokyo instead became even more firm in its criticism of the U.S. government and more resistant to any suggestion that a third non-official exchange take place.

9 Tokyo protests mistreatment of non-officials and the delay of the third exchange

Once the second U.S.–Japanese exchange was completed, the U.S. State Department immediately suggested a third. Tokyo was less interested than before, however, and delayed a third exchange by protesting the poor treatment of non-official Japanese nationals, especially at Tule Lake. As might be expected, many of the non-officials who had been repatriated to Japan during the first and second exchanges had either been housed in, or were even located by means of interviews conducted at the war relocation centers. Therefore, a larger percentage of the alleged infractions mentioned by the Japanese government during 1943 and 1944 took place in the war relocation centers. These accusations included mistreatment of the old and infirm, abuse of Japanese nationals in Hawaii, inadequate health care, mistreatment during transport, torture of Japanese nationals, and forced labor.

The U.S. government responded to these protests quickly and tried to show that they were unfounded. To do this, Washington early-on made a point of trying to distinguish the different types of evacuees: Japanese citizens loyal to Japan, American citizens of Japanese ancestry loyal to Japan, Japanese citizens loyal to the United States, and finally American citizens of Japanese ancestry loyal to the United States. Of these four groups, stated Washington, only the first was officially under the jurisdiction of the Japanese government. In particular, those Japanese who were American citizens but expressed loyalty to Japan could not be represented by any other foreign government. Therefore, the U.S. government made it clear that in its judgment the main criterion was citizenship, with a secondary criterion being loyalty; a person's ethnic background was not sufficient in and by itself. On this basis, the U.S. government overturned many of Japan's protests. The Japanese government's views, however, were based on race, not nationality.

The State Department also did its best to investigate the events behind the other Japanese accusations. While admitting on occasion that the underlying facts were consistent with the protest in question, at which point corrective measures were taken, in most cases additional information served to undermine the validity of the Japanese argument. For example, the Japanese government protested the use of Japanese labor to construct a swimming pool near a relocation center in Missoula, Montana. A later investigation clarified the pool was being built for the benefit of the Japanese-American evacuees themselves and not for the center's administrator or staff. Swimming pools for evacuees apparently had not occurred to the Japanese government, whose own internment camps became famous for their high mortality rates, not their recreational facilities.

In the end, these protests and counter-protests served mainly to increase diplomatic tensions between the Japanese and American governments. Such tensions reduced the possibility of a third U.S.–Japanese exchange until fighting near the Japanese home islands made any further exchanges impossible. Also, Japan saw little profit in continuing the exchanges, since it had secured the return of all of its officials. Allegations against U.S. mistreatment actually covered up the fact that Japan did not want the Tule Lake Segregation Center people back. Any additional expense Japan could make the U.S. pay to investigate and correct these supposed faults would also divert scarce U.S. resources away from the war effort.

Mistreatment of the elderly and infirm

Following the first U.S.–Japanese exchange, Tokyo officials interviewed the non-official participants and compiled a list of complaints. The first subsection of the October 1942 Japanese protest was called "Arrest and Internment." As a Confucian society, which followed a strict hierarchy by age, the Japanese accorded great respect to the elderly. Tokyo's first complaint was that older "internees are treated equally with those who are in the prime of life in respect of housing, food and discipline, and no special consideration for their age is accorded to them." This situation was exacerbated, according to the Japanese government, because so many of the evacuees were elderly, and "the average age of Japanese subjects interned is fifty-four or fifty-five at many an internment camp."[1]

According to the U.S. government response of December 1942: "Japanese subjects have been detained for investigation only when there existed special reasons of a serious nature necessitating their detention." This process included a formal hearing and these persons "have been ordered interned only when it has been determined after a thorough hearing at which the persons in question have been permitted to appear and to produce evidence in their own defense that there are grave reasons for holding them." Following such formal hearings, a "number of older persons who were detained temporarily on the outbreak of hostilities were released." Other older Japanese, who were arrested, "have subsequently been released following reviews of their cases." Furthermore, special medical care and even hospitalization when needed were provided by the U.S. government for the "sick infirm and aged."[2]

Almost a year later, immediately following the completion of the second U.S.–Japanese exchange, the U.S. government responded in greater detail to this note and aggressively challenged the specific accusations. In a detailed memorandum dated 21 October 1943, the State Department stated that, contrary to Japanese accusations that many elderly people were arrested: "A careful study made by the Immigration and Naturalization Service, which is charged with the internment of dangerous or potentially dangerous enemy civilians in the continental United States, shows that only two Japanese aged eighty or over have been in the custody of that Service and that but one Japanese of eighty years of age is held at the present time." Contrary to the Japanese government's accusations that the "average age of Japanese subjects held in many internment camps in the United States is fifty-four or fifty-five": "The same study shows that the average age of internees of Japanese nationality is now forty-five."[3]

Special treatment for the elderly was deemed unnecessary because the "treatment of all the persons held is so uniformly considerate." Such treatment was accorded only to the "sick or infirm," at which point "they are hospitalized and given proper medical treatment and special diets." However, the U.S. memorandum noted: "It has been the experience of the detaining authorities that older Japanese have often been anxious to join their friends and relatives in the general quarters rather than remain in hospitals as the detaining authorities would have preferred."[4]

The State Department assured Tokyo that even in the camps in Hawaii, which were operated by the Department of War, "special consideration is accorded" to old and infirm internees and "special medical care by competent physicians is provided for even the most minor ailments." For more serious illnesses: "Hospitalization when necessary is provided in Army hospitals or in hospitals established solely for the internees where the standard of equipment and professional service is equal to that in the hospitals of the United States Army."[5] This 21 October note followed soon after the second exchange. There can be little doubt that the State Department timed the delivery of its response so as not to interfere with the second U.S.–Japanese exchange.

Japanese protests of poor treatment in Hawaii

Hawaii in the early 1940s was a territory, not a state. Therefore, the alleged mistreatment of Japanese nationals in Hawaii equated—in Tokyo's eyes at least—with Japan's own mistreatment of American nationals in its imperial colonies, such as China, Indochina, the Philippines, and elsewhere. According to the Japanese government, the treatment of Japanese detainees in Hawaii was particularly harsh, which thus gave them the right to treat Americans with equal harshness in return.

A Japanese protest from April 1943 accused U.S. authorities on Oahu of regularly arresting and handcuffing Japanese nationals. According to reports from those who had been repatriated, some 200 were then housed in a "room with a capacity for only about eighty persons," where they were forced to remain without a chance to exercise. The only exception was mealtimes, when there was another humiliation, since the meals "were served, regardless of weather, on the lawn in the compound under the strict watch of soldiers with fixed bayonets posted about two feet apart."[6]

At the Sand Island Camp, in particular, the Japanese government claimed that Japanese civilians were treated just like prisoners of war, and were forced to erect tents for themselves and for German and Italian internees, build fences, do laundry, and grow "vegetables to be supplied to the soldiers." Later, when being transferred to the continental U.S. they were locked in a "room near the ship's bottom" covered by metal mesh and were "forbidden to go out of the room except for meals or lavatory."[7] A separate protest accused the U.S. authorities at Sand Island of making Japanese nationals dig up "blind shells," or duds, that "even the guards did not dare to approach." Later, when Japanese nationals were boarding a ship to the continental U.S. on the "pretext of a shortage of life-boats they were compelled to bring lifebuoys with them."[8]

The Japanese government also protested searches of Japanese civilians and the seizure of their personal possessions. Some detainees were searched as many as "nine times in all after their arrest until their departure from the United States": "The Japanese were forced to undergo the search on their arrival at, and departure from, the camp and also on their embarkation on, and disembarkation from, the vessel for transfer or for repatriation." When being transferred, detainees were also reportedly "obliged to get from their families about fifty dollars per head for miscellaneous expenses to cover the journey." However, the money had to be deposited with "military authorities" and these "authorities ignored the repeated requests from the Japanese for the return of the money in question as well as the money seized on their arrival," thus leaving them "in great hardship owing to the total lack of money."[9]

The Department of State's communiqués did not immediately answer these Japanese charges. In one note from October 1943, the U.S. government did explain that the Office of Immigration and Naturalization was not in charge of all Japanese nationals. Notable exceptions were in the: "Jurisdiction over the investigation, apprehension, and internment of Japanese nationals on the Hawaiian Islands, Alaska, and the Panama Canal Zone."[10] Therefore, the State Department had to investigate these accusations separately by working with the Department of War.

After checking with the Department of War, the U.S. government did respond to the Japanese protest on 25 March 1944. According to the investigation, "in no instance was it found necessary to use handcuffs during the apprehension and transportation of Japanese internees to custody." Housing for internees was the same as for U.S. soldiers, and meals were provided in a "roofed inclosure and were not subjected to elements as alleged." As for overcrowding, they could identify only one case when some 161 civilian internees arrived on the West Coast and: "This group was temporarily held while awaiting procession in bedroom with 192 beds, and was fed in new mess hall seating 250 persons."[11]

Regarding accusations of enforced labor, it was true that at Sand Island detention camp "within first few weeks after December 7, 1941 large number of aliens were taken into custody," and that "Japanese civilian internees were instructed to erect and align their tents." This treatment was the same as accorded to German and Italian internees, however, and: "No order was given as far as is known that Japanese should erect tents of Germans and Italians." As for building a fence, after asking the "leaders of Japanese internees" a number of "young Japanese" were found who were willing to assist in "the construction of a fence around their inclosure." Meanwhile, laundry work on behalf of army personnel was either voluntary or was reimbursed at a "rate of eighty cents per day." Finally, not only were the vegetables being grown so as to "enable Japanese who desired fresh vegetables to supply themselves therewith," but the U.S. government furnished both "implements" and "seeds."[12]

The State Department admitted that internees and their luggage were searched upon arrival, and once again before departing for the continental U.S. to "assure that no forbidden articles were taken aboard ship." Valuables were indeed collected and receipts provided, although "any article which might have been considered a possible lethal weapon was confiscated." All such "personal valuables except money were returned upon departure of internees for Mainland." The money was deposited in Hawaiian banks and "books were set up to show amounts credited to each internee." When an internee was sent to the continental U.S. then the "money was forwarded to provost marshal general Washington D.C. for credit to internees account at Mainland Internment camp to which he was transferred." According to records, $26,679.65 was transferred in this manner from Hawaii to Washington.[13]

During transfer, shipboard accommodations were not only "adequate" and not at all restrictive, but were "superior to those furnished either ships crew or transit troops"; for example, toilets were "furnished within room or were readily accessible." Once they arrived on the West Coast, the internees were housed in adequate facilities and "no complaints were lodged during any transfer." Finally, the State Department concluded, throughout the "process of investigation apprehension and detention Japanese civilians were treated humanely and were protected against violence insults and public curiosity."[14]

In a second note dated 21 July 1944, further information was provided on several of the Japanese accusations. For example, after investigating reports that Japanese detainees had to dig up "blind shells" the U.S. government reported: "Investigation has failed disclose any occasion when internees Sand Island required handle ammunition of any kind, including what are commonly referred to as duds or what Japanese Government refers to as blind shells." As for a variety of other accusations, including perhaps the one about having to bring extra life jackets because of a lack of lifeboats, the State Department concluded: "United States Government having thoroughly examined reports of these Japanese repatriates considers that these additional allegations reported to Japanese

Government are without foundation in fact and that these Japanese nationals were treated with humanity and consideration."[15]

The Japanese government was not satisfied with the U.S. response to its protests. On 13 January 1945, only eight months before Japan surrendered, it protested again against the "unjustifiable insults and inhuman maltreatment to which the United States authorities have subjected innocent Japanese civilians." This time, it gave specific names—including Tokuye Takahashi, Seigan Saito, and Minetaro Hori—who were handcuffed when they were arrested. It also repeated that Japanese nationals had been forced to live in crowded conditions and had to take their meals "on the lawn irrespective of the weather." This protest tacitly admitted that the internees were allowed out of their rooms to exercise when they were allowed to walk to "the place where they took meals three times a day." Finally, while repeating that at the Sand Island camp labor was compulsory during the first two weeks after the outbreak of war, when the camp was being constructed, the Japanese government then acknowledged that after that time it came to be of a "voluntary nature."[16]

Tokyo's second set of protests concerning problems transporting Japanese nationals was also much weaker. Criticism of the poor conditions on the ship was repeated, but this time it became clear that it was merely one wall and the door that were made of metal mesh, not the entire room or ceiling as had been suggested before. A guard was supposed to let the Japanese out every four hours to use the lavatory, but he "shirked his duty and often failed to appear at the appointed time." Instead, two garbage cans and several small buckets were, at the request of the detainees, turned into chamberpots. In sharp opposition to earlier protests, which had made the conditions sound unbearable, the Japanese government now merely argued that "afterwards they had to take the vessels out and dispose of their contents," and that: "They were provided with no facilities for washing their faces, nor was any water supplied for the purpose."[17]

As these later Japanese protests revealed, the alleged mistreatment of Japanese non-officials in Hawaii had been exaggerated in Tokyo's first series of protests. Sometimes these discrepancies were embarrassing. For example, a State Department investigation looking into one accusation that the U.S. government made Japanese nationals sleep two or even three to a bed revealed that the room in question contained three-tiered bunk beds, so that housing two to three people per "bed" was perfectly normal. These types of cultural misunderstandings, however, continued to plague U.S.–Japanese negotiations. The Japanese government refused to agree to a third exchange so long as it was not satisfied with the State Department's responses to its protests. Such delays condemned the Japanese-American evacuees to remain in the centers in the meantime.

Inadequate health care

The Japanese government also cited health care issues as a concern. In particular, the protest mentioned by name Japanese evacuees who had died or been injured while being moved from Los Angeles to Missoula, Montana. One man, named Shigekazu Hazama, was recovering from cancer at the time, and the three-day railway journey "rapidly aggravated" his illness and he died on 1 March 1942. Another evacuee, Fusaichi Katoh, supposedly lost his eyesight because he was not allowed to see an oculist quickly enough.[18] The Japanese government held the U.S. government directly responsible for these cases of death and injury.

As the Japanese government protest of October 1942 claimed, examples such as these were proof that in the evacuation process the U.S. government was not paying the "slightest regard to their age or condition of health." By contrast, the Japanese claimed, elderly United States citizens in Japan were being given "generous consideration to their age and health, and only a very few who are aged over sixty have been interned and that only for special reasons." In conclusion, the Japanese repeated that the U.S. government had "committed an act of inhumanity by interning a large number of Japanese civilians of advanced age or suffering from serious illness" and called on Washington to "immediately release those aged and invalid internees."[19]

Responding to the specific cases of Seiichiro Itoh, Kamaki Kinishita, Shigekazu Hazama, and Fusaichi Katoh, the U.S. State Department conducted a full-scale investigation. After intensive study, it concluded during October 1943 that Itoh, who died of hypostatic pneumonia on 3 February 1942, was "visited professionally by three Japanese physicians who indicated their satisfaction with the treatment he was receiving." Likewise, Kinishita was first reported to have contracted bronchial pneumonia on 20 March 1942, received treatment, but died on 1 April 1942 of "heart failure due to pneumonia and senility."[20] In both cases, the deaths could easily be attributed to the advanced ages of the patient, and both had received adequate health care prior to their death.

Meanwhile, according to their information Hazama was taken into custody on 8 December 1941. When his illness was discovered, he was sent to St. Patrick's Hospital in Missoula, Montana, where he died on 1 March 1942 of cancer of the colon. The State Department acknowledged one part of the Japanese protest, but gave a perfectly reasonable explanation: "It is probably true that the windows of the train in which Mr. Hazama traveled from Los Angeles to Missoula were shut and that the blinds were lowered as this precaution has often been taken to protect Japanese from possible injury and from being exposed to public curiosity."[21]

Finally, Katoh did in fact receive eye surgery at the Los Angeles General Hospital on 10 March 1942. When he was released on 12 March the attending physician recommended that the "patient may be discharged so far as his eye is concerned ... his eye is no longer painful."[22] In this case, as with the others mentioned above, all that could reasonably be expected to be done had been done. However, no amount of medical care could take every possible symptom or side effect into account.

When responding to Japanese accusations concerning the "suspicious" suicide of Dr. Rikita Honda, the State Department reported that Honda was "apprehended" on 7 December 1941 and placed with three other detainees in a large, 16' x 28' room at Terminal Island Immigration Station in San Pedro, California. On 14 December 1941, he committed suicide by "slashing his wrists and one arm." Although a physician was immediately called, it was too late.[23]

Because Honda was the president of the Los Angeles Naval Association, the Japanese government protested this case, arguing that there was "most grave suspicion as to the circumstances leading to his suicide." Tokyo demanded that "the United States Government ... furnish a detailed report concerning the circumstances which led to the death of Mr. Rikita Honda."[24] After a State Department investigation, it became clear that Honda had not had any personal disputes either with the U.S. government officials in charge or with any of the other detainees. He was never questioned, with the exception of being asked to "execute the alien enemy questionnaire required of all enemy aliens." Finally, based on testimony from Honda's roommates and the guards "there is no reason to think that anyone entered the bathroom or bedroom during the night of December 13–14 who might [have] attacked Dr. Honda."[25]

In fact, after this investigation was initiated, it became clear that Honda had previously served in the Japanese military, which was perhaps the basis of the Japanese belief that his suicide was suspicious. Exactly contrary to Tokyo's suggestion that Honda may have been murdered, a State Department study of "the notes prepared by Dr. Honda prior to his death" showed that "he considered suicide his duty as a Japanese officer."[26] Assuming that this description was accurate, then Honda's suicide was due not to mistreatment by American authorities, but to his feelings of loyalty to Japan. It is ironic, therefore, that this case of "honorable suicide" became the focus of a Japanese protest against America's alleged poor treatment of Japanese nationals. This protest—in turn—merely served to contribute to the delay of a third exchange that might have more quickly repatriated other Japanese loyalists to Japan, including those with medical problems.

Mistreatment during internment and transport

In addition to criticism over how the U.S. government had treated the elderly and infirm, evacuees in Hawaii, and health care in general, the Japanese government criticized U.S. authorities for general mistreatment of all of the Japanese nationals during the internment process. Their examples included the use of handcuffs on one Japanese national so that he could be "chained to the motor-car," being put in "narrow and filthy detention rooms," and being "beaten and kicked." Other Japanese evacuees being held at the San Francisco Immigration Office were denied exercise, and Tokyo claimed they "were allowed to have a walk outdoors for only an hour once in ten days."[27]

Over-crowding was one of the most frequently cited complaints in the Japanese protests. In Los Angeles, for example, Tokyo claimed that some 13 Japanese subjects were crowded into a cell meant for two, while others were housed with common criminals. In addition to not being given adequate food and clothing, they were "not allowed either to see the sunlight or to go out into the open air."[28] Other problems were reported after evacuees were already interned and were being sent from facility to facility. When transporting evacuees from one relocation center to another, a staff member of the Japanese Consulate in Los Angeles was "handcuffed and chained to bed as if he were a hard criminal."[29]

In other cases, soldiers with guns escorted evacuees through town while "crowds of people looked on." In contrast to these examples, the Japanese swore that the American citizens held by Japan had "been careful not to take any other measures than are necessary for restraining their personal liberty: they have never been handcuffed, nor have they been ever examined or treated like criminals." Therefore, the "Japanese Government lodge a most emphatic protest against the insulting and inhuman treatment according to Japanese civilians by the United States authorities."[30]

The U.S. government investigated all of these reported incidents. During internment, at sites such as the Immigration and Naturalization Service's San Francisco detention center, Japanese internees were in fact allowed two outdoor recreation periods per day, not once every ten days. Although on clear days each period was to last one and a half hours, on rainy days it was only 30 minutes. The State Department did acknowledge that: "According to the statistics of the United States Weather Bureau, there was an unusually long period of inclement weather during the months of December 1941 and January 1942." Japanese internees at Terminal Island, California, were never mixed with common criminals, as reported, but were "quartered in a section of the institution separate from that occupied by the other inmates."[31]

As for the story about handcuffing a Japanese national to a train, a State Department investigation determined that this was probably referring to Ken Nakezawa, who was treated for influenza at Fort Missoula from 13 to 17 April 1942. After he was released, Nakezawa was escorted to White Sulphur Springs, West Virginia, by an Immigration Officer. Since the two were sharing a sleeping car, with one in the top berth and one in the bottom, some method had to be devised to ensure security: "During the night each man wore a shackle around one wrist. The two shackles were attached to the ends of a lightweight chain five feet in length. ... The connecting chain hung loosely and away from public view behind the curtains of the upper and lower berth." In sharp contrast to the Japanese condemnation of this event: "Mr. Nakezawa expressed his amusement at the procedure rather than his displeasure and at no time was he chained to his berth."[32]

When investigating accusations of mistreatment during transport, the State Department reported that it had found only "one case where a Japanese subject was actually handcuffed." And, according to the report, in this particular case, the "use of handcuffs was necessary to prevent the man from destroying himself until a doctor could administer a hypodermic."[33]

Finally, although the U.S. guards were indeed armed, they carried their weapons inconspicuously and: "In no way is there intended to be a display of armed strength to embarrass or intimidate the internees." The only incident where "it might be said that the display of arms exceeded that necessary for proper protection," took place in Santa Fe, New Mexico, on 14 March 1942. After investigation, however, the State Department reported that: "sentiment at the time ran extremely high in New Mexico against the Japanese since many of the New Mexico National Guardsmen had been at bataan, and the display of firearms on this occasion was advisable for the protection of the internees."[34]

Contrary to the many Japanese accusations of mistreatment, therefore, Washington's explanation of these events would tend to confirm that its actions were in line with the U.S.–Japanese exchange agreement. In particular, the guards escorting the Japanese evacuees were armed precisely so as to protect the Japanese, not to threaten them, which was a requirement the Japanese had themselves insisted on early in the negotiations. However, the Japanese protests did not stop and Japan later accused the U.S. government of systematically torturing Japanese nationals and other Japanese-American evacuees during transportation and at the war relocation centers.

Alleged torture of Japanese nationals

According to Tokyo, Japanese nationals at a relocation center at Fort Missoula, Montana, were "beaten, kicked, forced to keep standing for hours running, and given no food," to the point where they "fell unconscious." And at Fort Lincoln, a U.S. official knocked down a Japanese man and broke his "two upper front teeth." The Japanese government demanded an "explanation of these outrages" and made a "further demand [on] the United States Government to take adequate and effective measures in order to prevent the recurrence of such events."[35]

The U.S. State Department investigated and submitted a report on these incidents. Although the State Department's memorandum challenged most parts of the Japanese protest from the year before, it did not try to whitewash real problems that it had uncovered. Repeating information that was included in a 6 August 1942 memorandum, it admitted that mistreatment of Japanese nationals had occurred at Fort Lincoln and at Fort Missoula. Corrective actions were immediately taken, however, and "the two Korean interpreters involved in the incident at Fort Lincoln were dismissed." At Fort Missoula, not only were "Inspector Bliss and Special Inspector Herstrom ... expelled from the Service," but the "commander of Fort Missoula was removed."[36]

These disciplinary actions did not satisfy Tokyo. Later, on 29 February 1944, the Japanese government sent an even more forceful protest. Referring to information obtained from "Japanese subjects who returned home through the second Japanese–American exchange," they lodged "a most emphatic protest with the United States Government against the injuries inflicted on Japanese subjects by the United States authorities." In addition to demanding "the punishment of the persons responsible and that adequate steps be taken to prevent the recurrence of similar incidents in future," they insisted that "the treatment of Japanese internees be substantially improved."[37]

The first example they provided was of a purported shooting of two Japanese men, Shiro Kobata and Hirtota Isomura, near the Lordsburg Internment Camp, New Mexico, for attempting to escape on 27 July 1942. The Japanese government argued that the two men were almost 60 years old, were in bad health, and were under armed escort. Therefore, it "is inconceivable that aged invalids hardly able to walk should while under military escort have attempted to escape." Other shootings reportedly took place at this internment camp between April and June, 1943, including: "At one time a captain fired his revolver to urge the internees to hasten their work, at another time an internee who was requesting a sentry to fetch golf ball which had fallen out of the fence was fired at from the watchtowers, and on a third occasion an internee was fired at while within twenty feet of the fence."[38]

The Japanese government lodged a similar protest for actions taken at the Manzanar Relocation Center. According to the reports given to it by returning Japanese nationals, the assistant commandant of this camp, named Campbell, was guilty of corruption in the distribution of sugar. To cover up evidence against him, he had Yoshio Ueno, the secretary of the "Kitchen Workers' Union," arrested on 5 December 1942 on the trumped up charge of attacking Fred Tayama, who positively identified Ueno as one of the three assailants who attacked him.[39]

When a large group of internees gathered to protest Ueno's arrest, according to one account there "arose a heavy gale" and the troops "were evidently taken by surprise by the sound of the wind and the noise made by the stepping internees." As a result, they "threw tear gas and fired machine-guns at the assembled people," killing one Nisei immediately and wounding ten others (one of whom, named Kanagawa, died two days later). Turmoil in the camp continued until mid-January 1943, when Campbell was dismissed.[40] Many years later, when Ueno was interviewed and his story was published, he gave a dramatically different story about the sugar shortages being an act of official corruption: "Of course a lot of it was the fault of the Japanese, too. I found out after I was sent to Leupp that some of the bunch was stealing the stuff when they transported it from the Lone Pine station to the camp."[41]

A group of less serious problems included cases where a Japanese internee had been improperly assessed income tax, and was forced to pay "immediately before the departure of the exchange ship, and was threatened with a refusal to be allowed to embark unless he paid it." Poor food was evidently a problem at the Kenedy and Santa Fe Internment Camps, leading to the loss of eyesight, with "about ten persons put under the necessity of using spectacles." The confiscation of "money and other belongings" from Japanese internees being transferred from Alaska meant that they were "hard up for pocket money." Finally, Japanese evacuated from Virginia to Philadelphia during July 1943 were given insufficient notice to "arrange their household affairs," had to pay the "expense of evacuation" and were not given "any assistance in obtaining employment," all of which, stated the Japanese government, meant that the "United States Government must bear the responsibility for the injury sustained by these individuals compulsorily evacuated from Virginia."[42]

In a follow-up protest dated 16 May 1944, the Japanese government described two shootings at the Gila River Relocation Center. The first victim, named Kensaburo Oshima, was shot on 12 May 1942 while reportedly approaching the barbed wire fence in violation of orders. Oshima "whose mind had been deranged," was killed at close range by a bullet in his skull. On 11 April 1943, an internee identified merely as Wakasa was shot and killed while still 6' within the boundary fence. The Japanese government condemned this action as an "atrocity," especially condemning the guard for too hastily concluding that Wakasa was "attempting escape and to shoot and kill him on spot without attempting any more appropriate measure."[43]

While many of the examples provided in the Japanese protest appeared to be based on real events, the U.S. State Department's investigations time after time revealed that there were many extenuating circumstances in each case that suggested that there was no widespread pattern of abuse. Therefore, with the exception of isolated incidents at Fort Lincoln and Fort Missoula, where the perpetrators were quickly reprimanded and removed from authority, or at Lordsburg or Manzanar, where thorough investigations were conducted, the vast majority of examples cited in the Japanese protests proved to be either exaggerated or invalid. It was also ironic that in one protest Tokyo even acknowledged that Japanese nationals were able to practice playing golf inside the relocation centers. This information would certainly suggest that conditions within the centers were not overly oppressive.

Requirements to conduct labor in the camps

A final section of the Japanese protest concerned forced labor, which was treated under a section entitled "Compulsory labor at internment camps." According to the Japanese government, Japanese evacuees at Fort Missoula were forced to work without compensation doing upkeep work within the camp, as well as work outside of the camp, including cleaning "the stable in which horses owned by the camp officials were kept." At a camp in Santa Fe, New Mexico, U.S. authorities tried to make evacuees build barracks "in spite of their opposition." At other camps, evacuees were made to clean the "offices of the camp officials" or to cook and provide "table service for these officials." One especially serious complaint was that Japanese at Fort Missoula were supposedly forced to help build a swimming pool outside of the immediate detention area.[44]

All of the examples cited in the Japanese government protest supposedly violated the Geneva Convention of 1929 which allowed for internees to labor only for the "administration, management, and maintenance of internment camps." In particular, labor outside of the camp compounds was expressly forbidden. As a result, the Japanese government insisted that the U.S. government "immediately cease the enforcement of the above-mentioned labour imposed on the Japanese civilian internees and pay adequate compensation to those who have hitherto been put to such labour."[45]

During December 1942, the U.S. government made its first response to the Japanese accusations concerning forced labor, pointing out that "in all detention and internment camps the distribution of labor necessary for the maintenance of the facilities by the internees is made by spokesmen elected by the internees themselves." As such, U.S. officials were not in charge of assigning labor, but: "These [elected] spokesmen take into consideration the distribution of the labor of their fellow detainees and internees, their age and physical condition."[46]

As for the specific examples listed by Tokyo, the U.S. note clarified that all "camp authorities have further been instructed that any other employment of the labor of persons held in their camps must be upon a voluntary basis, must not be in violation of article 31 of the convention and must be compensated with reference to the employment of internees in the maintenance of gardens, swimming pools, etcetera outside of the camp enclosures." Sometimes, this compensation was money, but other times it was "compensation in goods." With regard to swimming pools, "the internees were permitted to use the swimming pools." With regard to gardens and other enterprises, like bakeries, the "produce from the gardens and bakeries were consumed by them in the camps."[47]

Memoirs from various detainees show how difficult it was to draw the line between work and leisure. For example, at the Manzanar relocation center, several men decided to build a big pond near the mess hall: "When we were halfway finished, the people in the block found out that we were trying to make a big pond. Then everyone pitched in to help. They brought in big rocks. They borrowed an Army truck with a cable on it and a trailer and went up to the hills. Some of the rocks were about two tons, so the people could sit on them around the edge of the pond and wait for the signal to line up for the mess hall."[48] Japanese officials simply could not believe that all of this labor was voluntary, and that the building of swimming pools, ponds, etc., was being carried out at the discretion of the Japanese-Americans themselves.

In a later U.S. government communication dated August 1944, more information was provided regarding the Japanese protest that evacuees were forced to work. This U.S. note stated that the Japanese protest showed "a fundamental misunderstanding of the program of the war relocation authority." In fact, the relocation program was not primarily a "detention program" but was intended for the "relocation into normal life so far as practical of persons of Japanese ancestry who were evacuated from the West Coast in the early stages of the war as a matter of military necessity."[49]

In fact, as a direct result of efforts by the relocation authorities, many American citizens of Japanese ancestry were successfully relocated to other parts of the United States, away from the West Coast, where they were now "free to go about their business on the same basis as other American citizens." Meanwhile, the "relocated aliens"—in other words those evacuees who were Japanese citizens—were "subject only to the restrictions which apply to [an]other enemy aliens."[50]

During October 1943, immediately after the second exchange was completed, the State Department provided detailed information proving that many of the Japanese accusations were false. For example, the stable upkeep at Fort Missoula was justified because it was "located inside the compound" and was used "for recreation and storage purposes by the Japanese." At the internment camp at Santa Fe, "Japanese internees were requested to assist in the construction of barracks for their own use," but when they "declined because of possible difficulty with a labor union," which presumably wanted the job for its own workers, the "request of the American authorities was not pressed."[51]

At the Tuna Canyon camp, it was discovered that rather than being forced to "clean offices and perform cooking and table service for camp officials," five Japanese internees were "permitted at their own request to clean the administrative offices, serve at the officers' table in the messhall in the event of emergency meals and assist in preparing bunks and changing linen and towels." Instead of being forced to work without compensation, the internees "were compensated by the officers for this work, such compensation being paid to the spokesman of the camp to be distributed among destitute internees."[52]

Finally, Japanese protests over building a "swimming pool" were greatly exaggerated. In fact, "work performed by the Japanese in connection with the swimming pool project was limited to cutting away bushes along the bank of the near-by river so that they could go swimming." After a thorough "investigation," the "Japanese spokesman at Fort Missoula has testified that the work was performed voluntarily and that everyone was anxious to assist in the project."[53]

As this detailed information shows, the forced labor that Tokyo accused the U.S. government of making the Japanese nationals perform was intended not for the good of camp administrators or outsiders, but for the benefit of the Japanese themselves. This type of labor did not violate the 1929 Geneva accords. Nevertheless, Japan's protests increased rather than decreased over time.

Stopping Japanese-Americans from requesting repatriation

A final series of Japanese protests claimed that administrators at the war relocation centers were pressuring Japanese-Americans not to request repatriation. According to one such document, because of repeated questioning about loyalty and repatriation, the Japanese government accused the U.S. government of trying to "unduly" influence "their expression of intention as to repatriation," and to refuse "to accept their applications for repatriation."[54]

After denying the Japanese allegation that U.S. officials had put pressure on evacuees not to request repatriation, the U.S. government explained:

> There has never been any attempt to influence any person either to decline or to request repatriation. No officer of this government has ever been

authorized to refuse to accept communication from a Japanese national regarding his wishes for repatriation or for nonrepatriation. Decisions by individual Japanese were freely reached in all cases with the exception of some case in which Japanese aliens attempted to force Americans of Japanese extraction to elect to go to Japan.

In fact, the question of "allegiance to Japan has at no time and in no way been associated with the eligibility of Japanese nationals for repatriation to Japan" and the "records affecting the repatriation status of Japanese nationals contain no entries regarding replies to the so-called allegiance question."[55]

From the Japanese protests it is clear that they felt there was a mismatch between those people that the Japanese government wanted back, as opposed to those Japanese citizens and American citizens of Japanese ancestry who had requested repatriation to Japan. The U.S. government explained:

> The persons included in the lists submitted by the Japanese Government had named them for repatriation and that they were requested to indicate whether they desired to accept or decline. Such persons have been completely free to make their own decisions. In this connection it may be pointed out that of all of the persons whose names were submitted in the Winter of 1942 and Spring of 1943 approximately ninety percent stated that they did not desire to return to Japan. Even though they were informed that the Japanese Government had named them they indicated that they desired to remain in the United States. On the other hand thousands of applications have been received from persons who were not named by the Japanese Government indicating their wish to go to Japan. These names have been reported to the Japanese Government and the Japanese Government is aware that the Government of the United States has made every effort to arrange for their inclusion in American–Japanese exchanges.

As this statement shows, the war relocation centers were full of Japanese citizens and U.S. citizens of Japanese ancestry who had requested to be repatriated to Japan, but the Japanese government refused to accept them.[56]

Interviews and questionnaires were perhaps conducted so frequently because U.S. officials were accused by Japan of miscalculating the number of Japanese nationals who had requested repatriation. It was in the U.S. government's interest to acquire an accurate count of those requesting repatriation, since it was hoped that these "volunteers" would soon be traded for American citizens being housed in Japanese camps. However, the Japanese government time after time professed to misunderstand Washington's intentions and protested that U.S. officials were attempting instead to coerce the internees, especially at the Tule Lake Segregation Center, to force them *not* to request repatriation. This accusation was particularly hard to justify, especially since it was Tokyo that refused to authorize their rapid return, even though the United States government repeatedly expressed its willingness to let them leave.

The American response to this Japanese protest assured the Japanese government that the Spanish representatives had been given ample opportunity to assess the situation, and that they had been allowed to visit Tule Lake "several times" and "At no time have the representatives of the Embassy been denied access to the any of the centers." In particular, those Japanese nationals "whether at large or confined" were given every opportunity to report to the Spanish Embassy "their wishes and their changes of wish with respect to repatriation."[57]

The task of determining who wanted repatriation was not always easy, since there were "individuals who have changed their minds as many as four or five times and on consecutive days." But, whenever this happened, the Spanish representative was notified, and was given "free access to all Japanese nationals ... to verify ... the repatriation wishes of Japanese nationals," and often there were written statements from these nationals directly to the Spanish embassy. The U.S. memo also challenged Japan: "The United States Government would welcome any investigation by any authority into the individual cases of any Japanese to verify the accuracy of the foregoing statements."[58]

Contrary to the Japanese protests that the relocation centers were a punishment, this U.S. government document argued that they were in fact a "privilege" and that the "war relocation authority extends liberal assistance to those who desire to avail themselves of the opportunity." However, if Japanese-American who were loyal to the U.S. chose not to leave the relocation centers, that was also their right: "It is not and never has been the policy of the war relocation authority to force any evacuees to leave the relocation centers against their will so long as the restrictions remain in effect which prohibit them from returning to their former homes."[59]

Conclusions

In order to assist ongoing negotiations for a third exchange, Washington was eager to prove to Tokyo that it was treating all Japanese evacuees in line with the 1929 Geneva Convention. In particular, the U.S. government specially asked the Spanish embassy to

> inform the Japanese Government that in the American Government's opinion the best proof of the readiness of a belligerent to accord to enemy aliens in territories controlled by it the full benefit of the humanitarian provisions of applicable treaties conventions and agreements as well as of international law is afforded by the readiness of that belligerent to permit representatives of the protection power to have access to all places where enemy aliens are held." In line with this, the U.S. government would continue to provide Spanish representatives the opportunity to visit all places in which Japanese subjects are held ... by the American authorities.[60]

Meanwhile, stories of Japanese mistreatment of American citizens in Japanese camps were much more horrifying than any of the above-mentioned examples. Therefore, the U.S. response went on to note, the "American Government has itself received from American Nationals repatriated from Japan and Japanese controlled territory report[s] so shocking mistreatment cruelties and insults inflicted upon these American Nationals by officers and agents of the Japanese Government."[61] Washington made it clear, therefore, that "the best assurance that Japan is fulfilling its undertaking in respect to American nationals ... would be afforded by the granting of permission for representatives of the Swiss Government in charge of American interest[s] in Japan and Japanese controlled territory to visit all places without exception in which American nationals are held." Also, it expressed the hope that the "Japanese Government on its part will desire to make a thorough investigation of the complaints of American citizens regarding their mistreatment by its officers and agents with a view to taking the necessary steps to avoid the repetition in the future of abuses and to taking appropriate disciplinary action."[62]

In the end, these U.S.–Japanese diplomatic protests and counter-protests did little to dispel the distrust that had pervaded the preliminary negotiations for a third exchange. By delaying the realization of a third exchange, Tokyo virtually guaranteed that its nationals would have to remain living in the various war relocation centers—like the Tule Lake Segregation Center. Thus, the end result of Tokyo's protests was exactly the opposite of what the Japanese government claimed was its prime goal. Tokyo's protests could perhaps best be seen as Japanese attempts to "save face" by trying to prove that the U.S. government's generally excellent treatment of the Japanese nationals was as equally horrendous as Japanese mistreatment of American nationals in Japan, Manchuria, occupied China, and the Philippines. There is ample documentary evidence, however, proving that this was not the case.[63]

10 Negotiating safe passage and the sinking of *Awa Maru*

It is difficult to imagine how the United States government and the Japanese government succeeded in safely exchanging thousands of officials and non-officials even while the Pacific War was at its height. The ships involved in the exchange were largely navigating in disputed waters and were always at risk of accidental attack. During the formal U.S.–Japanese negotiations, therefore, many questions pertaining to the physical safety of the exchange ships were discussed. In February 1942 it was determined that "the Portuguese Government shall be requested to act as guarantor for the execution of the exchange on Portuguese territory at Lourenço Marques."[1] Later, as the war made navigation far from the Japanese islands even more difficult, the Portuguese port of Marmagao in western India was selected for the second exchange.

Japan initially proposed that hospital ships be used to conduct the exchanges. However, Washington disagreed that the exchange ships be marked "as hospital ships under the Geneva Agreement of 1907" and expressed its hope that instead "the Japanese Government will select another method of marking the vessel." In addition, the U.S. government stated that it would "mark distinctively the vessel to be used carrying Japanese Official personnel" and that it "is agreed that the markings of the vessel shall be such as to ensure the greatest possible visibility and that particulars of colors and markings shall be notified in due time before the departure of the voyage."[2] On 19 February 1942, the Japanese government formally agreed to these proposals.[3]

Even though two U.S.–Japanese exchanges were safely conducted on this basis, similar agreements to ensure the safety of hospital ships and relief vessels were not foolproof. The Japanese government later accused American forces of attacking several hospital ships. With the sea lanes too dangerous to ensure safety, for a time the United States government proposed an overland exchange of U.S. and Japanese citizens. This plan envisioned sending people through Russian Siberia where the vast distances would have restricted such an exchange to very small numbers of exchangees. While talks on this new phase of the exchange were still going on in early 1945, Tokyo protested the 1 April 1945 sinking of the Japanese relief ship, *Awa Maru*, by an American submarine, the USS *Queenfish*. Although Washington immediately apologized for this incident,

Awa Maru's sinking was the final deathblow for the wartime exchange program as U.S.–Japanese diplomatic tensions escalated catastrophically.

Marking the exchange ships

By the end of February 1942, Japanese and American negotiators had determined that civilian vessels should be used in the exchange. The German-owned, Swedish-operated *Gripsholm* was chosen for the American side. They had also agreed on the basic markings that the ships would bear. In mid-March, a U.S. government communication noted that "the Japanese Government will mark in a distinctive manner but not as a hospital ship the vessel or vessels to be used for the exchange and will in due course communicate to the United States Government natures of the marking decided upon."[4] Once the names and descriptions of the exchange ships were exchanged, then they were supposed to be immune from attack. A huge sign, reading D-I-P-L-O-M-A-T was hung from the ship's side.[5]

The U.S.–Japanese exchanges were dangerous. By spring 1942, American submarines and surface ships were already active throughout the Pacific Ocean attempting to sink Japanese cargo ships, merchantmen, and naval vessels. The sea routes were not secure. In order to ensure the safety of the exchange ships, their schedules and markings had to be transmitted to the American fleet in a timely fashion. On 11 May 1942, it was determined that four special lights in the pattern green–red–green–red should mark the ships as exchange vessels.[6]

Thereafter, on 8 June 1942, the United States government granted safe conduct for *Asama Maru* and *Conte Verde*, but warned Tokyo that due to the "lateness of notification given by the Japanese Government" this could not take effect until 10 June at the earliest. In particular: "If the *Conte Verde* is carrying Americans from Shanghai to Japan, that vessel must not leave Shanghai before June 10th." As for future exchange ships, such as *Tatuta Maru* and *Kamakura Maru*, "it is requested that the Japanese Government notify this Government of sailing dates and itinerary of these vessels as least ten days in advance of their sailing."[7]

This arrangement was understandably of great concern to the ships involved in the exchange. During June 1942, Minister Shigemitsu wrote to Hisanobu Terai, President of the Nippon Yusen Kaisya, which was entrusted with the task of navigating the Italian-registered S.S. *Conte Verde* between Shanghai, various ports in Japan, and Lourenço Marques. The Japanese government and the U.S. government agreed on the following six points:

1   In order to indicate that the vessel is an exchange boat, she shall bear special markings.
2   The vessel shall follow the given route.
3   The vessel shall be neither escorted nor armed.

4   A member of the staff of the Spanish Legation in Tokyo shall embark on the ship, and he shall be allowed to dispatch and receive communications in plain language.

5   No other passenger shall be allowed to dispatch or receive any communications.

6   The passengers and cargoes shall be limited to those designated.[8]

These provisions worked well for the two sets of exchange vessels, and there were no incidents worth noting during the 1942 and 1943 exchanges.

Understandably, the Japanese government was eager to take advantage of the U.S.–Japanese exchange program for reasons not related to the actual exchange of each others' citizens. These included delivering much-needed supplies and transporting Japanese diplomats to their new postings. These extraneous activities were arguably more important for Japan than for the United States, because the American and British navies virtually cut Japan off from Europe by sea, and because after June 1941 the war front between the Soviet Union and Germany was largely impassable. Therefore, the exchange ships soon became one of the only dependable transportation routes for sending Japanese diplomats to Europe and to other neutral countries.

The Japanese government hoped to use the exchange vessels to deliver their diplomats and other officials to their new postings, especially in European countries that had proclaimed their wartime neutrality. Spain and Switzerland, the very countries helping to organize the exchange, were two good examples. Originally, it had been agreed that "all officials who were at the time when Japan began hostilities against the United States enroute to any posts or away from posts to which they were accredited be included in the block exchange and be repatriated with all other officials."[9] This would have meant the return of all Japanese diplomats to Japan.

However, the Japanese government later reconsidered this point. On 19 February 1942 an official communication stated: "The Japanese Government are unable to concur in with the view of the United States Government to the effect that complication will ensue if some of the official personnel are permitted to proceed directly to their new posts in neutral countries. They therefore desire that the United States government will reconsider this matter." In particular, some of the Japanese diplomats in Latin America were to be assigned to new posts, and: "In this connection the Japanese Government desire that as some of these officials are ordered to proceed to their new posts, the United States Government will not place obstacle in their taking up posts elsewhere."[10]

In the American response, dated 17 March 1942, Washington disagreed, stating that "travel otherwise than in accordance with the stipulated movement to Lourenço Marques of officials accredited to third countries would in the opinion of the United States Government raise numerous complicating questions of safe conduct and of physical travel facilities which could not be settled within a reasonable time and without further undesirable delay." However, the U.S.

government concluded that it "would not be in a position to comment upon any redistribution of personnel which the Japanese Government might undertake to make from Lourenço Marques."[11]

Although Washington tried its best to ignore this issue, the Japanese government continued to pressure it to relent. The Swiss government, in particular, seems to have played an important role in bringing around a breakthrough on this issue. On 5 August 1942, the Swiss Minister to Japan wrote a note to Haruhiko Nishi, Vice-Minister of Foreign Affairs. In this letter, he stated that "according to my suggestion" the Swiss government had called the Swiss Minister in Washington soon after receiving his cable, date 1 August 1942. As a result of Swiss intervention, the U.S. government granted safe conduct for "23 Japanese diplomats who are to [be] sent abroad from Japan or from Lourenço-Marques."[12]

Evidently, the U.S. government telegraphed immediately to Lourenço-Marques with these orders, an action that "has likewise been confirmed in writing to the Spanish Embassy at Washington." Showing his personal interest in this case, the Swiss Minister ended his note by stating: "I am very glad indeed that the 23 Japanese diplomats are thus enabled to leave for their new posts; more particularly that Mr. Sakamoto can now proceed without delay to Berne."[13]

As these communications make clear, without the exchange program the Japanese government would have encountered great difficulty transporting its diplomats to Europe. Another example of the Japanese items transported by the exchange ships appears to have been medical supplies. According to a "Note Verbale" from the Royal Swedish Legation, dated 16 September 1943, a total of "four cases" were given to the master of *Gripsholm* for delivery to *Teia Maru*. These cases included "medical supplies and tinned provisions." This arrangement was made at Japan's request on 25 August 1943.[14] Although no additional details were provided, the delivery of these medicines was accomplished through an extremely circuitous route.

Proposals for overland exchanges through Russia

As the sea route to Japan became increasingly dangerous, during the summer of 1944 the State Department proposed adding an additional land route through Russia to conduct further exchanges. Russia's vast Siberian territories were thought to be ideal, and since the Soviet Union and Japan were still at peace, even while the United States was sending lend-lease aid to the USSR to fight Germany, there were ready transportation and communication links. For a variety of reasons this proposal never came to fruition.

On 25 July 1944, Secretary of State Hull wrote to the American Legation at Berne, Switzerland, to explain in greater detail a 27 June 1944 proposal to adopt a new type of exchange to the Japanese government. According to Hull:

The proposal for repatriation of nationals, using overland transportation, was made by Department in consideration of the possibility that the agreement of the Japanese Government might be obtained to an exchange of nationals in which railroad transportation would be used to and from some Siberian frontier point such as Manchouli or points on Asiatic mainland. Any Japanese nationals to be repatriated could be taken to a Siberian port on a vessel under neutral supervision; they could be released in Soviet territory at a point agreed upon in advance simultaneously with Americans to be repatriated. Thereafter, the exchanged groups would proceed to their respective countries over the reverse of the route traversed by the other group to the point of exchange.[15]

Hull emphasized that this proposed exchange would be "meant to *supplement*—not replace—the United States Government's other repatriation suggestions." Although the total numbers of citizens exchanged might be small, such "a development would appear to be necessary for keeping up the morale of nationals of the United States and Japanese Governments who are held by these Governments." In particular, Hull pointed out to Tokyo "the serious situation of great numbers of young children of both sides now confined behind barbed wire."[16]

To the embassy personnel in Berne, however, Hull pointed out that this new proposed exchange was mainly intended to create "facilities and a line or procedure be established so that continuing exchange (even if very restricted as to numbers) may be effected." In fact, what Hull was clearly trying to do was to keep the Japanese government engaged and talking about future exchanges. This was especially important as U.S. military forces approached closer to the Japanese islands, and the threat to the interned Americans necessarily became greater.[17]

A second plan was to transfer much-needed supplies through Siberia. On 16 February 1944, the Acting Secretary of State wrote to the American Embassy in Moscow to discuss this plan. Relief supplies would be shipped from the United States to the USSR, and then trans-shipped to American civilians being held in Japanese camps. The reason for these ships was that the "conditions under which nationals of the Allied countries are held, according to all reports, have deteriorated so greatly that the already high death rate will increase if assistance cannot be extended to these persons promptly." As part of this plan, Japanese nationals would be put on a ship with relief supplies. This ship would be manned by a Soviet crew and would "sail under safe conduct from a West Coast port in the United States to a Russian Pacific port, which the Soviet Government would designate." The crew would either remain the same, or be switched to a Japanese crew for the trip to Japan, at which point American civilians would be returned by the same route. If Japan refused to allow their return to the U.S., Washington was willing for them to remain in the USSR and sit out the rest of the war there.[18]

Japan's only response to this overture was to make accusations about the sinking of Japanese hospital ships, general mistreatment of Japanese in the United States, as well as about U.S. press stories of Japanese atrocities. On 30 March 1944, Secretary of State Hull wrote back to the Japanese, explaining that the Spanish representatives could at any time visit and report on the conditions in the U.S. relocation centers. Hull concluded that "therefore, as the United States Government has taken all possible measures to dispel the concern which the Japanese Government has stated was its reason for delaying consideration of additional exchanges and shipment of relief supplies, it hopes that the Japanese authorities will now give consideration immediately to the proposal under reference for the exchange of nationals on a reciprocal basis, to the shipment of relief supplies and to the proposal for the forwarding of the relief supplies which are at present being kept at Vladivostock."[19]

The Japanese government finally agreed, not to a third exchange, but to allowing the U.S. supplies from Vladivostock to be sent to Japanese internment camps. These supplies had been shipped by the U.S. government all the way from the continental United States. By December 1944, approximately 2,000 tons of food was rotting on the docks at Vladivostock. But, Japan would agree to deliver these supplies only if the ships involved were given safe passage in both directions. This meant that any Japanese ship delivering supplies would also be guaranteed a safe passage back to its home port. Desperate to transfer supplies to its citizens, Washington agreed to these terms.

The sinking of *Awa Maru*

Even as U.S.–Japanese negotiations for a third exchange were grinding to a halt, by spring 1945 the war was coming to an end, even though nobody knew it at the time. Although a third exchange was still being discussed, Tokyo kept delaying its departure, citing supposed American mistreatment of Japanese nationals. Any possibility of a third exchange of Japanese and American citizens was interrupted for good, however, by the U.S. sinking of the Japanese ship *Awa Maru* on 1 April 1945.

By late 1944 many of the Americans in the Japanese camps were ill and underfed. Many had lost from 40 to 50 pounds in weight due to the poor diet. If they could not be exchanged soon then their prospects were grim. As early as 23 December 1943, Washington protested their meager diet and the Japanese insistence that the Americans pay for their own food: "It is in direct contrast to the treatment accorded Japanese subjects in United States who are provided hygenic quarters with adequate space for individual needs, sufficient wholesome food in preparation of which allowance is made for national differences in taste and in addition allowances of money for tobacco, sweets and toiletries."[20]

By contrast with Japan's camps, where conditions were deteriorating rapidly, the war relocation centers were generally considered quite luxurious. As just one example of the relative luxury taken for granted by Japanese-American interns, during December 1943 the Chief Supply Officer for the relocation center in Missoula, Montana, tried and failed to buy "Large Sardines" for a particular Japanese dish from the Seattle Fish Market, hundreds of miles from Montana. Even though "no fresh sardines are being secured by the fishing industry on the West coast incident to its restriction from fishing areas in which the sardines are normally found," the Japanese government still protested this incident as a violation of the U.S. promise to treat the Japanese-Americans well. Even after U.S. diplomats explained that the item in question was simply not available for purchase, this fact "appeared to him [the Japanese representative] irrelevant to our meeting his request."[21] Meanwhile, another Japanese-American interned in Montana repeatedly complained all the way to Tokyo about the unwarranted delays he encountered receiving his golf clubs from a U.S. government storage warehouse.[22]

By late 1944, Tokyo began to warn Washington that it did not have enough food to provide for the American civilians located in its own camps. At great expense, the U.S. government offered to send food and medical supplies from the continental United States, half a world away. In December 1944, some 2,000 tons of food were sent through Siberia to Russian ports on the Pacific. On 12 September 1944, 13 December 1944, and 13 February 1945 Washington promised Tokyo that the ships assigned to deliver these supplies "will not be subject to attack, visit, or any interference whatever" either "on the outward or homeward voyages."[23]

Several Japanese ships, including *Awa Maru*, were assigned to take these supplies to the southern part of the Japanese empire, including as far south as the Dutch Indies. Tokyo plotted *Awa Maru*'s course from the Russian port of Nakhodka to the south and back. The U.S. Navy was given orders not to sink it. Evidently, the southward journey went as planned and the food aid was delivered. However, for the northward journey the route was altered just days before the ship left port; it is not clear whether these changes were transmitted to the U.S. submarines in the Pacific in time. Either way, the submarine *Queenfish* sank *Awa Maru* on 1 April 1945 in the Taiwan strait, resulting in the loss of its cargo and the death of over a thousand Japanese passengers.

Evidence suggests that *Awa Maru* was carrying contraband items, including petroleum products, on its return journey to Japan. Because of the immunities provided for the exchange ships, the Japanese government was eager to use the exchanges for other purposes, such as sending diplomatic missions abroad and carrying economic necessities. Perhaps with these programs as their guide, the Japanese over-stretched the immunity agreement with *Awa Maru*. The presence of contraband theoretically negated the American promise of "free passage." Granted, at the time the cargo of *Awa Maru* was probably not known, and so the sinking was most likely a true mistake. Either way, once this relief ship was sunk by a U.S. submarine, then safe passage for any future exchange ship was to become a major stumbling block that actively interfered with the negotiation of any future exchange.

Immediately after *Awa Maru* was sunk, this incident was roundly denounced by the Japanese government as treachery. To protest Washington's "most outrageous act of treachery," Japan absolutely refused to send a third exchange. Although the United States government apologized, and even offered to compensate Japan for the loss, the Japanese government would not be mollified. No further exchanges were now contemplated. Only the end of the war saved thousands of American citizens from almost certain death through starvation. If the war had not ended quickly, and if a third exchange had never been organized, then many more Americans would have died in the final months of the war.

U.S.–Japanese exchange negotiations after the sinking of *Awa Maru*

Washington reported *Awa Maru's* sinking to Japan on 17 April 1945, and while stating that it "deeply regrets the occurrence," the captain of the submarine reported that "no lights or special illumination were visible at any time." As a result of the dearth of information, the "question of primary responsibility for this incident has not yet been determined."[24] Japan responded by protesting that *Awa Maru* had been "deliberately and willfully attacked" even after receiving three U.S. assurances of safe passage. Tokyo called it "the most outrageous act of treachery unparalleled in the world history of war," and demanded that Washington take full responsibility for this "disgraceful act."[25]

Later, Washington admitted fault. Even though there was a heavy fog, and *Awa Maru* was eight miles off course and 32 miles ahead of its reported schedule, "the burden of establishing identity was that of commander of American submarine and in view of his failure to do so the United States Government acknowledges responsibility for sinking of vessel." Washington promised that "Disciplinary action is being taken with respect to commander of American submarine concerned," and it even offered to pay an indemnity. The U.S. government wanted to wait to negotiate the amount after the war, during which time the U.S. "will approach question with an attitude of complete fairness and without regard to the political situation then existing."[26] After the war, Captain Charles Elliot Loughlin was tried and found guilty of negligence in obeying orders.

Tokyo used the sinking of *Awa Maru* as a final excuse to cut negotiations on a third exchange. By contrast, Washington tried to use it to jumpstart the negotiations, pointing out that the survivors from *Awa Maru* were being cared for by U.S. authorities until "arrangements are perfected for further exchanges of nationals between Japan and the allies."[27] When Japan refused to reopen talks, during June 1945 Washington sent Tokyo a final warning: "By refusing to permit repatriation of American nationals, it has further obligated itself to safeguard them from starvation and death."[28] Since the existence of the A-bomb was still a secret, it appeared to many that the war might go on for several more years.

Therefore, the fate of Americans in the Japanese camps looked bleak. Again, Tokyo refused to reopen talks.

There has been an on-going mystery connected with the sinking of *Awa Maru*. A 1997 book by Roger Dingman reported that *Awa Maru* was loaded with Dutch treasure.[29] Tokyo perhaps decided to use *Awa Maru* for this task because it supposedly had an iron-clad guarantee that it would not be attacked by U.S. submarines. Other reports suggest that the ship was secretly carrying much-needed petroleum products back to the Japanese home islands, an item that would have also been banned from an exchange vessel.

One obvious answer to this apparent mystery is that Tokyo from the very beginning hoped to use U.S. food shipments as a "cover" for its own purposes. This is supported by certain events after the war, when negotiations were held to determine the indemnity. Interestingly, although Washington had admitted fault and had offered to pay an indemnity, as a result of these post-war negotiations the U.S. never paid Japan anything for sinking *Awa Maru*.

After *Awa Maru's* sinking, Tokyo appears to have intensified its on-going policy of relocating American citizens to Japanese military installations. Washington protested this, and even accused Japan of trying to use them as "human shields" to halt further American bombing. On 22 September 1944, the U.S. protested Japan moving American citizens from the Los Banos camp to Fort McKinley, "where a major ammunition dump for central Luzon is maintained." This violated the 1929 Geneva Convention, since the civilians were "used to give protection from bombardment to certain points or certain regions by his presence."[30] On 12 July 1945, Washington protested the movement of Americans in Shanghai to areas "subject to bombardment."[31]

While the status of American non-officials under the Geneva Convention was somewhat vague, the Japanese policy of putting American citizens in harm's way applied to POWs as well; for example, on 5 July 1945, Washington protested the housing of American POWs in Bangkok warehouses, pointing to their "close proximity to docks, railroad yards and other military objectives."[32] This Japanese policy violated all formal rules of warfare, including most especially the 1929 Geneva Convention. This policy meant that either the U.S. bombers had to be sent in knowing that they might kill Americans, or the bombing raids would have to stop, which of course was Tokyo's goal. Fortunately, the war ended before the full impact of this policy could be felt.

Conclusions

During the final years of the war every attempt was made by the United States government to continue the exchange program. However, by early 1945, there were fewer and fewer Americans held in Japanese camps to exchange. The original estimate for the number of American internees was 10,000. Some 2,700 had been returned during the two exchanges, while by early 1945 another 5,500 had been liberated from camps, mainly in Southeast Asia and the Philippines. An estimate of 500 deaths in the camps, due to starvation, mistreatment, and disease, reduced the total number even more. This left an estimated 1,300 American citizens under Japanese control, with 200 of these in Japan proper, about 1,000 scattered throughout northern China, and perhaps another 100 in camps further to the south. This number was barely sufficient to fill even one exchange ship, making the chances for any future U.S.–Japanese exchanges less likely.[33]

Luckily for those last remaining American inmates of the Japanese camps, the A-bomb was finished during summer 1945 and Truman authorized its use. Unexpectedly, the war did not drag on as many had feared, with estimates of U.S. casualties in the hundreds of thousands, if not millions. After Japan agreed to surrender and the war ended, all of the surviving U.S. citizens in Japan's internment camps were quickly returned home.

For the Japanese-Americans living in the U.S. war relocation centers, however, it would take a significantly longer time before their war-ravaged country was ready to welcome them home. For many, the prospect of returning to a war-torn Japan was no longer quite so appealing, in particular because there were no jobs and the threat of starvation was widespread. In the end, the vast majority of the more than 20,000 Japanese-Americans who had requested repatriation to Japan remained in the United States.

Conclusions

As this book has tried to show, there were intimate links between the diplomatic negotiations leading to the U.S.–Japanese exchange of officials and non-officials and the formation, daily activities, and long-term responsibilities of the Japanese-American war relocation centers. These links have never previously been clarified in histories of either the war relocation program or the wartime exchanges. The few books that do mention this connection in passing usually condemn it; for example, one author has referred to the Latin-American Japanese involved in the exchanges as "pawns in a human traffic Washington hoped to continue" throughout the war.[1]

The present work, by contrast, has sought to show the positive effects of the exchange program, in particular the successful repatriation of approximately 3,000 Japanese nationals in return for 3,000 citizens of Western Hemisphere nations. It must be emphasized that this repatriation on the part of the Japanese-Americans in the United States was completely voluntary, and that no adult who expressed a desire to remain in the United States was forced to return to Japan.

It is particularly important to reiterate that long before the U.S. government ever ordered Japanese-Americans to leave the West Coast, or ordered the creation of the war relocation centers, the Japanese government had provided detailed lists that included specific categories of Japanese citizens that it wanted the U.S. government to find, collect in one place, protect, and repatriate. Locating such a large number of people in a timely manner required establishing processing centers, which, it was hoped by officials in Washington, would make possible the repatriation of the largest possible number of American citizens from Japanese detention camps.

From Washington's viewpoint, the war relocation centers could serve and assist it in its role of guaranteeing the health and well-being of United States citizens being held by Japan under life-threatening conditions, in particular, by identifying as many candidates as possible for repatriation to Japan. In return for every Japanese citizen or American citizen of Japanese ancestry who elected to repatriate to Japan, one American citizen from Japan's detention camps could be returned to the United States. Some 3,000 Japanese loyalists were eventually able to return to Japan during the war in exchange for an equal number of North and

South American citizens, with more to follow after the war ended. It was hoped at the time that many thousands more could be exchanged during the war, but this proved to be impossible, not because of U.S. resistance, but because Japan refused to continue the exchanges.

Clearly, obtaining the safe return of interned Americans was part of the U.S. government's sworn responsibility to place the highest value on guaranteeing the security of its citizenry. As a direct result of the U.S.–Japanese exchanges, thousands of interned American citizens were able to return home safely. Furthermore, almost all of the Japanese-Americans survived the war under U.S. care. By contrast, large numbers of Americans who remained in the Japanese camps died. Given the intolerable conditions the American civilians were forced to endure in the Japanese camps, for the United States government not to have actively negotiated with Japan to exchange non-official citizens would have opened it up to accusations of negligence and dereliction of duty. The war relocation centers proved to be an essential part of this process.

The documentation presented in this book reveals the firm link between the Japanese government's demands to repatriate specific Japanese nationals and the creation and functions of the war relocation centers. Tokyo at first gave only general guidelines as to the types of people it wanted returned, but later it provided detailed lists naming specific Japanese citizens. However, the lists often did not include the current addresses of these people, which made it virtually impossible to find them on a one-by-one basis. What would at first glance appear to be the simple task of locating, assembling, and interviewing these selected Japanese to determine whether they wanted to return to Japan proved, in reality, to be a daunting task; this task was impeded by the serious manpower shortages due to the two-front war both in Europe and in the Pacific.

In addition to trying to locate those people on the Japanese lists, a secondary reason for establishing the war relocation centers was to find appropriate "substitutes" for those Japanese civilians on Tokyo's lists who could not be located, did not desire to be repatriated to Japan, or were deemed by U.S. security organizations to pose a serious risk to national security. While the numbers of security risks were initially quite large, totaling well into the thousands, by 1943 only slightly over 100 were involved. Eventually, the security organs dropped their reservations altogether. In the intervening negotiations, the thousands of volunteers at the war relocation centers were offered to Japan instead.

Seen in this perspective, the establishment of war relocation centers to collect and interview Japanese-Americans about their desire to be repatriated was a logical solution to fulfill a difficult task. In the end, the centers accomplished this task both expeditiously and accurately. Contrary to the commonly accepted explanation that it was the U.S. government's "racist" or revenge-motivated policies against the Japanese-American community that led to the creation of the war relocation centers, the centers served a very real purpose in forwarding the goals of the U.S.–Japanese exchange program. If a third exchange had ever been carried out, then the vast majority of the Japanese-Americans being repatriated would have come from the war relocation centers.

In sharp contrast to claims that the U.S. government created the war relocation centers as some sort of plot to humiliate the Japanese-American community, therefore, the evidence presented in this study suggests that it was largely the demands made by the Japanese government to provide security for its nationals that made the creation of the war relocation centers necessary. If these centers had not existed, then Tokyo's insistence on absolute reciprocity would have eventually made the organization of a similar system necessary in order to locate and repatriate Japanese nationals in return for American citizens being allowed to come home.

Seen in this light, the Japanese government was holding innocent Americans hostage, and the war relocation centers helped provide the "ransom" that Tokyo demanded for their release. This aspect of the war relocation program has perhaps been obscured because during the war only a small number of the residents of the war relocation centers were repatriated to Japan; most of the more than 20,000 Japanese citizens and American citizens of Japanese ancestry who had requested repatriation were destined to wait until the end of the war before their requests could be addressed.

Finally, in addition to serving as a primary means for liberating thousands of U.S. citizens held by Japan, the war relocation centers both protected their residents from any post-Pearl Harbor vigilantism, and also neutralized any security risk that selected members of the Japanese-American community might have posed to the United States. MAGIC intercepts show that this security risk was very real and this reason alone could have rationalized the establishment of the war relocation centers in the midst of war. However, this work has identified another even more pressing reason for creating the war relocation centers—the exchange of willing Japanese citizens and U.S. citizens of Japanese ancestry for American civilians being held by Japan.

* * *

To date, the most common criticism of the Japanese-American war relocation centers has been from members of the Japanese-American community, especially from those Japanese citizens or American citizens of Japanese ancestry who at the time vocally proclaimed their loyalty to the United States. Their resentment is understandable for they were torn from their homes, moved against their will into war relocation centers, and forced to undergo intensive questioning by U.S. government authorities to determine either their loyalty to the United States or their interest in being repatriated to Japan. In 1976, in recognition of their mistreatment, President Gerald R. Ford signed a proclamation stating of Executive Order 9066 "not only was that evacuation wrong, but Japanese Americans were and are loyal Americans."[2]

However, what is equally clear today is that not all of the Japanese-Americans were loyal; unfortunately, many were not. In fact, during the first few years of the war it proved remarkably easy to locate thousands of such volunteers, with over 20,000 Japanese-Americans applying for repatriation and approximately 6,000 volunteers housed at the Tule Lake Segregation Center awaiting repatriation in exchange for an equal number of American civilians; altogether this number of 20,000 seeking repatriation equaled almost one-fifth of the entire Japanese-American population who were affected by the war relocation program.

Even books that are highly critical of the war relocation program admit that the dominant view in "the WRA and the war department" was that "the people who remained at Tule Lake after the 'loyal' were cleared to leave for the other, less restricted camps had cast their lot with Japan for the future ... [and] many continued to resist in ways that tended to confirm the view of the administration and a hostile press that they preferred Japan: they participated in language schools, Japanese cultural practices, paramilitary drills, repatriation requests, and pro-Japan organizations."[3]

If the wartime exchanges had continued, many—if not all—of the Japanese citizens and U.S. citizens of Japanese ancestry at Tule Lake who had requested repatriation would have undoubtedly been living in Japan during the final years of the war. Fortunately for them, most of them were spared this unhappy fate. The Americans held against their will in the Japanese camps were not nearly as lucky, however, and many paid with their lives.

Because there were only two exchanges during the war, and only 318 of the Japanese-Americans from the war relocation centers were included, this has led to the false conclusion that such exchanges were illegal. According to one such account: "no amount of legal gymnastics would permit exchange of Japanese Americans for those Americans under Japanese military control."[4] The evidence presented in this book does not support this conclusion. As this work also shows, the Japanese government, not the U.S. government, opposed conducting any further exchanges during the war, despite the best efforts of the Department of State to change their minds.

Much self-righteous and indignant anger has also been directed at Washington by younger members of the Japanese-American community who were not yet born or were minors at the time the war relocation centers were established. Such criticism has largely overlooked the Japanese government's own role in these events. Meanwhile, the older members of the Japanese-American community know better. Many of them had friends or relatives who repatriated to Japan after the war, or at least knew of people who did. Clearly, this aspect of the war relocation program has not been communicated to the younger generation of Japanese-Americans.

Before one can understand the true history of the war relocation centers, therefore, one must recall that the Japanese government was the first to intern American citizens, beginning even before the war started, but intensifying dramatically within hours of the 7 December 1941 surprise attack on Pearl Harbor. Not only was interning civilians illegal according to the norms of international behavior at the time, but if Tokyo had immediately agreed to repatriate all internees without restriction then all American citizens being held in its detention camps could have returned home immediately.

Instead, by demanding reciprocity the Japanese government insisted that they be included in a one-for-one exchange where every American citizen was 'traded' for either a Japanese citizen or an American citizen loyal to Japan. It was this requirement that made it necessary for Washington to locate approximately 6,000 Japanese-Americans who wished to be repatriated to Japan. Therefore, in the final analysis responsibility for the U.S. decision to establish the war relocation centers must rest as much with Tokyo as it does with Washington.

* * *

In sharp contrast to earlier portrayals of the war relocation centers as an expression of U.S. racism or anti-Japanese anger, this study has attempted to show their purpose and relatively humane administration. This generally good treatment was provided under the trying conditions imposed by a world war fought by an enemy which abused its American internees and prisoners as a matter of policy, not to mention the civilian populations in the countries it invaded and occupied.

Under these circumstances, U.S.–Japanese negotiations leading to the exchange of government officials and non-officials began the very day after Pearl Harbor. Eventually, two sets of exchange vessels were organized. Unfortunately, because of the dangerous conditions caused by the Pacific War, as well as increasing diplomatic tensions between Japan and the United States, a third exchange was never successfully negotiated or carried out. As a result, a large number of the American citizens who remained in Japanese detention camps died of malnutrition, illness, or mistreatment during the war.

As soon as the war ended, an additional three sailings were arranged by the War Relocation Authority. On 25 November 1945, 423 internees departed, on 29 December 1945, 3,551 internees departed, and then on 23 February 1946, a final 432 departed. Of these 4,406 persons, an almost equal number were men (2,194) and women (2,212), while by far the largest number were U.S. citizens—1,767—the second largest were Japanese citizens—1,523—and then the third group—1,116—were referred to as "renunciants" or as "a former citizen whose formal application for renunciation of United States citizenship was approved by the Department of Justice."[5]

According to Executive Order 2655, signed by President Harry Truman soon after the war ended, all such "alien enemies" were "subject to removal from the U.S."[6] Meanwhile, in Canada, a similar program was adopted. While 10,000 Japanese-Canadians were originally scheduled to be repatriated forcibly to Japan, only about 4,000 of these left before the program was halted in January 1947.[7]

What is somewhat surprising about the U.S. statistics is that some 2,883 of the total, or just over 65 percent, of those repatriated to Japan immediately after the war ended were either current or former U.S. citizens. One possible explanation was the U.S. government announcement in 1945 that its top priority was to send Nisei renunciants and other "enemy aliens" back to Japan. According to one memoir, most of these repatriates were single men without families, a group that included not only elderly farm laborers, but the younger Kibei who had lived and been educated mainly in Japan.[8]

According to an 18 December 1945 letter written by the Department of Justice, the only persons to be repatriated to Japan against their will would have to be "repatriable under standards which have been established for German alien enemies."[9] According to one account, a large number of Kibei were part of this order, including "those who are marked disloyal or troublemakers."[10] The status "enemy alien" continued to be used until the U.S. and Japan signed a formal peace treaty on 28 April 1952, when the conflict formally ended.

Meanwhile, the U.S. government decided that any first generation Issei non-citizens who elected not to be repatriated to Japan would be allowed to remain and relocate within the United States. As an added bonus, after the war the Issei were suddenly eligible for the first time to become naturalized American citizens, a privilege they were denied previously because of the gentlemen's agreement and the 1924 Immigration Law.[11] This decision to extend citizenship to the Issei is also not in keeping with the generally negative conclusions of those who see the U.S. war relocation centers only through the prism of racism.

By January 1945, therefore, there were over 5,000 Nisei—or second generation Japanese—who were listed on the War Relocation Authority rolls as having renounced their U.S. citizenship. But, on 26 October 1945, anyone who wanted to change their form from "Application of Repatriation" to "Application of Non-Repatriation" was urged to do so.[12] Harry U. Ueno, who had been adamant about returning to Japan, was told by the Tule Lake administrator: "Harry, those people who went back had a miserable time. There is not much food to eat. You don't want to expose your children to that." Following the October ruling, many of the 5,000 Nisei who had renounced their citizenship decided to invalidate their renunciations, and Ueno recounted: "Sometime late in December 1945, I changed my mind and decided to stay."[13]

Eventually, "all who wished to invalidate their renunciations were able to do so," and they were allowed to remain in the United States.[14] Interestingly, this decision was opposed by Japanese-American veterans of the 100th Infantry Battalion and the 442nd Regimental Combat Team, and at a 1946 meeting they argued that "they [the renunciants] be made to face the consequences of their former attitude."[15] According to one account, 5,766 Japanese-Americans had renounced their U.S. citizenship during the war, but of this number 5,409 later requested that it be restored and in 4,987 cases the government agreed to do so.[16]

Strange to say, after the war some Japanese citizens living in the U.S. even experienced trouble obtaining permission to return to Japan. Kiyoaki Murata, for example, had come to the United States on a student visa and had been forced to remain in a war relocation center for the duration. After the war, he applied to the Department of State for an exit permit to return to Japan, but was told that it would take several months to obtain permission from General MacArthur's headquarters in Tokyo. This was because the Americans in charge of the occupation did not want "to have even Japanese citizens enter the country if they were to prove to be inimical to the purpose of the Occupation, namely, the democratization of Japan."[17]

Meanwhile, there were also approximately 3,000 U.S.-born Nisei who had been stranded in Japan by the war. Once they were able to prove that they were American citizens, they were issued new passports and allowed to return to the United States. In some cases, however, they were then prosecuted for their activities during the war, for example working for the Japanese government as translators or radio announcers, like Iva Ikuko Toguri D'Aquino, better known as "Tokyo Rose."

After World War II ended, the Japanese-American community tried to regain a sense of normality. Of the 106,775 evacuees who were registered as being housed at the war relocation centers during 1942, a total of 49,517, or 47 percent, had returned to Washington, Oregon, or California by 31 January 1946, while the largest remaining groups settled in Colorado, Utah, and Idaho.[18] Ten years after the war, on 12 August 1955, even those Japanese-Americans who had renounced their U.S. citizenship and had been repatriated to Japan were given a second chance when the U.S. District Court for the Northern District of California decreed that such renunciants were entitled to regain their U.S. citizenship.[19] As a result, many of the U.S. citizens who had renounced their citizenship and repatriated to Japan after the war subsequently returned to live and work in the United States.[20]

Thus, according to the statistical evidence collected both by the U.S. government and by private sources, the overwhelming majority of Japanese-Americans interned in the war relocation centers elected to remain in the U.S. after the war, or later decided to return to the U.S. from Japan. In spite of whatever criticism they might have voiced against the war relocation centers and their internment experience during World War II, this statistic alone shows where the Japanese-American community as a whole felt the brightest future for themselves and their descendents would lie.

Notes

Introduction

1 According to WorldCat, there are 1,732 books that match the subject search terms "Japanese Americans" and "evacuation and relocation, 1942–1945." Fortunately, there are a number of useful bibliographies and guides to these materials, including Wendy L. Ng, *Japanese American Internment during World War II: A History and Reference Guide* (Westport, CT: Greenwood Press, 2002); Christine Corcos, *Japanese-American Internment and Relocation during World War II: A Selected Bibliography* (Case Western Reserve University, Law Library, 1991); Denice Lee Mills, *The Evacuation and Relocation of Japanese Americans During World War II: A Bibliography* (Vance Bibliographies, 1989); Leslie A. Ito, *Japanese Americans during World War II: A Selected, Annotated Bibliography of Materials Available at UCLA* (UCLA Asian American Studies Center Reading Room/Library; 2nd edition, 1997).

2 Mitchell T. Maki, Harry H. L. Kitano, and S. Megan Berthold, *Achieving the Impossible Dream: How Japanese Americans Obtained Redress* (Urbana, IL: University of Illinois Press, 1999), 1.

3 Lillian Baker, *American and Japanese Relocation in World War II: Fact, Fiction and Fallacy* (Medford, OR: Webb Research Group, 1990), 76–77; This reason was given by her critics to explain why Ms. Baker was so opposed to referring to the war relocation centers as "concentration camps." Arthur A. Hanson and Betty E. Mitson, *Voices Long Silent: An Oral Inquiry into the Japanese American Evacuation* (Fullerton, CA: Kulberg Publications, 1974), 178–179.

4 David D. Lowman, *MAGIC: The Untold Story of U.S. Intelligence and the Evacuation of Japanese Residents from the West Coast During WWII* (Utah: Athena Press, Inc., 2000), vii.

5 Michelle Malkin, *In Defense of Internment: The Case for "Racial Profiling" in World War II and the War on Terror* (Washington, D.C.: Regnery Publishing, Inc., 2004), xiv.

6 P. Scott Corbett, *Quiet Passages: The Exchange of Civilians between the United States and Japan during the Second World War* (Kent, OH: The Kent State University Press, 1987), 2.

7 Ibid., 1.

8 Baker, *American and Japanese Relocation*, vi.

9 William Minoru Hohri, *Repairing America: An Account of the Movement for Japanese-American Redress* (Pullman, WA: Washington State University Press, 1988), i.

10 Timothy J. Holian, *The German-Americans and World War II* (New York: Peter Lang, 1996), 1.

11 Arnold Krammer, *Undue Process: The Untold Story of America's German Alien Internees* (New York: Rowman & Littlefield Publishers, Inc., 1997), 142–143.

12 Stephen Fox, *The Unknown Internment: An Oral History of the Relocation of Italian Americans during World War II* (Boston, MA: Twayne Publishers, 1990), 186.

13 Memorandum from Elizabeth B. Smith, Chief, Japanese Repatriation Unit, Department of State, Special War Problems Division, 27 March 1945, U.S. National Archives, Record Group 59, Lot 58D8, Special War Problems Division, Box #196.

14 Note from the Swiss Minister to Japan, Camille Gorge, to Minister of Foreign Affairs Shigenori Togo, 10 December 1941; Japanese Foreign Ministry Archives (hereafter Gaimusho) A700, 9-24-1, 1.

15 "The Secretary of State (Hull) to the Chargé in Switzerland (Huddle)," 8 December 1941; *Foreign Relations of the United States* (hereafter FRUS) 1942: Volume 1, 377.

16 For a discussion of the importance of "reciprocity" in gift-giving and the effect this can have on gaining and losing "face," see S.C.M. Paine, *The Sino-Japanese War of 1894–1895: Perceptions, Power, and Primacy* (Cambridge, UK: Cambridge University Press, 2003), 333–366; Toshio Yatsushiro, *Politics and Cultural Values: The World War II Japanese Relocation Centers United States Government* (New York: Arno Press, 1978), 605.

17 Denis and Peggy Warner, *The Tide at Sunrise: A History of the Russo-Japanese War* (New York: Charterhouse, 1974), 451–452.

18 D. E. Collins, *Native American Aliens: Disloyalty and the Renunciation of Citizenship by Japanese Americans during World War II* (Westport, CT: Greenwood Press, 1985), 9.

19 Lowman, *MAGIC*, 375–377.

20 Thomas Connell, *America's Japanese Hostages: The World War II Plan for a Japanese Free Latin America* (Westport, CT: Praeger Press, 2002), 115, fn 6.

21 *The Evacuated People: A Quantitative Description* (Washington, D.C.: U.S. Government Printing Office, 1975), 196.

22 Ibid.

23 Corbett, *Quiet Passsages*, *passim*.

1 The origin of the Japanese–American exchange program

1 Except when they impinged directly on the American negotiations with Japan, the British exchanges will not be discussed in this work. See Bob Moore and Barbara Hately-Broad, *Prisoners of War, Prisoners of Peace: Captivity, Homecoming and Memory in World War II* (New York: Berg, 2005).

2 Roger Daniels, *Concentration Camps USA: Japanese Americans and World War II* (New York: Holt, Rinehart and Winston, Inc., 1972), 84.

3 Morton Grodzins, *Americans Betrayed: Politics and the Japanese Evacuation* (Chicago: The University of Chicago Press, 1949), 309.

4 "First proposal of the United States Government–telegram dated December 16, 1941, from the Foreign Office at Berne to the Swiss Minister at Tokyo," in "Documents regarding exchange of officials and nationals and their effects," National Archives, State Department, Record Group 59, Special War Problems Division, Box 131.

5 Note from the Swiss Minister to Japan to Minister of Foreign Affairs Shigenori Togo, 17 December 1941; Gaimusho A700, 9-24-1, 1; also see FRUS, 1942, Volume 1, 378–379.

6 Corbett, *Quiet Passage*, 31.

7 Tetsuden Kashima, *Judgment Without Trial: Japanese American Imprisonment During World War II* (Seattle, WA: University of Washington Press, 2003), 181.

8 Note from the Swiss Minister to Japan to Minister of Foreign Affairs Shigenori Togo, 17 December 1941; Gaimusho A700, 9-24-1, 1; also see FRUS, 1942, Volume 1, 378–379.

9 Ibid.

10 Ibid.
11 Note from the U.S. Government to the Japanese Minister of Foreign Affairs Shigenori Togo, 10 December 1941; Gaimusho A700, 9-24-1.
12 Early Japanese draft listing its preference for Japanese exchangees, 16 December 1941; Gaimusho A700, 9-24-1.
13 Open letter from Max Huber, President International Red Cross Committee, explaining terms of 1929 Geneva Convention, 17 December 1941; Gaimusho A700, 9-11-1 (1).
14 English translation of the Geneva Convention, 27 July 1929; Gaimusho A700, 9-11-1-1.
15 Ibid.
16 Note from the U.S. Government to the Japanese Minister of Foreign Affairs Shigenori Togo, 27 December 1942; Gaimusho A700, 9-11-1 (2).
17 Note from the Minister of Foreign Affairs Shigenori Togo to the American Government, 29 January 1942; Gaimusho A700, 9-11-1-1.
18 U.S. Government Note to the Japanese Government, 5 January 1942; Gaimusho A700, 9-24-1 (1).
19 American Reply to a Japanese Proposal, 12 February 1942; Gaimusho A700, 9-24-1 (1).
20 Japanese Note to the U.S. Government, 24 March 1942; Gaimusho A700, 9-11-3-2 (2).
21 Michi Weglyn, *Years of Infamy: The Untold Story of America's Concentration Camps* (New York: William Morrow and Company, Inc., 1976), 55.
22 Robert Harvey, *Amache: The Story of Japanese Internment in Colorado During World War II* (Dallas, TX: Taylor Trade Publishing, 2004), 58–59.
23 Roger Daniels, *Concentration Camps: North America Japanese in the United States and Canada During World War II* (Malabar, FL: Robert E. Krieger Publishing Company, 1981), 95.
24 Note from the Swiss Minister to Japan to Minister of Foreign Affairs Shigenori Togo, 17 December 1941; Gaimusho A700, 9-24-1, 1.
25 War Department, Washington, D.C., Public Proclamation No. WD 1, August 13, 1942, signed by Henry L. Stimson, Secretary of War, U.S. Wartime Civil Control Administration, Hoover Archives, Stanford University, Box 1.
26 Note from the Swiss Minister to Japan to Minister of Foreign Affairs Shigenori Togo, 5 January 1942 (EE.5); Gaimusho A700, 9-24-1, 1; also see FRUS, 1942, Volume 1, 382–385.
27 C. Harvey Gardiner, "The Latin-American Japanese and World War II," in Daniels, Taylor, Kitano, *Japanese Americans*, 142–5.
28 Note from the Swiss Minister to Japan to Minister of Foreign Affairs Shigenori Togo, 5 January 1942 (EE.5); Gaimusho A700, 9-24-1, 1; also see FRUS, 1942, Volume 1, 382–385.
29 Ibid.
30 Telegram from "Maderi" (Madrid) transmitting the American response to Japan's Memorandum 42, 9 February 1942 (No. 4371); Gaimusho, A700, 9-24-1, 7.
31 Japanese Communication entitled "Further Observations of the Japanese Government," 19 February 1942; Gaimusho, A700, 9-24-1, 7.
32 Telegram from Madrid transmitting U.S. Government to the Japanese Government, 17 March 1942 (No. 7859); Gaimusho A700, 9-24-1, 7.
33 Note from the Swiss Minister to Minister of Foreign Affairs Shigenori Togo, 14 March 1942 (CC.1.2.1./5.2.-ce.-); Gaimusho A700, 9-24-1, 7.
34 Note from the Swiss Minister to Japan to Minister of Foreign Affairs Shigenori Togo, 5 January 1942 (EE.5); Gaimusho A700, 9-24-1, 1; also see FRUS, 1942, Volume 1, 382–385.
35 Ibid.
36 Ibid.

37 Ibid.
38 Ibid.
39 Ibid.
40 Page Smith, *Democracy on Trial: The Japanese American Evacuation and Relocation in World War II* (New York: Simon & Schuster, 1995), 53.
41 Sidney L. Gulick, *The American Japanese Problem: A Study of the Racial Relations of the East and the West* (New York: Charles Scribner's Sons, 1914), 204–205.
42 Leonard Broom and Ruth Riemer, *Removal and Return: The Socio-Economic Effects of the War on Japanese Americans* (Berkeley, CA: University of California Press, 1949/Reprint 1973), 80–81.
43 S. Frank Miyamoto, "Dorothy Swaine as Director of JERS: Some Personal Observations," Yuji Ichioka, ed., *Views from Within: The Japanese American Evacuation and Resettlement Study* (Los Angeles, CA: Asian American Studies Center, 1989), 45.
44 Miyamoto, in Ichioka, 48.
45 Eileen Sunada Sarasohn, *The Issei: Portrait of a Pioneer, An Oral History* (Palo Alto, CA: Pacific Books, 1983), 225.

2 Non-officials and the U.S.–Japanese exchange agreement

1 FRUS, 1942, Volume 1, 386–388.
2 Telegram from "Maderi" (Madrid) transmitting the American response to Japan's Memorandum 42, 9 February 1942 (No. 4371); Gaimusho, A700, 9-24-1, 7.
3 Roger Daniels, *The Decision to Relocate the Japanese Americans* (New York: J.B. Lippincott Company, 1975), 111.
4 FRUS, 1942, Volume 1, 386–388.
5 FRUS, 1942, Volume 1, 388–390.
6 FRUS, 1942, Volume 1, 391.
7 Japanese Communication entitled "Further Observations of the Japanese Government," 19 February 1942; Gaimusho, A700, 9-24-1, 7.
8 Telegram from "Maderi" (Madrid) transmitting the American response to Japan's Memorandum 42, 9 February 1942 (No. 4371); Gaimusho, A700, 9-24-1, 7; FRUS, 1942, Volume 1, 391–397.
9 Lowman, *MAGIC*, 164.
10 Telegram from "Maderi" (Madrid) transmitting the American request to receive the names and addresses of non-official Japanese wishing to return to Japan, 12 February 1942 (No. 4550); Gaimusho, A700, 9-24-1, 7.
11 Japanese Communication entitled "Further Observations of the Japanese Government," 19 February 1942; Gaimusho, A700, 9-24-1, 7.
12 Telegram from Madrid transmitting request of Japanese representatives in the U.S. to the Japanese Government, 14 March 1942 (No. 7556); Gaimusho A700, 9-24-1, 7.
13 Ibid.
14 Letter from the Japanese Foreign Minister to the Swiss Minister in Tokyo, responding to his letter No. EE.5.1.-ce from 24 March 1942, 2 April 1942; Gaimusho A700, 9-24-1, 7.
15 Lowman, *MAGIC*, 129; access to "governmental organizations of various characters, factories, and transportation facilities" was considered to be particularly important.
16 Telegram from Madrid transmitting request of Japanese representative in the U.S. to the Japanese Government, 14 March 1942 (No. 7545); Gaimusho A700, 9-24-1, 7.
17 FRUS, 1942, Volume 1, 446–449.
18 Louis Fiset, *Imprisoned Apart: The World War II Correspondence of an Issei Couple* (Seattle, WA: University of Washington Press, 1997), 69.

19 Telegram from Madrid transmitting request of Japanese representatives in the U.S. to the Japanese Government, 14 March 1942 (No. 7556); Gaimusho A700, 9-24-1, 7.
20 Telegram from Madrid transmitting request of Japanese representative in the U.S. to the Japanese Government, 16 March 1942 (No. 7752); Gaimusho A700, 9-24-1, 7.
21 Telegram from Madrid transmitting U.S. Government to the Japanese Government, 17 March 1942 (No. 7861); Gaimusho A700, 9-24-1, 7; FRUS, 1942, Volume 1, 404–406.
22 Ibid.
23 Ibid.
24 Ibid.
25 Gwen Terasaki, *Bridge to the Sun* (Chapel Hill, NC: The University of North Carolina Press, 1957), 98.
26 FRUS, 1942, Volume 1, 417.
27 "Copy of letter addressed to the American Ambassador [Joseph Clark Grew] by 198 American civilians on board the evacuation vessel [*Asama Maru*]," 21 July 1942, U.S. National Archives, Record Group 59, Lot 58D8, Special War Problems Division, Box #131.
28 Terasaki, *Bridge to the Sun*, 98.
29 Telegram from "Maderi" (Madrid) transmitting the Japanse opinion, 3 June 1942 (No. 15464); Gaimusho, A700, 9-24-1, 2.
30 Telegram from "Maderi" (Madrid) which included this list (No. 16063), 8 June 1942, Gaimusho, A700, 9-24-1, 2.
31 Ibid.
32 Klancy Clark de Nevers, *The Colonel and the Pacifist: Karl Bendetsen-Perry Saito and the Incarceration of Japanese Americans During World War II* (Salt Lake City, UT: The University of Utah Press, 2004), 167–8.
33 Telegram from "Maderi" (Madrid) transmitting this Japanese suggestion, 8 June 1942 (No. 16004); Gaimusho A700, 9-24-1, 2.
34 Note from the Swiss Legation to the Japanese Foreign Ministry, 16 June 1942 (E.E.5.1.7./ ce.-), Gaimusho A700, 9-24-1, 2.
35 Terasaki, *Bridge to the Sun*, 90–94.
36 Note from the Swiss Legation to Foreign Minister Shigenori Togo, 2 June 1942 (EE.5.2.4.1.1.- ce.-); Gaimusho A700, 9-24-1, 2.
37 Note from the Spanish Government forwarding the Japanese message to the U.S. Government, 15 June 1942 (No. 256); Gaimusho A700- 9-24-1, 2.
38 Note from the Swiss Legation to the Japanese Foreign Ministry, 16 June 1942 (E.E.5.1.7./ ce.-), Gaimusho A700, 9-24-1, 2.
39 Letter from the Japanese Foreign Ministry to the U.S. State Department, 16 June 1942; Gaimusho A700, 9-24-1, 2.
40 Ibid.

3 Exchanging journalists and non-officials from outside the U.S.

1 Telegram from Madrid transmitting U.S. Government to the Japanese Government, 17 March 1942 (No. 7856); Gaimusho A700, 9-24-1, 7.
2 Daniels, Taylor, Kitano, *Japanese Americans*, 143.
3 Telegram from Madrid transmitting U.S. Government to the Japanese Government, 17 March 1942 (No. 7856); Gaimusho A700, 9-24-1, 7.
4 Ibid.
5 Telegram from "Maderi" (Madrid) transmitting the American response to Japan's Memorandum 42, 9 February 1942 (No. 4371); Gaimusho A700, 9-24-1, 7.
6 Japanese Communication entitled "Further Observations of the Japanese Government," 19 February 1942; Gaimusho, A700, 9-24-1, 7.

7 Note from the Swiss Legation to Japanese Foreign Minister Shigenori Togo, 1 May 1942 (EE.5.2/EE.5.1.3.-ce); Gaimusho A700, 9-24-1, 2.
8 Note from the Swiss Legation to the Japanese Foreign Ministry, 20 May 1942; Gaimusho A700, 9-24-1, 2.
9 Note from Swiss Legation to the Japanese Foreign Minister Shigenori Togo, 27 May 1942 (EE.5.1.3.- ce.-); Gaimusho A700, 9-24-1, 2.
10 Ibid.
11 Note from the Swiss Legation to Japanese Foreign Minister Shigenori Togo containing the American offer, 17 April 1942 (EE.5.2.1.2.ca); Gaimusho A700, 9-24-1, 9.
12 Ibid.
13 Note from the Peruvian Minister to Japan, Ricardo Rivera Schreiber to Foreign Minister Shigenori Togo, 10 January 1942 (5-18-M/.2); Gaimusho A700, 9-24-1, 7.
14 Note from the Swiss Minister to Foreign Minister Shigenori Togo, 4 February 1942 (QQ.2.4.-ca.-); Gaimusho A700, 9-24-1, 7.
15 Note from the Swiss Minister to Foreign Minister Shigenori Togo, 30 January 1942 (NN.1.1.ca.); Gaimusho A700, 9-24-1, 7.
16 C. Harvey Gardiner, *Pawns in a Triangle of Hate: The Peruvian Japanese and the United States* (Seattle, WA: University of Washington Press, 1981), viii.
17 Connell, *America's Japanese Hostages*, 74.
18 Takeo Kaneshiro, compiler, *Internees: War Relocation Center Memoirs and Diaries* (New York: Vantage Press, 1976), 36.
19 Daniels, Taylor, Kitano, *Japanese Americans*, 145.
20 Note from Foreign Minister Shigenori Togo to the Peruvian Minister to Japan, Ricardo Rivera Schreiber, undated (No. 2/E3); Gaimusho A700, 9-24-1, 7.
21 Translated copy of a telegram, marked "extremely secret," of an American note transmitted from the Swiss Foreign Ministry in Berne to the Swiss Legation in Tokyo, 5 February 1942 (No. 116); Gaimusho A700, 9-24-1, 7; Note from the Swiss Minister to Foreign Minister Shigenori Togo, 5 February 1942; Gaimusho A700, 9-24-1, 7.
22 Telegram from "Maderi" (Madrid) transmitting the American response to Japan's Memorandum 42, 9 February 1942 (No. 4371); Gaimusho, A700, 9-24-1, 7; italic text here is underlined.
23 Japanese Communication entitled "Further Observations of the Japanese Government," 19 February 1942; Gaimusho, A700, 9-24-1, 7.
24 Telegram from Madrid transmitting request of Japanese representatives in the U.S. to the Japanese Government, 14 March 1942 (No. 7545); Gaimusho A700, 9-24-1, 7.
25 Telegram from Madrid transmitting U.S. Government to the Japanese Government, 17 March 1942 (No. 7859); Gaimusho A700, 9-24-1, 7.
26 Telegram from "Maderi" (Madrid) transmitting the American response to Japan's Memorandum 42, 9 February 1942 (No. 4371); Gaimusho, A700, 9-24-1, 7.
27 FRUS, 1942, Volume 1, 428–429.
28 Ibid., 400–401.
29 Letter from the Swiss Minister to Foreign Minister Shigenori Togo, 15 April 1942 (EE.5.1.[A.P.] ca.-); Gaimusho A700, 9-24-1, 7.
30 Letter from the Japanese Foreign Minister to the Swiss Minister, 27 April 1942 (No. 152/E3); Gaimusho A700, 9-24-1, 7.
31 FRUS, 1942, Volume 1, 412–414.
32 Note from the Swiss Legation to Foreign Minister Shigenori Togo, 26 May 1942 (EE.GG.5.1 [AP&JP]- ce.-); Gaimusho, A700, 9-24-1, 2.
33 FRUS, 1942, Volume 1, 412–414.
34 For the American list of these 484 Japanese officials, see 4 June 1942 telegram from "Maderi"; Gaimusho, A700, 9-24-1, 2.

35 For the American list of 527 non-officials from the United States and 131 non-officials from South and Central America (for a total of 658), see 4 June 1942 telegram from "Maderi"; Gaimusho, A700, 9-24-1, 2.
36 Note from the Swiss Legation to Japanese Foreign Minister Shigenori Togo, 29 May 1942 (EE.5.1.8.- ce.-); Gaimusho A700, 9-24-1, 2.
37 Note from Japanese Foreign Minister Shigenori Togo to the Swedish Foreign Minister, 2 June 1942 (No. 230); Gaimusho A700, 9-24-1, 2.
38 Kashima, *Judgment without Trial*, 181.
39 Telegram from Madrid transmitting message from the Japanese Minister to the Japanese Government, 15 April 1942 (No. 10534); Gaimusho A700, 9-24-1, 7.
40 Ibid.
41 Letter from the Swiss Minister to Foreign Minister Shigenori Togo, 21 April 1942 (EE.2.2.1.ce.-); Gaimusho A700, 9-24-1, 7.
42 Telegram from "Maderi" (Madrid) setting forth the American information, 21 May 1942; Gaimusho A700, 9-24-1, 2.
43 Note from the Swiss Legation to Japanese Foreign Minister Shigenori Togo, 18 May 1942 (EE.5.1.ca.-); Gaimusho A700, 9-24-1, 2.
44 Note from the Swiss Legation to Japanese Foreign Minister Shigenori Togo, 29 May 1942 (EE.5.1.8.- ce.-); Gaimusho A700, 9-24-1, 2.
45 Ibid.

4 Final U.S.–Japanese negotiations for the first exchange ship

1 Note from the Swiss Minister to Foreign Minister Shigenori Togo, 12 January 1942 (EE.5.2.-ca.-); Gaimusho A700, 9-24-1, 7.
2 Telegram from "Maderi" (Madrid) transmitting the American response to Japan's Memorandum 42, 9 February 1942 (No. 4371); Gaimusho, A700, 9-24-1, 7.
3 Japanese Communication entitled "Further Observations of the Japanese Government," 19 February 1942; Gaimusho, A700, 9-24-1, 7.
4 Ibid.
5 Telegram from Madrid transmitting U.S. Government to the Japanese Government, 17 March 1942 (No. 7859); Gaimusho A700, 9-24-1, 7.
6 Note from the Swiss Legation to Foreign Minister Shigenori Togo, 30 March 1942 (EE.5.2.1.2 ce); Gaimusho A700, 9-24-1, 9.
7 Note from the Swiss Legation repeating the American Protest, 24 August 1943. (EE.5.53/5.5.4.-dgu); Gaimusho A700, 9-24-1, 9.
8 Ibid.
9 "Instructions for Repatriates," undated but issued between the first and second exchanges, Japanese Relocation Papers, Bancroft Library, UC Berkeley, Microfilm reel #40.
10 Letter from R.D. Fitch, Special Agent, Department of State, to T. F. Fitch, Chief Special Agent, 6 September 1943, U.S. National Archives, Record Group 59, Lot 58D8, Special War Problems Division, Box #106.
11 Instructions for Repatriates," undated but issued between the first and second exchanges, Japanese Relocation Papers, Bancroft Library, UC Berkeley, Microfilm reel #40.
12 Note from the Swiss Minister to Foreign Minister Shigenori Togo, 12 January 1942 (EE.5.2.-ca.-); Gaimusho A700, 9-24-1, 7.
13 Telegram from "Maderi" (Madrid) transmitting the American response to Japan's Memorandum 42, 9 February 1942 (No. 4371); Gaimusho, A700, 9-24-1, 7; FRUS, 1942, Volume 1, 391–397.
14 Japanese Communication entitled "Further Observations of the Japanese Government," 19 February 1942; Gaimusho, A700, 9-24-1, 7.

15 Telegram from "Maderi" (Madrid) transmitting the American response to Japan's Memorandum 42, 9 February 1942 (No. 4371); Gaimusho, A700, 9-24-1, 7.
16 Japanese Communication entitled "Further Observations of the Japanese Government," 19 February 1942; Gaimusho, A700, 9-24-1, 7.
17 Japanese "Memorandum" to the U.S. Government, 16 July 1943; Gaimusho A700, 9-24-1, 9.
18 American "Memorandum" to the Japanese Government, undated (probably late July or early August 1943); Gaimusho A700, 9-24-1, 9.
19 Ibid.
20 Ibid.
21 Japanese Government protest to the U.S. Government, 27 October 1942; Gaimusho A700, 9-11-1-5.
22 Ibid.
23 U.S. Government 12 December 1942 reply to the Japanese October 1942 protest, 18 December 1942 (Nos. 32245, 32250, 32246, 32258); Gaimusho A700, 9-11-1-5.
24 Telegram from "Maderi" (Madrid) transmitting the American response to Japan's Memorandum 42, 9 February 1942 (No. 4371); Gaimusho, A700, 9-24-1, 7.
25 Ibid.
26 Japanese Communication entitled "Further Observations of the Japanese Government," 19 February 1942; Gaimusho, A700, 9-24-1, 7.
27 Telegram from Madrid to the Japanese Government (No. 6678), 6 March 1942; Gaimusho A700, 9-24-1, 7.
28 Telegram from Madrid transmitting U.S. Government to the Japanese Government, 17 March 1942 (No. 7859); Gaimusho A700, 9-24-1, 7.
29 Telegram from Madrid to the Japanese Government (No. 6564), 5 March 1942; Gaimusho A700, 9-24-1, 7.
30 Ibid.
31 Japanese "Memorandum" to the U.S. Government, 16 July 1943; Gaimusho A700, 9-24-1, 9.
32 American "Memorandum" to the Japanese Government, undated (probably late July or early August 1943); Gaimusho A700, 9-24-1, 9.
33 Japanese Note to the U.S. Government, 21 August 1943; Gaimusho A700, 9-24-1, 9.
34 Ibid.
35 American "Memorandum" to the Japanese Government, undated (probably late July or early August 1943); Gaimusho A700, 9-24-1, 9.
36 Ibid.
37 Japanese Note to the U.S. Government, 21 August 1943; Gaimusho A700, 9-24-1, 9.
38 Terasaki, *Bridge to the Sun*, 90–94.

5 Creating the Japanese-American war relocation centers

1 In 1973, two researchers from the California State University, Fullerton, Japanese American Oral History Project interviewed residents of Owens Valley, CA, where the Manzanar relocation center was situated. One such person interviewed was A. A. Brierly, who explained how bitter Americans were after Pearl Harbor and their conviction that the Japanese-Americans would have helped invading Japanese forces "In any way they could." Jessie A. Garrett and Ronald C. Larson, eds., *Camp and Community: Manzanar and the Owens Valley* (Van Nuys, CA: Delta Lithograph Co., 1977), 97–105.
2 Budd Fukei, *The Japanese American Story* (Minneapolis, MN: Dillon Press Inc., 1976), 56.

3 Jacobus tenBroek, Edward N. Barnhart, and Floyd W. Matson, *Japanese American Evacuation and Resettlement: Prejudice, War and the Constitution* (Berkeley, CA: University of California Press, 1958), 208.

4 Lowman, *MAGIC*, 377.

5 Note from the Swiss Legation, 3 August 1942 (EE. 5.5.1.ce): Gaimusho, A700, 9-24-1, 2.

6 Donald Pike and Roger Olmsted, "The Japanese in California," in Maisie & Richard Conrat, *Executive Order 9066: The Internment of 110,000 Japanese Americans* (Los Angeles, CA: Anderson, Ritchie and Simon, 1972), 19.

7 Audrie Girdner and Anne Loftis, *The Great Betrayal: The Evacuation of the Japanese-Americans During World War II* (Toronto: The Macmillan Company, 1969), 53–54.

8 Masakazu Iwata, *Planted in Good Soil: The History of the Issei in United States Agriculture* (New York: Peter Lang, 1992), 268.

9 James Oda, *Heroic Struggles of Japanese Americans: Partisan Fighters From America's Concentration Camps* (Los Angeles, CA: KNI, Inc., 1981), 237.

10 Dillon S. Myer, *War Relocation Authority: The Director's Account* (Berkeley, CA: Earl Warren Oral History Project, 1974), 6–7.

11 Yamato Ichihashi, *Japanese in the United States: A Critical Study of the Problems of the Japanese Immigrants and Their Children* (Stanford, CA: Stanford University Press, 1932), 309–310.

12 Yuji Ichioka, *The Issei: The World of the First Generation Japanese Immigrants, 1885–1924* (New York: The Free Press, 1988), 247.

13 Gordon K. Hirabayashi, "The Japanese Canadians and World War II," Roger Daniels, Sandra C. Taylor, Harry H. L. Kitano, eds., *Japanese Americans: From Relocation to Redress* (Salt Lake City, UT: University of Utah Press, 1986), 139–141.

14 Roger Daniels, "The Decisions to Relocate the North American Japanese: Another Look," in Charles McClain, *The Mass Internment of Japanese Americans and the Quest for Legal Redress* (New York: Garland Publishing, Inc., 1994), 1.

15 Peter Irons, *Justice at War: The Story of the Japanese American Internment Cases* (New York: Oxford University Press, 1983), 272.

16 Japanese protest opposing the loyalty oaths Japanese citizens and Japanese-Americans were asked to take, 18 April 1944 (No. 102); Gaimusho A700, 9-11-1-5-1.

17 Vice Admiral Yoji Koda, "The Russo-Japanese War: Primary Causes of Japanese Success," *Naval War College Review* (Spring 2005), Volume 58, Number 2, 11–44.

18 Lowman, *MAGIC*, 147–152.

19 Bill Hosokawa, *Out of the Frying Pan: Reflections of a Japanese American* (Niwot, CO: University Press of Colorado, 1998), 28–29.

20 "Factors making the Kibei a dangerous group," Colonel E. F. Cress to Commander K. D. Ringle, 27 May 1942, Japanese Relocation Papers, Bancroft Library, UC Berkeley, Microfilm reel #19.

21 Ibid.

22 Roger Daniels, *Concentration Camp USA: Japanese Americans and World War II* (New York: Holt, Rinehart and Winston, Inc., 1972), 107.

23 *The Fire Balloons*, http://www.vectorsite.net/avfusen.html; based on John McPhee, "Balloons of War," *New Yorker*, 29 January 1996, 52:60

24 Eleanor Hull, *Suddenly the Sun: A Biography of Shizuko Takahashi* (New York: Friendship Press, 1957), 113.

25 Headquarters Western Defense Command and Fourth Army, Public Proclamation No. 1, March 2, 1942, United States Wartime Civil Control Administration, Hoover Institution Archives, Stanford University, Box #1.

26 Dorothy Swaine Thomas and Richard S. Nishimoto, *The Spoilage: Japanese-American Evacuation and Resettlement During World War II* (Berkeley, CA: University of California Press, 1969), 101–102.

27 Daniels, *Concentration Camps USA,* 157.
28 Jeane Wakatsuki Houston and James D. Houston, *Farewell to Mansanar* (Boston, MA: Houghton Mifflin Company, 1973), 109–110.
29 Myer, *War Relocation Authority,* 47.
30 Japanese protest opposing the loyalty oaths Japanese citizens and Japanese-Americans were asked to take, 18 April 1944 (No. 102); Gaimusho A700, 9-11-1-5-1.
31 *Personal Justice Denied: Report of the Commission on Wartime Relocation and Internment of Civilians* (Washington, D.C.: 1982), 209.
32 Yatsushiro, 607–608.
33 John Christgau, "Collin versus the World: The Fight to Restore Citizenship to Japanese American Renunciants of World War II," Charles McClain, ed., *The Mass Internment of Japanese Americans and the Quest for Legal Redress* (New York: Garland Publishing, Inc., 1994), 349.
34 John D. Cook Collection, Hoover Institution Archives, Stanford University, Box #1.
34 Myer, *War Relocation Authority,* 27–28.
36 "American Civilian Internees in the Far East: Comparison of Reports of Numbers and Locations," 30 June 1944, U.S. National Archives, Record Group 59, Lot 58D8, Special War Problems Division, Box #132.
37 "Statistics of Japanese Population in the United States and Possessions," 23 January 1943, U.S. National Archives, Record Group 59, Lot 58D8, Special War Problems Division, Box #131.
38 Bill Hosokawa, *Thirty-Five Years in the Frying Pan* (New York: McGraw-Hill Book Company, 1978), 76; this incident was described by the author as one of the "still-unsolved evacuation-connected mysteries."
39 De Nevers, *The Colonel and the Pacifist,* 169.
40 "Confidential" letter from D.S. Myer to Paul Taylor, 27 March 1943, Japanese Relocation Papers, Bancroft Library, UC Berkeley, Microfilm reel #40.
41 Letter from D.S. Myer to "All Project Directors," undated but clearly prior to the second exchange in September 1943, Japanese Relocation Papers, Bancroft Library, UC Berkeley, Microfilm reel #40.
42 Letter from B. R. Stauber, War Relocation Authority, undated but clearly prior to the second exchange in September 1943, Japanese Relocation Papers, Bancroft Library, UC Berkeley, Microfilm reel #40.
43 *Evacuated People,* 196.
44 Harvey, *Amache,* 170–171.
45 "Restricted" letter from D.S. Myer to "All Project Directors," 11 September 1943, Japanese Relocation Papers, Bancroft Library, UC Berkeley, Microfilm reel #40.

6 Life in the war relocation centers

1 Japanese protest opposing the loyalty oaths Japanese citizens and Japanese-Americans were asked to take, 18 April 1944 (No. 102); Gaimusho A700, 9-11-1-5-1.
2 Spanish Report on the Tule Lake Relocation Center entitled "Visit to Japanese Internees or Detainees," written by Antonio R-Martin on 24 September 1943 and dispatched to Japan on 2 November 1943 (No. 419); Gaimusho A700, 9-11-1-5-1.
3 Bill Hosokawa, *Nisei: The Quiet Americans* (Niwot, CO: University Press of Colorado, 1969), 342.
4 Based on a 1994 telephone conversation with the Stanford University student housing office.
5 Spanish Report on the Tule Lake Relocation Center entitled "Visit to Japanese Internees or Detainees," written by Antonio R-Martin on 24 September 1943 and dispatched to Japan on 2 November 1943 (No. 419); Gaimusho A700, 9-11-1-5-1.
6 Ibid.

7 Ibid.
8 Thomas James, *Exile Within: The Schooling of Japanese Americans, 1942–1945* (Cambridge, MA: Harvard University Press, 1987), 84.
9 Spanish Report on the Tule Lake Relocation Center entitled "Visit to Japanese Internees or Detainees," written by Antonio R-Martin on 24 September 1943 and dispatched to Japan on 2 November 1943 (No. 419); Gaimusho A700, 9-11-1-5-1.
10 "Questions and Answers for Governing Administration and Policy of the Segregation Center," undated but most likely from July 1943, Japanese Relocation Papers, Bancroft Library, UC Berkeley, Microfilm reel #39.
11 Wartime Civil Control Administration, 4 August 1942, Memorandum: "Voting by Japanese Evacuees," United States Wartime Civil Control Administration, Hoover Institution Archives, Stanford University, Box #2.
12 Spanish Report on the Tule Lake Relocation Center entitled "Visit to Japanese Internees or Detainees," written by Antonio R-Martin on 24 September 1943 and dispatched to Japan on 2 November 1943 (No. 419); Gaimusho A700, 9-11-1-5-1.
13 War Relocation Authority, Bulletin No. 21, Supplement A "Disposition of Household and Personal Effects, and Other Evacuee Property," 4 November 1942, United States Wartime Civil Control Administration, Hoover Institution Archives, Stanford University, Box #2; italic text here is underlined in the original.
14 Spanish Report on the Tule Lake Relocation Center entitled "Visit to Japanese Internees or Detainees," written by Antonio R-Martin on 24 September 1943 and dispatched to Japan on 2 November 1943 (No. 419); Gaimusho A700, 9-11-1-5-1.
15 Alexander H. Leighton, *The Governing of Men: General Principles and Recommendations Based on Experience at a Japanese Relocation Camp* (Princeton, NJ: Princeton University Press, 1945), 130.
16 Yatsushiro, *Politics and Cultural Values*, 595.
17 James, *Exile Within*, 147.
18 Spanish Report on the Tule Lake Relocation Center entitled "Visit to Japanese Internees or Detainees," written by Antonio R-Martin on 24 September 1943 and dispatched to Japan on 2 November 1943 (No. 419); Gaimusho A700, 9-11-1-5-1.
19 Marnie Mueller, "A Daughter's Need to Know," in Erica Harth, ed. *Last Witnesses: Reflections on the Wartime Internment of Japanese Americans* (New York: Palgrave, 2001), 108.
20 Spanish Report on the Tule Lake Relocation Center entitled "Visit to Japanese Internees or Detainees," written by Antonio R-Martin on 24 September 1943 and dispatched to Japan on 2 November 1943 (No. 419); Gaimusho A700, 9-11-1-5-1.
21 Leighton, *Governing of Men*, 132.
22 Spanish Report on the Tule Lake Relocation Center entitled "Visit to Japanese Internees or Detainees," written by Antonio R-Martin on 24 September 1943 and dispatched to Japan on 2 November 1943 (No. 419); Gaimusho A700, 9-11-1-5-1.
23 Ibid.
24 Ibid.
25 Ibid.
26 Ibid.
27 Paul Bailey, *City in the Sun* (Los Angeles, CA: Westernlore Press, 1971), 104-105.
28 "War Relocation Authority, Washington: Administrative Instruction No. 65, Repatriation and Exchange, with Special Reference to Japan," 23 November 1942, U.S. National Archives, Record Group 59, Lot 58D8, Special War Problems Division, Box #158.
29 Letter from John J. McCloy, Assistant Secretary of War, to Dillon Myer, Director War Relocation Authority, 9 October 1942, U.S. National Archives, Record Group 59, Lot 58D8, Special War Problems Division, Box #176.

30 Letter from Fitch to Lyons, 24 November 1942, U.S. National Archives, Record Group 59, Lot 58D8, Special War Problems Division, Box #176.
31 Joseph D. Harrington, *Yankee Samurai (The Secret Role of Nisei in America's Pacific Victory)* (Detroit, MI: Harlo Press, 1979), 363–364.
32 Daniel I. Okimoto, *American in Disguise* (New York: Walker/Weatherhill, 1971), 32.
33 Sandra Taylor, *Jewel of the Desert: Japanese American Internment at Topaz* (Berkeley, CA: University of California Press, 1993), 151.
34 Douglas W. Nelson, *Heart Mountain: The History of an American Concentration Camp* (Madison, WI: Logmark Editions, 1976), 110–111.
35 Bailey, *City in the Sun*, 156.
36 Taylor, *Jewel of the Desert*, 152.
37 "Relocation Center Address," Japanese Relocation Papers, Bancroft Library, UC Berkeley, Microfilm reel #40.
38 Nelson, *Heart Mountain*, 99.
39 Miyamoto, in Ichioka, *Views from Within*, 44.
40 John Tateishi, *And Justice for All: An Oral History of the Japanese American Detention Camps* (New York: Random House, 1984), 113–123.
41 Sarasohn, *The Issei*, 209.
42 Anthony L. Lehman, *Birthright of Barbed Wire: The Santa Anita Assembly Center for the Japanese* (Los Angeles, CA: Westernlore Press, 1970), 64–65.
43 Donna K. Nagata, *Legacy of Injustice: Exploring the Cross-Generational Impact of the Japanese American Internment* (New York: Plenum Press, 1993), 12.
44 Letter from Frank Knox, Secretary of the Navy, to Harold Ickes, Secretary of the Interior, 17 April 1944, Japanese Relocation Papers, Bancroft Library, UC Berkeley, Microfilm reel #19.
45 Richard S. Nishimoto, *Inside an American Concentration Camp* (Tucson, AZ: The University of Arizona Press, 1995), 221.
46 John D. Cook Collection, Hoover Archives, Stanford University, Box #1.
47 Ibid.
48 "War Relocation Authority, Washington: Administrative Instruction No. 65, Repatriation and Exchange, with Special Reference to Japan," 23 November 1942, U.S. National Archives, Record Group 59, Lot58D8, Special War Problems Division, Box #158.
49 Ibid.
50 Japanese Relocation Papers, Bancroft Library, UC Berkeley, Microfilm reel #40.
51 Letter from George Hiroshi Sawamura, March 8, 1943, Bancroft Library, University of California, Berkeley, Reel #124.
52 Bailey, *City in the Sun*, 155.
53 Japanese Relocation Papers, Bancroft Library, UC Berkeley, Microfilm reel #124.
54 Bailey, *City in the Sun*, 157.
55 See http://www.pbs.org/wgbh/pages/frontline/shows/elian/etc/eliancron.html.
56 Japanese Relocation Papers, Bancroft Library, UC Berkeley, Microfilm reel #124.
57 National Archives, RG 59 Lot 55D, Special War Problems Division, Box 167.
58 "Supplemental Instructions for Agents going to Detention Centers for Japanese Repatriates," issued by T. F. Fitch, Chief Special Agent, undated but attached to documents dated 23 November 1942, U.S. National Archives, Record Group 59, Lot58D8, Special War Problems Division, Box #158.
59 "War Relocation Authority, Washington: Administrative Instruction No. 65, Repatriation and Exchange, with Special Reference to Japan," 23 November 1942, U.S. National Archives, Record Group 59, Lot58D8, Special War Problems Division, Box #158.

7 Tokyo protests mistreatment of officials and its impact on the second exchange

1 Japanese Government protest to the U.S. Government, 27 October 1942; Gaimusho A700, 9-11-1-5.
2 U.S. Government 12 December 1942 reply to the Japanese October 1942 protest, 18 December 1942 (Nos. 32245, 32250, 32246, 32258); Gaimusho A700, 9-11-1-5.
3 Ibid.
4 Japanese Protests over Alleged Poor Treatment off Officials, Family, and Staff in the First Exchange, undated (probably 1943); Gaimusho A700, 9-11-1-5.
5 Ibid.
6 Ibid.
7 Ibid.
8 Ibid.
9 Ibid.
10 Ibid.
11 Ibid.
12 U.S. Government Response to the Japanese Protest on 8-9 September 1942, 16 September 1943; Gaimusho A700, 9-11-1-5.
13 Ibid.
14 Ibid.
15 Ibid.
16 Ibid.
17 Ibid.
18 Ibid.
19 Ibid.
20 "Memorandum by the Assistant Chiefs of the Special Division (Keeley and Clattenburg) to President Roosevelt," 16 December 1942; FRUS, 1942, Volume 1, 446–449.
21 Ibid.
22 Ibid.
23 Ibid.
24 "Memo from B.L to SD," 6 July 1942, U.S. National Archives, Record Group 59, Lot 57D657, Box #85.
25 U.S. Government Memorandum to the Japanese Government, 6 August 1942; A700, 9-24-1(6).
26 Ibid.
27 Ibid.
28 Ibid. For unknown reasons, the number listed here was 564, not 466 or 636.
29 Memorandum from the State Department to the Spanish Embassy, 10 August 1942, U.S. National Archives, Record Group 59, Lot 57D6, Special War Problems Division, Box #86.
30 Japanese Government Response to U.S. Memorandum, 5 September 1942; A700, 9-24-1(6).
31 Ibid.
32 Department of State, Washington, "Memorandum: Japanese Exchange," December 16, 1942, Laurence Salisbury Papers, Hoover Institution Archives, Stanford University, Box #1.
33 Ibid. Italic text here is underlined in the original.
34 "Memorandum by the Assistant Secretary of State (Long)," 16 December 1942; FRUS, 1943, Volume 3, 867–868.
35 "Memorandum by the Assistant Chiefs of the Special Division (Keeley and Clattenburg) to President Roosevelt," 16 December 1942; FRUS, 1942, Volume 1, 446–449.

36 Ibid.

37 Ibid.

38 Memo from Joseph C. Green to Assistant Secretary of State Breckinridge Long, 6 July 1942, U.S. National Archives, Record Group 59, Lot 57D657, Box 85.

39 "Memorandum by the Assistant Secretary of State (Long)," 16 December 1942; FRUS, 1943, Volume 3, 867–868.

40 Ibid.

41 Letter from R. L. Bannerman, Special Agent, Department of State, to T. F. Fitch, Chief Special Agent, 30 January 1943, U.S. National Archives, Record Group 59, Lot 58D8, Special War Problems Division, Box #105.

42 "The Secretary of State to the Minister in Switzerland (Harrison)" 4 February 1943; FRUS, 1943, Volume 3, 868–871.

43 "Memorandum: The Spanish Embassy to the Department of State," 4 May 1943; FRUS, 1943, Volume 3, 872–874.

44 "Memorandum by the Chief of the Division of Far Eastern Affairs (Hamilton) to the Assistant Secretary of State (Long)," 7 May 1943; FRUS, 1943, Volume 3, 874–875.

45 Ibid.

46 "Effect on the exchange of objections by the agencies," attachment "e," page 3, Laurence Salisbury papers, Hoover Institution Archives, Stanford University, Box 1; in a 12-page letter to Stettinius dated 6 November 1943, Salisbury blamed all of the unwarranted delays on the "Senior Officer of the Department of State charged with negotiating the exchanges," who apparently was Breckinridge Long.

47 "Resolution Concerning Detention and Expulsion of Dangerous Axis Nationals" issued by the Third Meeting of the Ministers of Foreign Affairs of the American Republics, 5 June 1943, U.S. National Archives, Record Group 59, Lot 57D6, Special War Problems Division, Box #86.

48 "The Minister in Switzerland (Harrison) to the Secretary of State," 25 June 1943; FRUS, 1943, Volume 3, 882–883, see footnote 43.

49 "The Secretary of State to the Spanish Ambassador (Cardenas)," 24 June 1943; FRUS, 1943, Volume 3, 882–883.

50 "The Minister in Switzerland (Harrison) to the Secretary of State," 4 August 1943; FRUS, 1943, Volume 3, 891–892.

51 "Passenger List of Japanese From the United States who sailed aboard the M/V Gripsholm, 2 September 1943, for Mormugao, Portuguese India," 3 September 1943, U.S. National Archives, Record Group 59, Lot58D8, Special War Problems Division, Box #105.

52 "Passenger List of Japanese repatriates from Canada and Mexico who sailed aboard the M/V Gripsholm, 2 September 1943, for Mormugao, Portuguese India," 3 September 1943, U.S. National Archives, Record Group 59, Lot 58D8, Special War Problems Division, Box #105.

53 Daniels, Taylor, Kitano, *Japanese Americans*, 144.

54 "Relief Supplies Shipped on M.V. Gripsholm Transferred to Teia Maru–Scheduled for unloading at Manila," undated but probably August or September 1943, United States National Archives, Record Group 59, Lot 57D657, Box #85.

55 "The Secretary of State to the Spanish Ambassador (Cardenas)," 9 September 1943; FRUS, 1943, Volume 3, 923–924.

56 "The Secretary of State to the Minister in Switzerland (Harrison)," 4 September 1943; FRUS, 1943, Volume 3, 922–923.

57 "Individuals Named by the Japanese Government for Repatriation who have refused to go to Japan," U.S. National Archives, Record Group 59, Lot 57D6, Special War Problems Division, Box 86; an additional 23 Japanese apparently said "no" but subsequently died.

58 "The Spanish Embassy to the Department of State," 1 October 1943; FRUS, 1943, Volume 3, 938–939.
59 "The Department of State to the Spanish Embassy,"11 October 1943; FRUS, 1943, Volume 3, 939–941.
60 Ibid.
61 Ibid.
62 Second Japanese Protest to the U.S. Government following up on the protest dated 8-9 September 1943, 21 January 1944; Gaimusho A700, 9-11-1-5.
63 U.S. Government Response to 21 January 1944 Protest, 21 July 1944; Gaimusho A700, 9-11-1-5.

8 Rising tensions at the Tule Lake Segregation Center

1   Daisuke Kitagawa, *Issei and Nisei: The Internment Years* (New York: The Seabury Press, 1967), 142.
2   Japanese protest opposing the loyalty oaths Japanese citizens and Japanese-Americans were asked to take, 18 April 1944 (No. 102); Gaimusho A700, 9-11-1-5-1.
3   Spanish Report on the Tule Lake Relocation Center entitled "Visit to Japanese Internees or Detainees," written by Antonio R-Martin on 24 September 1943 and dispatched to Japan on 2 November 1943 (No. 419); Gaimusho A700, 9-11-1-5-1.
4   Japanese protest opposing the loyalty oaths Japanese citizens and Japanese-Americans were asked to take, 18 April 1944 (No. 102); Gaimusho A700, 9-11-1-5-1.
5   "The Segregation Program of WRA," a foreword by Dillon S. Myer, 30 July 1943, Japanese Relocation Papers, Bancroft Library, UC Berkeley, Microfilm reel #39.
6   Spanish Report on the Tule Lake Relocation Center entitled "Visit to Japanese Internees or Detainees," written by Antonio R-Martin on 24 September 1943 and dispatched to Japan on 2 November 1943 (No. 419); Gaimusho A700, 9-11-1-5-1; this report included in a separate annex a list of those individuals who had formally applied for repatriation to Japan.
7   "Letter to those evacuees to be segregated who are to remain at Tule Lake," signed by K. K. Best, project director, undated, Bancroft Library, University of Berkeley, Microfilm reel #172.
8   Kitagawa, *Issei and Nisei*, 143.
9   Thomas and Nishimoto, *The Spoilage*, 315.
10 19 February 1943 interview with Junichi Nimura, John D. Cook Papers, Hoover Institution Archives, Stanford University, Box 1.
11 "Registration Questionnaire," Japanese Relocation Papers, Bancroft Library, UC Berkeley, Microfilm reel #40.
12 Spanish Report on the Tule Lake Relocation Center entitled "Visit to Japanese Internees or Detainees," written by Antonio R-Martin on 24 September 1943 and dispatched to Japan on 2 November 1943 (No. 419); Gaimusho A700, 9-11-1-5-1.
13 McClain, *Mass Internment*, 347.
14 "The Segregation Program of WRA," a foreword by Dillon S. Myer, 30 July 1943, Japanese Relocation Papers, Bancroft Library, UC Berkeley, Microfilm reel #39.
15 "Special Problems in Regard to Evacuee Attitudes and the Segregation Program," Notes taken at the 26 July 1943 Denver meeting by John Embree, Japanese Relocation Papers, Bancroft Library, UC Berkeley, Microfilm reel #39.
16 Spanish Report on the Tule Lake Relocation Center entitled "Visit to Japanese Internees or Detainees," written by Antonio R-Martin on 24 September 1943 and dispatched to Japan on 2 November 1943 (No. 419); Gaimusho A700, 9-11-1-5-1.
17 Japanese protest opposing the loyalty oaths Japanese citizens and Japanese-Americans were asked to take, 18 April 1944 (No. 102); Gaimusho A700, 9-11-1-5-1.

18 Letter from Charles F. Ernst, Project Director, Topaz, Utah, to Mr. Dillon S. Myer, Director, War Relocation Authority, Washington, Mojiro Ono to the State Department, April 10, 1944, Bancroft Library, University of California, Berkeley, Reel #124.

19 "Analysis Chart on Attitudes of Selected Group Re Future Plans," April 27, 1944, Bancroft Library, University of California, Berkeley, Reel #124.

20 "Reasons for Repatriation," April 27, 1944, Bancroft Library, University of California, Berkeley, Reel #124.

21 Ibid.

22 Letter from Mojiro Ono to the State Department, March 3, 1945, Bancroft Library, University of California, Berkeley, Reel #172.

23 "Reported Absences on Leave by Centers For Weeks Ending August 7 and August 14, 1943 By Type of Leave, Net Change, and Population Remaining," 14 August 1943, U.S. War Relocation Authority, Stanford Institution Archives, Stanford University, Box #1.

24 Departures for School, John D. Cook Collection, Hoover Institution Archives, Stanford University, Box #1.

25 *Directory of American Students of Japanese Ancestry in the Higher Schools, Colleges and Universities of the United States of America* (National Japanese American Student Relocation Council, 1943), 2–3.

26 Allan W. Austin, *From Concentration Camp to Campus: Japanese American Students and World War II* (Urbana, Illinois: University of Illinois Press, 2004), 151.

27 Ibid., 151.

28 Stephen S. Fugita, David J. O'Brien, *Japanese American Ethnicity: The Persistence of Community* (Seattle, WA: University of Washington Press, 1991), 119.

29 "Hirabayashi vs. United States," June 21, 1943, United States Supreme Court, Hoover Institution Archives, Stanford University, Box #1.

30 "Memorandum, Strictly Confidential, Executive Meeting of Members of the United States Congress and Representatives from the Three Pacific Coast States," 2 December 1943, U.S. National Archives, Record Group 59, Lot 58D8, Special War Problems Division, Box #131.

31 Ibid.

32 Ibid.

33 Kitagawa, *Issei and Nisei*, 136.

34 Japanese protest opposing the loyalty oaths Japanese citizens and Japanese-Americans were asked to take, 18 April 1944 (No. 102); Gaimusho A700, 9-11-1-5-1.

35 Ibid.

36 Ibid.

37 Ibid.

38 Ibid.

39 Kitagawa, *Issei and Nisei*, 144–148.

40 Weglyn, *Years of Infamy*, 161.

41 Dillon S. Myer, *Uprooted Americans: The Japanese Americans and the War Relocation Authority during World War II* (Tucson, AZ: The University of Arizona Press, 1971), 29.

42 Weglyn, *Years of Infamy*, 170.

43 Japanese protest opposing the loyalty oaths Japanese citizens and Japanese-Americans were asked to take, 18 April 1944 (No. 102); Gaimusho A700, 9-11-1-5-1.

44 Ibid.

45 U.S. response to Japanese protests of April 1944 opposing the loyalty oaths Japanese citizens and Japanese-Americans were asked to take, 10 August 1944 (Nos. 12382, 12395, 12407, 12408, 12411, 12412, 12413, 12453); Gaimusho A700, 9-11-1-5-1.

46 Letter from John H. Provinse, Acting Director, to Secretary-of-State Cordell Hull, 27 January 1944; Gaimusho A700, 9-11-1-5-1.
47 U.S. response to Japanese protests of April 1944 opposing the loyalty oaths Japanese citizens and Japanese-Americans were asked to take, 10 August 1944 (Nos. 12382, 12395, 12407, 12408, 12411, 12412, 12413, 12453); Gaimusho A700, 9-11-1-5-1.
48 Letter from Henry L. Stimson, Secretary of War, to the Secretary-of-State, stamped 10 March 1944; Gaimusho A700, 9-11-1-5-1.
49 U.S. response to Japanese protests of April 1944 opposing the loyalty oaths Japanese citizens and Japanese-Americans were asked to take, 10 August 1944 (Nos. 12382, 12395, 12407, 12408, 12411, 12412, 12413, 12453); Gaimusho A700, 9-11-1-5-1.
50 Letter from Henry L. Stimson, Secretary of War, to the Secretary-of-State, stamped 10 March 1944; Gaimusho A700, 9-11-1-5-1.
51 U.S. response to Japanese protests of April 1944 opposing the loyalty oaths Japanese citizens and Japanese-Americans were asked to take, 10 August 1944 (Nos. 12382, 12395, 12407, 12408, 12411, 12412, 12413, 12453); Gaimusho A700, 9-11-1-5-1.
52 Myer, *Uprooted Americans*, 29.
53 Weglyn, *Years of Infamy*, 171.
54 U.S. response to Japanese protests of April 1944 opposing the loyalty oaths Japanese citizens and Japanese-Americans were asked to take, 10 August 1944 (Nos. 12382, 12395, 12407, 12408, 12411, 12412, 12413, 12453); Gaimusho A700, 9-11-1-5-1.
55 Letter from Henry L. Stimson, Secretary of War, to the Secretary-of-State, stamped 10 March 1944; Gaimusho A700, 9-11-1-5-1.
56 U.S. response to Japanese protests of April 1944 opposing the loyalty oaths Japanese citizens and Japanese-Americans were asked to take, 10 August 1944 (Nos. 12382, 12395, 12407, 12408, 12411, 12412, 12413, 12453); Gaimusho A700, 9-11-1-5-1.
57 Ibid.
58 Letter from Henry L. Stimson, Secretary of War, to the Secretary-of-State, stamped 10 March 1944; Gaimusho A700, 9-11-1-5-1.
59 Ibid.
60 Letter from the Spanish representative stating "les thres quartas partes de los internados son eiudadanos Americanos y una cuarte parte nactionales Japoneses," 27 January 1944 (Enero 27 de 1944); Gaimusho A700, 9-11-1-5-1.
61 Weglyn, *Years of Infamy*, 169.
62 U.S. response to Japanese protests of April 1944 opposing the loyalty oaths Japanese citizens and Japanese-Americans were asked to take, 10 August 1944 (Nos. 12382, 12395, 12407, 12408, 12411, 12412, 12413, 12453); Gaimusho A700, 9-11-1-5-1.
63 Letter from John H. Provinse, Acting Director, to Secretary-of-State Cordell Hull, 27 January 1944; Gaimusho A700, 9-11-1-5-1.
64 Letter from Henry L. Stimson, Secretary of War, to the Secretary-of-State, stamped 10 March 1944; Gaimusho A700, 9-11-1-5-1.
65 Letter from John H. Provinse, Acting Director, to Secretary-of-State Cordell Hull, 27 January 1944; Gaimusho A700, 9-11-1-5-1.
66 Letter from Henry L. Stimson, Secretary of War, to the Secretary-of-State, stamped 10 March 1944; Gaimusho A700, 9-11-1-5-1.
67 Japanese protest opposing the loyalty oaths Japanese citizens and Japanese-Americans were asked to take, 18 April 1944 (No. 102); Gaimusho A700, 9-11-1-5-1.
68 Ibid.
69 Ibid.
70 U.S. response to Japanese protests of April 1944 opposing the loyalty oaths Japanese citizens and Japanese-Americans were asked to take, 10 August 1944 (Nos. 12382, 12395, 12407, 12408, 12411, 12412, 12413, 12453); Gaimusho A700, 9-11-1-5-1.
71 Ibid.
72 Ibid.

73 Ibid.

74 Ibid.

75 Ibid.

76 Ibid.

77 Letter from John H. Provinse, Acting Director, to Secretary-of-State Cordell Hull, 27 January 1944; Gaimusho A700, 9-11-1-5-1.

9 Tokyo protests mistreatment of non-officials and the delay of the third exchange

1 Japanese Government protest to the U.S. Government, 27 October 1942; Gaimusho A700, 9-11-1-5.

2 U.S. Government 12 December 1942 reply to the Japanese October 1942 protest, 18 December 1942 (Nos. 32245, 32250, 32246, 32258); Gaimusho A700, 9-11-1-5.

3 U.S. Government response to the Japanese October 1942 protest, 21 October 1943; Gaimusho A700, 9-11-1-5.

4 Ibid.

5 Ibid.

6 Japanese Government protest to the U.S. Government, 9 April 1943; Gaimusho A700, 9-11-1-5.

7 Ibid.

8 Second Japanese Protest to the U.S. Government following up on the protest dated 8-9 September 1942, 21 January 1943; Gaimusho A700, 9-11-1-5.

9 Japanese Government protest to the U.S. Government, 9 April 1943; Gaimusho A700, 9-11-1-5.

10 U.S. Government response to the Japanese October 1942 protest, 21 October 1943; Gaimusho A700, 9-11-1-5.

11 U.S. Government Response to Japanese Protests over Alleged Poor Treatment in Hawaii, 7 April 1943; Gaimusho A700, 9-11-1-5.

12 Ibid.

13 Ibid.

14 Ibid.

15 U.S. Government Response to 21 January 1944 Protest, 21 July 1944; Gaimusho A700, 9-11-1-5.

16 Japanese Government protest to the U.S. Government, 13 January 1945; Gaimusho A700, 9-11-1-5.

17 Ibid.

18 Japanese Government protest to the U.S. Government, 27 October 1942; Gaimusho A700, 9-11-1-5.

19 Ibid.

20 U.S. Government response to the Japanese October 1942 protest, 21 October 1943; Gaimusho A700, 9-11-1-5.

21 Ibid.

22 Ibid.

23 Ibid.

24 Japanese Government protest to the U.S. Government, 27 October 1942; Gaimusho A700, 9-11-1-5.

25 U.S. Government response to the Japanese October 1942 protest, 21 October 1943; Gaimusho A700, 9-11-1-5.

26 Ibid.

27 Japanese Government protest to the U.S. Government, 27 October 1942; Gaimusho A700, 9-11-1-5.

28 Ibid.

29 Ibid.

30 Ibid.
31 U.S. Government response to the Japanese October 1942 peorwar, 21 October 1943; Gaimusho A700, 9-11-1-5.
32 Ibid.
33 Ibid.
34 Ibid.
35 Japanese Government protest to the U.S. Government, 27 October 1942; Gaimusho A700, 9-11-1-5.
36 U.S. Government response to the Japanese October 1942 protest, 21 October 1943; Gaimusho A700, 9-11-1-5.
37 Japanese Government protest to the U.S. Government, 29 February 1944; Gaimusho A700, 9-11-1-5.
38 Ibid.
39 Arthur A. Hansen and Betty E. Mitson, eds., *Voices Long Silent: An Oral Inquiry into the Japanese American Evacuation* (Fullerton, CA: Kulberg Publications, 1974), 42.
40 Japanese Government protest to the U.S. Government, 29 February 1944; Gaimusho A700, 9-11-1-5.
41 Sue Kunitomi Embrey, Arthur A. Hansen, Betty Kulberg Mitson, *Manzanar Martyr: An Interview with Harry Y. Ueno* (Anaheim, CA: Shumway Family History Services, 1986), 70.
42 Japanese Government protest to the U.S. Government, 29 February 1944; Gaimusho A700, 9-11-1-5.
43 Japanese Government protest to the U.S. Government, 16 May 1944; Gaimusho A700, 9-11-1-5.
44 Japanese Government protest to the U.S. Government, 27 October 1942; Gaimusho A700, 9-11-1-5.
45 Ibid.
46 U.S. Government 12 December 1942 reply to the Japanese October 1942 protest, 18 December 1942 (Nos. 32245, 32250, 32246, 32258); Gaimusho A700, 9-11-1-5.
47 Ibid.
48 Embrey, Hansen, Mitson, *Manzanar Martyrs*, 29.
49 U.S. response to Japanese protests of April 1944 opposing the loyalty oaths Japanese citizens and Japanese-Americans were asked to take, 10 August 1944 (Nos. 12382, 12395, 12407, 12408, 12411, 12412, 12413, 12453); Gaimusho A700, 9-11-1-5-1.
50 Ibid.
51 U.S. Government response to the Japanese October 1942 protest, 21 October 1943; Gaimusho A700, 9-11-1-5.
52 Ibid.
53 Ibid.
54 Japanese protest opposing the loyalty oaths Japanese citizens and Japanese-Americans were asked to take, 18 April 1944 (No. 102); Gaimusho A700, 9-11-1-5-1.
55 U.S. response to Japanese protests of April 1944 opposing the loyalty oaths Japanese citizens and Japanese-Americans were asked to take, 10 August 1944 (Nos. 12382, 12395, 12407, 12408, 12411, 12412, 12413, 12453); Gaimusho A700, 9-11-1-5-1.
56 Ibid.
57 Ibid.
58 Ibid.
59 Ibid.
60 U.S. Government 12 December 1942 reply to the Japanese October 1942 protest, 18 December 1942 (Nos. 32245, 32250, 32246, 32258); Gaimusho A700, 9-11-1-5.
61 Ibid.
62 Ibid.

63 See, for example, Anton Bilek, *No Uncle Sam: the Forgotten of Bataan* (Kent, OH: Kent State University Press, 2003).

10 Negotiating safe passage and the sinking of *Awa Maru*

1 Telegram from "Maderi" (Madrid) transmitting the American response to Japan's Memorandum 42, 9 February 1942 (No. 4371); Gaimusho, A700, 9-24-1, 7.
2 Ibid.
3 Japanese Communication entitled "Further Observations of the Japanese Government," 19 February 1942; Gaimusho, A700, 9-24-1, 7.
4 Telegram from Madrid transmitting U.S. Government to the Japanese Government, 17 March 1942 (No. 7859); Gaimusho A700, 9-24-1, 7.
5 Baker, *American and Japanese Relocation*, 76; quoting from the 3 September 1943 *New York Times*.
6 U.S. Government Memorandum discussing Exchange Vessels, 11 May 1942; Gaimusho A700, 9-24-1(2).
7 Telegram from "Maderi" (Madrid) transmitting the American message, 8 June 1942; Gaimusho A700, 9-24-1, 2.
8 Translated letter from Minister Shigenori Togo to Hisanobu Terai, President of the Nippon Yusen Kaisya, June 1942 (no day given), marked Translation; Gaimusho, A700, 9-24-1, 2.
9 Telegram from "Maderi" (Madrid) transmitting the American response to Japan's Memorandum 42, 9 February 1942 (No. 4371); Gaimusho, A700, 9-24-1, 7.
10 Japanese Communication entitled "Further Observations of the Japanese Government," 19 February 1942; Gaimusho, A700, 9-24-1, 7.
11 Telegram from Madrid transmitting U.S. Government to the Japanese Government, 17 March 1942 (No. 7859); Gaimusho A700, 9-24-1, 7.
12 Note from the Swiss Minister to Japan to Mr. Haruhiko Nishi, Vice-Minister of Foreign Affairs, 5 August 1942 (AA.5.1.27.-ce); Gaimusho A700, 9-24-1, 2.
13 Ibid.
14 "Note Verbale" from the Royal Swedish Legation to the Japanese Foreign Ministry, Tokyo, 16 September 1943; Gaimusho A700, 9-24-1, 9.
15 Paraphrase of Telegram Sent from Secretary of State Hull to American Legation at Berne, 25 July 1944, U.S. National Archives, Record Group 59, Lot 55D400/401/402, Special War Problems Division, Box #193.
16 Ibid. Italic text here is underlined in original.
17 Ibid.
18 Paraphrase of Telegram Sent from Acting Secretary of State to American Embassy at Moscow, 16 February 1944, U.S. National Archives, Record Group 59, Lot 55D400/401/402, Special War Problems Division, Box #193.
19 Paraphrase of Telegram Sent from Secretary of State Hull to American Legation at Berne, 30 March 1944, U.S. National Archives, Record Group 59, Lot 55D400/401/402, Special War Problems Division, Box #193.
20 Note from the Swiss Minister to Japan's Ministry of Foreign Affairs, 23 December 1943; Gaimusho A700, 9-11-6 (4).
21 Note from the Swiss Minister to Japan's Ministry of Foreign Affairs including a report from "Lloyd Fortune, Chief Supply Officer, Missoula, Montana," 16 December 1943; Gaimusho A700, 9-11-1-10-1 (2).
22 Complaint of Katsuji Onishi, 15 December 1943; Gaimusho, A700, 9-11-1-10-1(2).
23 Note from the Swiss Minister to Japan's Ministry of Foreign Affairs, 27 April 1945; Gaimusho A700, 9-11-4 (3).
24 Note from the Swiss Minister to Japan's Ministry of Foreign Affairs, 17 April 1945; Gaimusho A700, 9-11-4 (2).

25 Note from the Swiss Minister to Japan's Ministry of Foreign Affairs, 27 April 1945; Gaimusho A700, 9-11-4 (3).
26 Note from the Swiss Minister to Japan's Ministry of Foreign Affairs, 18 May 1945; Gaimusho A700, 9-11-4 (1).
27 Ibid.
28 Note from the Swiss Minister to Japan's Ministry of Foreign Affairs (CC.2.1.3, F6C), 27 June 1945; Gaimusho A700, 9-11-4 (1).
29 Roger Dingman, *Ghost of War: The Sinking of the "Awa Maru" and Japanese–American Relations, 1945-1995* (Annapolis, MD: Naval Institute Press, 1997).
30 Note from the Swiss Minister to Japan's Ministry of Foreign Affairs, 22 September 1944; Gaimusho A700, 9-11-6 (1).
31 Note from the Swiss Minister to Japan's Ministry of Foreign Affairs (CC.2.1.3.-FFc), 12 July 1945; Gaimusho A700, 9-11-4 (1).
32 Note from the Swiss Minister to Japan's Ministry of Foreign Affairs (CC.1.3.6, F6C), 5 July 1945; Gaimusho A700, 9-11-4 (1).
33 "Americans in Far East," Note from Maurice Pate, American Red Cross Headquarters, to Eldred D. Kuppinger, Special War Problems Division, 26 February 1945, U.S. National Archives, Record Group 59, Special War Problems Division, Box #91.

Conclusion

1 Daniels, Taylor, Kitano, *Japanese Americans*, 144.
2 Yoshiko Uchida, *Desert Exile: The Uprooting of a Japanese American Family* (Seattle, WA: University of Washington Press, 1982), 146.
3 James, *Exile Within*, 143.
4 Connell, *America's Japanese Hostages*, 100.
5 Evacuated People, 196. Another source lists this number as 4, 724.
6 McClain, *Mass Internment*, 351.
7 Daniels, Taylor, Kitano, *Japanese Americans*,141.
8 Embrey, Hansen, Mitson, *Manzanar Martyr*, 92.
9 Toru Matsumoto, *Beyond Prejudice* (New York: Arno Press, 1978), 133.
10 Kaneshiro, *Internees*, 86.
11 Ibid., 101.
12 Ibid., 85.
13 Embrey, Hansen, Mitson, *Manzanar Martyr*, 92.
14 Nagata, *Legacy of Injustice*, 13–14.
15 Eric L. Muller, *Free to Die For Their Country: The Story of the Japanese American Draft Resisters in World War* II (Chicago, IL: The University of Chicago Press, 2001), 180.
16 McClain, *Mass Internment*, 374.
17 Kiyoaki Murata, *An Enemy Among Friends* (Tokyo: Kodansha International, 1991), 226.
18 Matsumoto, *Beyond Prejudice*, 135.
19 Minoru Kiyota, *Beyond Loyalty: The Story of a Kibei* (Honolulu, HI: The University of Hawai'i Press, 1997), 226.
20 Minoru Kiyota, ed., *The Case of Japanese Americans During World War II: Suppression of Civil Liberty* (Lewiston, NY: The Edwin Mellen Press, 2004), 22, 102–3.

Bibliography

Primary sources

Primary research for this book has been conducted at the Japanese Foreign Ministry Archives (Gaimusho), Tokyo, Japan, at the U.S. National Archives, College Park, MD, at the Hoover Institution Archives, Stanford, CA, and at the Bancroft Library, University of California at Berkeley, in Berkeley, CA. In addition, the War Relocation Authority published over a dozen books and pamphlets documenting the progress of the program, including *Relocation of Japanese-Americans* (Washington, DC: War Relocation Authority, 1943), *The Wartime Handling of Evacuee Property* (Washington, DC: War Relocation Authority, 1946), *Wartime Exile: The Exclusion of the Japanese Americans from the West Coast* (Washington, DC: War Relocation Authority, 1946), *Impounded People: Japanese-Americans in the Relocation Centers* (Washington, DC: War Relocation Authority, 1946), and *WRA: A Story of Human Conservation* (Washington, DC: War Relocation Authority, 1946). Several other WRA reports were reprinted in the 1970s by AMS Press, including *The Evacuated People: A Quantitative Description* (New York: AMS Press, 1975), *Community Government in War Relocation Centers* (New York: AMS Press, 1975), *The Relocation Program* (New York: AMS Press, 1975), and *Administrative Highlights of the WRA Program* (New York: AMS Press, 1975). The director of the WRA later published two books on the topic, including Dillon S. Myer, *Uprooted Americans: The Japanese Americans and the War Relocation Authority during World War II* (Tucson, AZ: The University of Arizona Press, 1971), and Dillon S. Myer, *War Relocation Authority: The Director's Account* (Berkeley, CA: Earl Warren Oral History Project, 1974). Although most of the documents discussed in this book were taken from archival sources, some new documents, as well as some reprints of archival documents, were published either in whole or in part in various volumes from the on-going U.S. Department of State series *Foreign Relations of the United States*. Finally, one organizational pamphlet was referenced: *Directory of American Students of Japanese Ancestry in the Higher Schools, Colleges and Universities of the United States of America* (National Japanese American Student Relocation Council, 1943).

Secondary sources

Allan W. Austin, *From Concentration Camp to Campus: Japanese American Students and World War II* (Urbana, IL: University of Illinois Press, 2004).
Paul Bailey, *City in the Sun* (Los Angeles, CA: Westernlore Press, 1971).

Lillian Baker, *American and Japanese Relocation in World War II: Fact, Fiction and Fallacy* (Medford, OR: Webb Research Group, 1990).

Anton Bilek, *No Uncle Sam: the Forgotten of Bataan* (Kent, OH: Kent State University Press, 2003).

Jacobus tenBroek, Edward N. Barnhart, and Floyd W. Matson, *Japanese American Evacuation and Resettlement: Prejudice, War and the Constitution* (Berkeley, CA: University of California Press, 1958).

Leonard Broom and Ruth Riemer, *Removal and Return: The Socio-Economic Effects of the War on Japanese Americans* (Berkeley, CA: University of California Press, 1949/Reprint 1973).

Donald E. Collins, *Native American Aliens: Disloyalty and the Renunciation of Citizenship by Japanese Americans During World War II* (Westport, CT: Greenwood Press, 1985).

Thomas Connell, *America's Japanese Hostages: The World War II Plan for a Japanese Free Latin America* (Westport, CT: Praeger Press, 2002).

Maisie and Richard Conrat, *Executive Order 9066: The Internment of 110,000 Japanese Americans* (Los Angeles, CA: Anderson, Ritchie & Simon, 1972).

P. Scott Corbett, *Quiet Passages: The Exchange of Civilians between the United States and Japan during the Second World War* (Kent, OH: The Kent State University Press, 1987).

Christine Corcos, *Japanese-American Internment and Relocation During World War II: A Selected Bibliography* (Case Western Reserve University, Law Library, 1991).

Roger Daniels, *Concentration Camp USA: Japanese Americans and World War II* (New York: Holt, Rinehart and Winston, Inc., 1972).

—— , *The Decision to Relocate the Japanese Americans* (New York: J.B. Lippincott Company, 1975).

—— , *Concentration Camps: North America Japanese in the United States and Canada During World War II* (Malabar, FL: Robert E. Krieger Publishing Company, 1981).

Roger Daniels, Sandra C. Taylor, Harry H. L. Kitano, eds., *Japanese Americans: From Relocation to Redress* (Salt Lake City, UT: University of Utah Press, 1986).

Roger Dingman, *Ghost of War: The Sinking of the "Awa Maru" and Japanese–American Relations, 1945-1995* (Annapolis, MD: Naval Institute Press, 1997).

Sue Kunitomi Embrey, Arthur A. Hansen, and Betty Kulberg Mitson, *Manzanar Martyr: An Interview with Harry Y. Ueno* (Anaheim, CA: Shumway Family History Services, 1986).

Louis Fiset, *Imprisoned Apart: The World War II Correspondence of an Issei Couple* (Seattle, WA: University of Washington Press, 1997).

Stephen Fox, *The Unknown Internment: An Oral History of the Relocation of Italian Americans during World War II* (Boston, MA: Twayne Publishers, 1990).

Stephen S. Fugita and David J. O'Brien, *Japanese American Ethnicity: The Persistence of Community* (Seattle, WA: University of Washington Press, 1991).

Budd Fukei, *The Japanese American Story* (Minneapolis, MN: Dillon Press Inc., 1976).

C. Harvey Gardiner, *Pawns in a Triangle of Hate: The Peruvian Japanese and the United States* (Seattle, WA: University of Washington Press, 1981).

Jessie A. Garrett and Ronald C. Larson, eds., *Camp and Community: Manzanar and the Owens Valley* (Van Nuys, CA: Delta Lithograph Co., 1977).

Audrie Girdner and Anne Loftis, *The Great Betrayal: The Evacuation of the Japanese-Americans During World War II* (Toronto: The Macmillan Company, 1969).

Morton Grodzins, *Americans Betrayed: Politics and the Japanese Evacuation* (Chicago, IL: The University of Chicago Press, 1949).

Sidney L. Gulick, *The American Japanese Problem: A Study of the Racial Relations of the East and the West* (New York: Charles Scribner's Sons, 1914).

Arthur A. Hansen and Betty E. Mitson, eds., *Voices Long Silent: An Oral Inquiry into the Japanese American Evacuation* (Fullerton, CA: Kulberg Publications, 1974).

Joseph D. Harrington, *Yankee Samurai (The Secret Role of Nisei in America's Pacific Victory)* (Detroit, MI: Harlo Press, 1979).

Erica Harth, ed., *Last Witnesses: Reflections on the Wartime Internment of Japanese Americans* (New York: Palgrave, 2001).

Robert Harvey, *Amache: The Story of Japanese Internment in Colorado During World War II* (Lanham, MD: Taylor Trade Publishing, 2004).

William Minoru Hohri, *Repairing America: An Account of the Movement For Japanese-American Redress* (Pullman, WA: Washington State University Press, 1988).

Timothy J. Holian, *The German-Americans and World War II* (New York: Peter Lang, 1996).

Bill Hosokawa, *Nisei: The Quiet Americans* (Niwot, CO: University Press of Colorado, 1969).

——, *Thirty-Five Years in the Frying Pan* (New York: McGraw-Hill Book Company, 1978).

——, *Out of the Frying Pan: Reflections of a Japanese American* (Niwot, CO: University Press of Colorado, 1998).

Jeane Wakatsuki Houston and James D. Houston, *Farewell to Mansanar* (Boston, MA: Houghton Mifflin Company, 1973).

Eleanor Hull, *Suddenly the Sun: A Biography of Shizuko Takahashi* (New York: Friendship Press, 1957).

Yamato Ichihashi, *Japanese in the United States: A Critical Study of the Problems of the Japanese Immigrants and Their Children* (Stanford, CA: Stanford University Press, 932).

Yuji Ichioka, *The Issei: The World of the First Generation Japanese Immigrants, 1885-1924* (New York: The Free Press, 1988).

——, ed., *Views from Within: The Japanese American Evacuation and Resettlement Study* (Los Angeles, CA: Asian American Studies Center, 1989).

Peter Irons, *Justice at War: The Story of the Japanese American Internment Cases* (New York: Oxford University Press, 1983).

Leslie A. Ito, *Japanese Americans During World War II: A Selected, Annotated Bibliography of Materials Available at UCLA* (UCLA Asian American Studies Center Reading Room/Library; 2nd edition, 1997).

Masakazu Iwata, *Planted in Good Soil: The History of the Issei in United States Agriculture* (New York: Peter Lang, 1992).

Thomas James, *Exile Within: The Schooling of Japanese Americans, 1942-1945* (Cambridge, MA: Harvard University Press, 1987).

Takeo Kaneshiro, compiler, *Internees: War Relocation Center Memoirs and Diaries* (New York: Vantage Press, 1976).

Tetsuden Kashima, *Judgment without Trial: Japanese American Imprisonment During World War II* (Seattle, WA: University of Washington Press, 2003).

Daisuke Kitagawa, *Issei and Nisei: The Internment Years* (New York: The Seabury Press, 1967).

Minoru Kiyota, *Beyond Loyalty: The Story of a Kibei* (Honolulu, HI: The University of Hawai'i Press, 1997).

——, ed., *The Case of Japanese Americans During World War II: Suppression of Civil Liberty* (Lewiston, NY: The Edwin Mellen Press, 2004).

Arnold Krammer, *Undue Process: The Untold Story of America's German Alien Internees* (New York: Rowman & Littlefield Publishers, Inc., 1997).

Anthony L. Lehman, *Birthright of Barbed Wire: The Santa Anita Assembly Center for the Japanese* (Los Angeles, CA: Westernlore Press, 1970).

Alexander H. Leighton, *The Governing of Men: General Principles and Recommendations Based on Experience at a Japanese Relocation Camp* (Princeton, NJ: Princeton University Press, 1945).

David D. Lowman, *MAGIC: The Untold Story of U.S. Intelligence and the Evacuation of Japanese Residents from the West Coast During WWII* (Utah: Athena Press, Inc., 2000).

Charles McClain, ed., *The Mass Internment of Japanese Americans and the Quest for Legal Redress* (New York: Garland Publishing, Inc., 1994).

Mitchell T. Maki, Harry H. L. Kitano, and S. Megan Berthold, *Achieving the Impossible Dream: How Japanese Americans Obtained Redress* (Urbana, IL: University of Illinois Press, 1999).

Michelle Malkin, *In Defense of Internment: The Case for "Racial Profiling" in World War II and the War on Terror* (Washington, DC: Regnery Publishing, Inc., 2004).

Toru Matsumoto, *Beyond Prejudice* (New York: Arno Press, 1978).

Denice Lee Mills, *The Evacuation and Relocation of Japanese Americans During World War II: A Bibliography* (Vance Bibliographies, 1989).

Eric L. Muller, *Free to Die For Their Country: The Story of the Japanese American Draft Resisters in World War* II (Chicago, IL: The University of Chicago Press, 2001).

Kiyoaki Murata, *An Enemy Among Friends* (Tokyo: Kodansha International, 1991).

Donna K. Nagata, *Legacy of Injustice: Exploring the Cross-Generational Impact of the Japanese American Internment* (New York: Plenum Press, 1993).

Douglas W. Nelson, *Heart Mountain: The History of an American Concentration Camp* (Madison, WI: Logmark Editions, 1976).

Klancy Clark de Nevers, *The Colonel and the Pacifist: Karl Bendetsen-Perry Saito and the Incarceration of Japanese Americans during World War II* (Salt Lake City, UT: The University of Utah Press, 2004).

Wendy L. Ng, *Japanese American Internment During World War II: A History and Reference Guide* (Westport, CT: Greenwood Press, 2002).

Richard S. Nishimoto, *Inside an American Concentration Camp* (Tucson, AZ: The University of Arizona Press, 1995).

James Oda, *Heroic Struggles of Japanese Americans: Partisan Fighters From America's Concentration Camps* (Los Angeles, CA: KNI, Inc., 1981).

Daniel I. Okimoto, *American in Disguise* (New York: Walker/Weatherhill, 1971).

S.C.M. Paine, *The Sino-Japanese War of 1894–1895: Perceptions, Power, and Primacy* (Cambridge, UK: Cambridge University Press, 2003).

Eileen Sunada Sarasohn, *The Issei: Portrait of a Pioneer, An Oral History* (Palo Alto, CA: Pacific Books, 1983).

Page Smith, *Democracy on Trial: The Japanese American Evacuation and Relocation in World War II* (New York: Simon & Schuster, 1995).

John Tateishi, *And Justice for All: An Oral History of the Japanese American Detention Camps* (New York: Random House, 1984).

Sandra Taylor, *Jewel of the Desert: Japanese American Internment at Topaz* (Berkeley, CA: University of California Press, 1993).

Gwen Terasaki, *Bridge to the Sun* (Chapel Hill, NC: The University of North Carolina Press, 1957).

Dorothy Swaine Thomas and Richard S. Nishimoto, *The Spoilage: Japanese-American Evacuation and Resettlement During World War II* (Berkeley, CA: University of California Press, 1969).

Yoshiko Uchida, *Desert Exile: The Uprooting of a Japanese American Family* (Seattle, WA: University of Washington Press, 1982).

Denis and Peggy Warner, *The Tide at Sunrise: A History of the Russo-Japanese War* (New York: Charterhouse, 1974).

Michi Weglyn, *Years of Infamy: The Untold Story of America's Concentration Camps* (New York: William Morrow and Company, Inc., 1976).

Toshio Yatsushiro, *Politics and Cultural Values: The World War II Japanese Relocation Centers United States Government* (New York: Arno Press, 1978).

Index

Printed in the United States
by Baker & Taylor Publisher Services